RACE, TRANSNATIONALISM, AND NINETEENTH-CENTURY AMERICAN LITERARY STUDIES

Inspired by Toni Morrison's call for an interracial approach to American literature, and by recent efforts to globalize American literary studies, *Race, Transnationalism, and Nineteenth-Century American Literary Studies* ranges widely in its case-study approach to canonical and noncanonical authors. Leading critic Robert S. Levine considers Cooper, Hawthorne, Stowe, Melville, and other nineteenth-century American writers alongside less well-known African American figures such as Nathaniel Paul and Sutton Griggs. He pays close attention to racial representations and ideology in nineteenth-century American writing, while exploring the inevitable tension between the local and the global in this writing. Levine addresses transatlanticism, the Black Atlantic, citizenship, empire, temperance, climate change, black nationalism, book history, temporality, Kantian transnational aesthetics, and a number of other issues. The book also provides a compelling critical frame for understanding developments in American literary studies over the past twenty-five years.

ROBERT S. LEVINE is Distinguished University Professor of English at the University of Maryland, College Park. He is the author of *Conspiracy and Romance* (1989), *Martin Delany, Frederick Douglass, and the Politics of Representative Identity* (1997), *Dislocating Race and Nation* (2008), and *The Lives of Frederick Douglass* (2016), and the editor of over twenty volumes. He is General Editor of *The Norton Anthology of American Literature*. Levine has received fellowships from the National Endowment for the Humanities and the Guggenheim Foundation. In 2014 the American Literature Section of the Modern Language Association awarded him the Hubbell Medal for Lifetime Achievement in American Literary Studies.

RACE, TRANSNATIONALISM, AND NINETEENTH-CENTURY AMERICAN LITERARY STUDIES

ROBERT S. LEVINE

University of Maryland

CAMBRIDGE
UNIVERSITY PRESS

CAMBRIDGE
UNIVERSITY PRESS

University Printing House, Cambridge CB2 8BS, United Kingdom

One Liberty Plaza, 20th Floor, New York, NY 10006, USA

477 Williamstown Road, Port Melbourne, VIC 3207, Australia

314–321, 3rd Floor, Plot 3, Splendor Forum, Jasola District Centre, New Delhi – 110025, India

79 Anson Road, #06–04/06, Singapore 079906

Cambridge University Press is part of the University of Cambridge.

It furthers the University's mission by disseminating knowledge in the pursuit of education, learning, and research at the highest international levels of excellence.

www.cambridge.org
Information on this title: www.cambridge.org/9781107095069
DOI: 10.1017/9781316154939

First published 2018

Printed in the United States of America by Sheridan Books, Inc.

A catalogue record for this publication is available from the British Library.

Library of Congress Cataloging-in-Publication Data
NAMES: Levine, Robert S. (Robert Steven), 1953– author.
TITLE: Race, transnationalism, and nineteenth-century American literary studies / Robert S. Levine.
DESCRIPTION: New York : Cambridge University Press, 2017. | Includes bibliographical references and index.
IDENTIFIERS: LCCN 2017030491 | ISBN 9781107095069 (hardback)
SUBJECTS: LCSH: American literature – 19th century – History and criticism. | Race in literature. | Transnationalism in literature. | African Americans in literature. | American literature – African American authors – History and criticism. | Blacks in literature. | Black nationalism in literature.
CLASSIFICATION: LCC PS217.R28 L48 2017 | DDC 810.9/355–dc23
LC record available at https://lccn.loc.gov/2017030491

ISBN-978-1-107-09506-9 Hardback

To Nina Baym
and in memory of
Joan Levine (1931–2015)

Contents

Acknowledgments

The Department of English at the University of Maryland has been my academic home for over thirty years, and I want to thank my chair, Amanda Bailey, and former chairs Theresa Coletti, Charles Caramello, Kent Cartwright, and William Cohen for their generous support of my research. My thanks as well to my colleagues at Maryland, with special thanks to Jonathan Auerbach, Ralph Bauer, Tita Chico, Neil Fraistat, Ted Leinwand, Marilee Lindemann, Peter Mallios, Carla Peterson, Sangeeta Ray, Martha Nell Smith, Mary Helen Washington, and Edlie Wong. I did the bulk of my research at the Library of Congress and the University of Maryland's McKeldin Library, and I thank the expert librarians at both institutions, particularly McKeldin's Patricia Herron, research librarian par excellence. For their helpful responses to sections of the book, I am grateful to Christopher Castiglia, Russ Castronovo, Jeannine DeLombard, Elizabeth Duquette, Susan Gillman, Sandra Gustafson, Gordon Hutner, Carrie Hyde, Caroline Levander, Sam Otter, Joel Pfister, Elizabeth Renker, Larry Reynolds, Xiomara Santamarina, Cindy Weinstein, and the editors listed in the next paragraph. My special thanks to Leonard Cassuto, who offered editorial assistance at key moments over the years, and to my wife, Ivy Goodman, who read the entire book in manuscript and remains my very best reader.

This book draws on previously published work. In all cases I've updated and revised, and in some cases I've dramatically changed arguments or simply gone in new directions. I'm grateful to my colleagues in the field for continually challenging my thinking. I'm also grateful to the editors of the following books and journals for providing me with useful early forums: *American Literary History* (1990), ed. Gordon Hutner; *Temperance and American Literature* (1997), eds. David Reynolds and Debra Rosenthal; *"Genius in Bondage": Literature of the Early Black Atlantic* (2001), eds. Vincent Carretta and Philip Gould; *The Cambridge Companion to the African American Slave Narrative* (2007), ed. Audrey Fisch; *States of*

Emergency: The Object of American Studies (2009), eds. Russ Castronovo and Susan Gillman; *Melville and Aesthetics* (2011), eds. Samuel Otter and Geoffrey Sanborn; *The Oxford Handbook of Nineteenth-Century American Literature* (2012), ed. Russ Castronovo; *Jim Crow, Literature, and the Legacy of Sutton E. Griggs* (2013), eds. Tess Chakkalakal and Kenneth W. Warren; and *The Cambridge Companion to Slavery in American Literature* (2016), ed. Ezra Tawil.

My warm thanks to Ray Ryan, my wonderfully supportive editor at Cambridge University Press, for inviting me to do this book and offering helpful advice along the way. For her assistance with the manuscript, I'm also grateful to Sharon McCann. My thanks as well to Edgar Mendez; to my project manager at Integra, Anubam Vijayakrishnan; to my skillful copyeditor Plaegian Alexander; and to my indexer, Robert Swanson (Arc Indexing).

I dedicate this book to Nina Baym, whose work I've been learning from and admiring since my graduate-student years. Whether writing on Hawthorne or women writers, Nina taught me and many others to pay close attention to literary form and historical context, while resisting historical reductionism. Nina also became my mentor, coeditor, and friend as we worked together on *The Norton Anthology of American Literature*. I couldn't have had a kinder or more knowledgeable guide to American literary history. Her scholarship continues to instruct and inspire.

I also dedicate this book to my mother, the late Joan Levine, whose love made so much possible.

Introduction

In the mid-1980s, during an excursion to Harvard Square, I visited my favorite used bookstore and stumbled across a first edition of Harriet Beecher Stowe's *Dred: A Tale of the Great Dismal Swamp*. Published in two volumes in 1856, *Dred*, I was later to learn, was Stowe's second antislavery novel. At the time I hadn't heard of the novel, and I suspect the owners of the used bookstore were similarly in the dark about Stowe's post–*Uncle Tom's Cabin* career, for the two pristine volumes (which I've long since marked up) were priced at ten dollars, which was cheap even back then.

I bought the books, and when I returned to Maryland I put them in my "to-read" pile and for a while didn't give them a second thought. But a few years later, while doing research on Frederick Douglass for a book on temperance and nineteenth-century American literature, I found amidst Douglass's temperance writings in *Frederick Douglass' Paper* a number of columns celebrating *Uncle Tom's Cabin*. I had been taught that black writers were always at odds with – or "signifying" on – white writers, so I was intrigued by Douglass's enthusiastic response to a novel that James Baldwin and other twentieth-century African American writers so disdained.[1] While reading Douglass's newspaper on microfilm, I also found a number of letters and essays by Martin Delany, who had unflattering things to say about Stowe and Douglass. Who was Martin Delany? And would *Dred* help me to better understand the relationships among Douglass, Stowe, and Delany?

I finally cracked open my volumes of *Dred* and immediately noticed how different the novel was from *Uncle Tom's Cabin*, particularly in its conception of race. In *Uncle Tom's Cabin*, Stowe, working as a romantic racialist, presents dark-skinned blacks as domestic and nonviolent, but in *Dred* the eponymous dark-skinned revolutionary hero is prepared to kill for black freedom. In her second antislavery novel, Stowe also turns against the African colonizationist ending of *Uncle Tom's Cabin*. Instead, she

I

depicts fugitive slaves who choose to emigrate to Canada or escape to New York City, where they find a new home. Did Stowe, a subscriber to *Frederick Douglass' Paper*, conceive of her second antislavery novel partly in response to the criticism of the colonizationist ending of *Uncle Tom's Cabin* voiced by Delany and Douglass in that newspaper? And did Delany's serialized novel of black revolutionary conspiracy, *Blake* (1859, 1861–62), set in the United States, Canada, Africa, and Cuba, emerge partly in response to his reading of Stowe's antislavery novels, which, while mainly set in the United States, had sections set in Africa and Canada? My attempt to answer the questions that emerged from buying a used copy of a Stowe novel soon led to the abandonment of my temperance project and the decision to begin a new one that addressed, among other things, race and transnationalism in Douglass, Delany, and Stowe.[2]

I rehearse this narrative of the scholarly journey to my second book, *Martin Delany, Frederick Douglass, and the Politics of Representative Identity* (1997), as a way of considering the dramatic changes that took place in the field of nineteenth-century American literary studies from the mid-1980s to the 1990s. These changes had a decisive impact on my research agenda and those of many other Americanists. To be sure, as I discuss in Chapter 1, significant work on race and American literary studies had been published before the 1980s, and the field had changed as a result of the Civil Rights and women's movements (which had a role in revitalizing Stowe studies).[3] But even with the increased interest in race and gender, many of us were still working to reproduce the literary-nationalist exceptionalism that helped to create the field of American literature studies in the first place. Perhaps I'm overstating the influence of F. O. Matthiessen-inflected antebellum American literary studies, but the fact is that graduate education in nineteenth-century American literature during the 1970s and early 1980s meant reading Matthiessen, Richard Chase, R. W. B. Lewis, Leo Marx, and many others (all very much worth our continued attention) who did their major work well before the 1970s. My own first book, *Conspiracy and Romance* (1989), which I began in the late 1970s, certainly addressed race and transnationalism by examining Charles Brockden Brown, James Fenimore Cooper, Nathaniel Hawthorne, and Herman Melville in relation to such discursive contexts as international freemasonry, European revolutions of the 1830s, transatlantic socialism, and slave revolts at sea.[4] But the book was inspired by a desire to revise and enlarge Chase's notion of the American romance, not to dislodge and move beyond it. My debt to Chase's *The American Novel and Its Tradition* (1957) remained central to my initial ambition to follow up with a book on temperance and nineteenth-century American literature. But as critics in the field began to ask new questions, I did, too.

The 1980s was a time of critical ferment. I want to highlight three developments from the mid-1980s to the early 1990s that had an especially large impact on nineteenth-century American literary studies. First, the New Historicism that had become so central to early modern studies quickly migrated to American literature studies. The trajectory running from Sacvan Bercovitch's 1978 *The American Jeremiad*, one of the most influential Americanist works of the 1970s, to Walter Benn Michaels's 1987 *The Gold Standard and the Logic of Naturalism*, one of the most influential Americanist works of the 1980s, reveals a field that was moving away from a concern with "Americanness" (and its reproduction) in order to explore the enmeshment of literature in economic and other social and cultural discourses.[5] The New Historicism brought scholars back to the archives to assess literature not as a transcendent category but as a discourse in a world of interconnected discourses. When I finally got around to reading *Dred*, I had no inclination to try to fit the novel into a master narrative of nineteenth-century American literature, hermetically understood. Instead, partly under the sway of the New Historicism, I was interested in reading the novel synchronically in relation to an archive of contemporaneous discourses about slavery and race. That archive included the writings of Douglass and Delany.

A second key development in the field from the mid-1980s to the early 1990s was that race theory, slavery studies, and African American studies came into their own. Especially influential were the essays on race in special issues of *Critical Inquiry* published in 1985 and 1986 and then brought out as a book, *"Race," Writing, and Difference* (1986), edited by Henry Louis Gates Jr. This collection included work by Gates, Anthony Appiah, Hazel V. Carby, and Houston A. Baker Jr., critics who over the next several decades would be among the scholarly leaders in the study of race, slavery, and African American and African diasporic literature. Gates's collection had an immediate impact on the field, teaching us that "race" itself was a contested term that could and should play an important role in literary and cultural interpretation. If race, as the volume's authors contended, was a rhetorically constructed category, one of the challenges facing literary critics was to better understand how race came to inform literary production at particular historical moments. Dana D. Nelson addressed precisely these questions in *The Word in Black and White: Reading "Race" in American Literature, 1638–1867* (1992), and Eric J. Sundquist followed with his landmark *To Wake the Nations: Race in the Making of American Literature* (1993).[6]

Nelson's and Sundquist's books emerged not only from new developments in race theory but also from compelling work on slavery and African American literature. William Andrews's 1986 book on the slave narrative, *To Tell a Free Story*, brought African American literature more to the center of American literary studies, and slavery moved from background to foreground in many literary analyses. Drawing on developments in the New Historicism, critical race theory, and the ever more sophisticated scholarship on slavery coming out of history departments, Deborah McDowell and Arnold Rampersad's coedited book *Slavery and the Literary Imagination* (1989) threw down the gauntlet and challenged Americanists of all period specializations to consider the relationship of slavery to the nation's literary history. The volume included Hortense Spillers's tour de force "Changing the Letter," which put Stowe and the contemporary writer Ishmael Reed into conversation.[7] Taking in these critical developments as I thought about Stowe in conversation with Douglass and Delany, I began to ask why Stowe changed her views on race from the 1852 *Uncle Tom's Cabin* to the 1856 *Dred*, what were the consequences of such a shift for the form and conception of her second antislavery novel, and how her antislavery novels responded to African American writing of the period.

One way I addressed such questions was to learn about racial representation and the history of the antislavery movement through archival and secondary research. Another way was to read Stowe in relation to Douglass, Delany, and other antebellum black writers. I felt encouraged in such a comparative approach by Toni Morrison's reflections on race and American literature, which, of all of the critical work I encountered during the 1980s and early 1990s, had perhaps the greatest impact on my own scholarship. I discuss Morrison in Chapter 1, so I'll be relatively brief here. In her 1989 lecture/essay, "Unspeakable Things Unspoken: The Afro-American Presence in American Literature," and her short, powerful 1992 book, *Playing in the Dark: Whiteness and the Literary Imagination*, Morrison called for a complete rethinking of the American literary tradition, starting with how scholars typically approach the canonical writings of white authors. Those writings, she argued, were "haunted" by the "dark and abiding presence" of African Americans – as slaves, free people, and writers – and thus needed to be considered differently from the ahistorical US romance tradition established by Richard Chase. For Chase, who emphasized the centrality of allegory and melodrama to the American novel, "blackness" signified something like evil or the sublime.[8] But for

Morrison, blackness in US writings had much, if not everything, to do with slavery and race, which she claimed white writers typically sought to evade, but in ways that contributed to their art. Morrison's argument was thus both political and aesthetic, for she maintained that the black presence had a shaping impact on American authors and was a crucial constituent of their writing. Among the many aspects of Morrison's work that I admired at the time, and continue to admire, was her dismantling of the idea of distinct white and black literary traditions. I also appreciated that Morrison didn't mandate a particular method for reading white and black texts together. She trusted critics to develop their own methods for doing so.

Morrison's work inspired Henry Wonham's edited collection, *Criticism and the Color Line: Desegregating American Literary Studies* (1996), which included Shelley Fisher Fishkin's wide-ranging essay "Interrogating 'Whiteness,' Complicating 'Blackness': Remapping American Culture." Morrison, Fishkin, and other critics of the time helped to shape my efforts to read Stowe's *Dred* through the lens of race and African American culture. Because Stowe's novel is about slavery and features black characters, it is not exactly "haunted" by blackness; it directly addresses slavery and race. But exploring cross-influences among Stowe, Douglass, and Delany allowed me to see what Morrison termed the racial "miscegenation" at the heart of American literary history. Morrison's call to read canonical white authors in relation to the African American presence eventually led to my coedited collection *Frederick Douglass and Herman Melville: Essays in Relation* (2008).[9] Her influence can also be seen in the essays in this volume (Chapters 5, 9, and 10 in particular) that read white and black writers together in national and transnational contexts.

This discussion brings me to a third critical development from the 1980s to the early 1990s: the increasing importance of transnationalism to nineteenth-century American literary studies. Again, this development was not entirely new to this critical moment, as Americanists had long been interested in studying connections between British and American literature, though typically with an emphasis on what makes US literature distinctively different from British literature. But as slavery and race emerged as central concerns of nineteenth-century American literature studies, the British-US dyad came to seem limited. It seemed particularly limited with respect to black writers, who, because of their historical and genealogical ties to the international slave trade, inevitably had a complicated relationship to US or British nationalism. Recognizing the need for a critical paradigm that would address these complications, Paul Gilroy, in

The Black Atlantic (1993), developed a provocative revisionary perspective on the transnational dimension of black writing, arguing that "different nationalist paradigms for thinking about cultural history fail when confronted by the intercultural and transnational formation" that he termed "the black Atlantic." For Gilroy, the Middle Passage and the triangular slave trade demanded a new way of thinking about the place of Europe, the United States, Africa, and the Caribbean in black writing. *The Black Atlantic* vitalized African American and African diasporic studies, and it contributed, as well, to the development of oceanic studies. At the time of its publication, the book supplied fresh tools for working on Delany, to whom Gilroy devoted a major section. As he elaborated in *The Black Atlantic*, Delany doesn't fit easily into US nationalist paradigms. His travels between the United States, Canada, Central America, England, and Africa reveal a man in motion who is perhaps best understood through transcultural, international formations. Gilroy's insights were crucial for my reading of Delany's *Blake* in relation to Stowe's *Dred*, as he helped me to better understand not only Delany's but also Stowe's transnational orientations. His work has remained crucial to much scholarship on African diasporic studies, and it informs my discussion of the circulatory routes of Nathaniel Paul's black nationalism in Chapter 3, below.[10]

Equally influential on the transnational turn in American literary studies was the publication, also in 1993, of Amy Kaplan and Donald E. Pease's edited collection, *Cultures of United States Imperialism*. Gilroy forcefully linked black writing to diasporic histories which were inevitably tied to British, French, and US colonialism and imperialism. Kaplan and Pease's collection addressed these and other contexts, stimulating new interest in US literature's international engagements. Their collection made clear that imperialism had long been part of the national project and that the nation's literature was often implicated. As I discuss in Chapter 9, one of the most popular stories in American literary history, Edward Everett Hale's "The Man without a Country" (1863), was regularly adduced by Hale and others to support US imperialism and expansionism. Numerous essays in Kaplan and Pease's collection also demonstrated how central race was to the imperialist imagination; their collection included essays on imperialism in white and black culture. *Cultures of United States Imperialism* and Kaplan's later *The Anarchy of Empire in the Making of U.S. Culture* (2002) gave rise to a new emphasis on imperialism in nineteenth-century American literary studies, which has been eye-opening but at times has risked its own form of exceptionalism (the United States as *the* imperialistic nation). That said, imperialism as a topic for literary investigation soon became important to my own work in nineteenth-century American literary studies; I engage the topic in *Dislocating Race and Nation* (2008) and in several essays in this volume (see Chapters 2, 7, 8, and 9).[11]

In 1993, Gilroy, along with Kaplan and Pease, suggested the potential of transnational American studies for developing new frames of analysis in larger geographical contexts. That potential was highlighted by Carolyn Porter's provocative review-essay of 1994, "What We Know That We Don't Know: Remapping American Literary Studies," which addressed José David Saldívar's *The Dialectics of Our America* (1991) and other works on the literatures of the Americas. Stirred by the hemispheric vision central to such scholarship, Porter declared that it was imperative for Americanists to "rupture the nationalist myths" in order to create a "field reconstellated by a historical politics of location."[12] There was a flurry of work from the mid-1990s into the twenty-first century that reconceived American literary studies in relation to the Americas, Europe, and Africa.[13] Certainly one of the significant consequences of the transnational turn for Americanists, who had long thought of US literature mainly in relation to the nation-state, has been a rethinking of scale. Porter's essay, for instance, celebrated and further prompted work on hemispheric studies; my coedited *Hemispheric American Studies* (2008) owed much to Porter's instigations. Hemispheric studies, transatlanticism, globalization, and concerns about the planet (which I take up in Chapter 4 of this volume), along with the recent interest in temporality, provided new critical frames for Americanists,[14] while raising some nagging questions: What about the local? And what happens when US literary studies is reframed in relation to larger geographical contexts? Does the United States remain at the center, and, if so, have we really moved beyond exceptionalism?

Given the sometimes excessive enthusiasm for transnational approaches,[15] it is not surprising that skeptics have recently emerged to tell us that transnational American literary studies continues to do what American literary studies has always done: assume or advance US exceptionalism. For instance, in an acerbic essay titled "On the Redundancy of 'Transnational American Studies,'" Jared Hickman asserts that the very term "transnational American studies" "is a logically incoherent formulation" because the idea of American nationality at the nation's founding, according to Thomas Paine and others, was precisely its status as "the first trans-nation." Thus Hickman maintains that "American studies' transnational turn is not merely mimetic of contemporary US hegemony but a profound and predictable return to the very wellspring of American exceptionalism – the Enlightenment localization of the universal in America." Equally acerbic is Winfried Fluck, who asserts that the "forms of transnationalism that are currently dominant in American studies are not a new beginning." Thus he questions what many see as one of the more positive developments of transnational study: the field's fuller engagement with African American and other minority writings. Convinced that current modes of such engagement are symptomatic of "the American rhetoric of consensus," Fluck concludes that the new transnationalism ultimately perpetuates the old way of doing American literary studies. As he chidingly puts it: "What American revisionists do not want to acknowledge . . . is the crucial role ethnicity and minorities have played in redefining and thereby reviving American exceptionalism."[16]

How odd that efforts to broaden American literary studies could be seen as falling into the exceptionalist trap! As I sketched out at the beginning of this introduction, American literary studies from the 1940s to the early 1980s was all too often about reproducing the terms of the field as established by mid-century Americanists, and at least one of those terms was an American distinctiveness that had virtually nothing to do with racial diversity and the history of slavery. Taking a longer view of the *practice* of American literary studies, which for most of the twentieth century had nothing to do with a Paine-like devotion to the trans-nation, I would suggest that newly prevalent forms of transnational analysis (hemispheric, transatlantic, diasporic, global) have done precisely what Carolyn Porter called for in 1994: helped us to become more aware of what we know we don't know about nineteenth-century American literature. In this sense, transnationalism is at least in part about epistemology. As Yogita Goyal has recently remarked, "[T]here is nothing intrinsically radical or complicit about a transnational turn"; instead, it offers "an occasion for examination and critique."[17] In this formulation, transnationalism is less a specific method than a heuristic that presses us to continue the work of trying to understand the nation in all of its complexity, at least in part by exploring intertwined histories of slavery, race, and the nation from a variety of locations and perspectives.

Recent critical work has played a large role in these revisionary analyses. But as I suggest in all of the chapters of *Race, Transnationalism, and Nineteenth-Century American Literary Studies*, nineteenth-century writers themselves bring various national and transnational perspectives to their work. Attending to their perspectives allows us to see more clearly the complexity of their approaches to race and nation, for their vision was invariably *not* hermetically national. Cooper, Hawthorne, Nathaniel Paul, Melville, María Amparo Ruiz de Burton, and a number of other nine-teenth-century authors looked well beyond the nation or considered the nation in sometimes overlapping geographical contexts. Even as I draw on a range of critical approaches, I emphasize the need to take fuller account of nineteenth-century authors' representational strategies and insights. We still have much to learn about nineteenth-century American literary history, and one of our most neglected resources, I argue in the book's opening chapter, are the canonical authors themselves.

The chapters that follow take a variety of approaches to race and transnationalism and have been shaped in part by the critical developments that I've been describing. Most of the chapters draw on previously published essays, which have been significantly revised, updated, and in some cases expanded in order to respond to issues that have come up since their initial publication. For instance, Chapter 8, on "antebellum Rome" and *The Marble Faun*, a version of which was first published in 1990, contains new material on transatlanticism and race, and from beginning to end addresses post-1990s criticism on Hawthorne. Because most of the chapters emerged from essays published over a long period of time, the book does not seek to develop one large (overdetermined) argument. Winfried Fluck, in the same essay warning Americanist revisionists about the danger of reviving American exceptionalism, remarks on the value of monographs on American literary history in which the "organizing principles seem to rest on primarily practical considerations and remain, theoretically speaking, relatively arbitrary."[18] In some respects, *Race, Transnationalism, and Nineteenth-Century American Literary Studies* is that sort of book. It's "practical" insofar as it addresses critical problems staked out less in this introduction than in each chapter's opening interpretive frame. The book can be regarded as a selective guide to conversations about race, transnationalism, and American literary studies over the past few decades, as well as a critical work on these topics. Or it may be best to view it as a casebook, by which I mean that each chapter poses a critical question and then attempts to model ways of building an argument from literary and historical evidence.

As heterogeneous or even "arbitrary" as these chapters may seem, several key issues provide a through-line to the volume: interracialism, tensions between nationalism and transnationalism (or the local and the global), book history, literary form, the complicated and shifting nature of race, and the importance of close reading. An interest in authorial agency or intention may be unfashionable, but I emphasize authorial perspectives in many of the chapters, whether I'm analyzing Cooper's views on race and empire (Chapter 2) or slave narrators' efforts to situate themselves in relation to an American revolutionary tradition (Chapter 5). The writers I discuss in this book typically know what they're doing; they have a deep understanding of their culture, and they have much to teach readers about the nineteenth century and beyond.[19] At this point it is hardly revolutionary to say that Melville can illuminate the topics of race and transnationalism, but it is somewhat revolutionary to say the same about Cooper (as I do in Chapters 1 and 2). Nathaniel Paul helped to establish the terms of black nationalism (Chapter 3); Poe and Hawthorne anticipated some of our current concerns about climate change (Chapter 4); William Wells Brown examined connections between race and corporeality (Chapter 6); Melville engaged transnational aesthetics in his "minor" novel *Israel Potter* (Chapter 7); Hawthorne, as I've said, addressed transatlanticism in ways that anticipate today's critical interest in the subject (Chapter 8); and Edward Everett Hale and Sutton Griggs explored interconnections among citizenship, race, nation, and the oceanic (Chapter 9).

I begin *Race, Transnationalism, and Nineteenth-Century American Literary Studies* with a theoretical chapter on Toni Morrison, race, canonicity, authorial knowledge, and reading. The issues raised in that chapter recur throughout the book, and in effect frame the volume. The subsequent chapters are arranged in a loose chronological order based on the publication dates of the works under consideration. At a critical moment in which chronology, periodization, and historical contextualization are under suspicion,[20] I continue to see value in literary-historical analyses that take account of continuities and differences and tell stories over time. Perhaps the most compelling story that unfolds across the ten chapters that follow is of the nation's failure over one hundred years to live up to its egalitarian revolutionary ideals. This is a story told in various ways by white and black writers alike, by such figures as Paul, writers of slave narratives, Brown, Melville, and Griggs. There are apprehensions running from Cooper to Hale about the contingency and vulnerability of the nation, and even about the end of humankind (see Chapter 4). The book also tells a story about geographical scale, but that particular story doesn't have a clear beginning, middle, and end. Still, it's worth noting that all of the authors discussed in this volume, however local their concerns, looked beyond the nation in their writings. Mid-twentieth-century critics of US literature may have developed an exceptionalist vision of that literature, but it's difficult to find a corresponding exceptionalism in most nineteenth-century US writers.

Race, Transnationalism, and Nineteenth-Century American Literary Studies concludes with a chapter on Douglass in fiction from Stowe to James McBride, and thus takes us full circle from my opening reflections on *Dred*, a novel that Douglass helped to inspire. One of the large goals of this final chapter is to develop the argument, which is implicit in most of the other chapters, that writers are to some extent literary critics and theorists.[21] Stowe and Douglass learned from one another, and not just as literary artists: they learned as they engaged each other's critical perspectives. I discuss María Amparo Ruiz de Burton and Sutton Griggs as literary critics of Douglass (both had problems with his writings). But the chapter mainly looks at post-1960s novelists, such as John Updike, Chimamanda Ngozi Adichie, and Russell Banks, whom I approach not just as novelists but as critics who engage race and transnationalism. These novelists join another novelist, Toni Morrison, in helping us to better understand race in US history and literature. And they do so by exploring and interrogating Douglass, one of the nation's most profound thinkers on race and transnationalism. The chapter shows how writers as critics have continued to learn from Douglass, even as they sometimes challenge him. We could use more such dialectical exchanges between critics and nineteenth-century American writers; such dialogues would contribute to the ongoing recovery of aesthetics in nineteenth-century American literary studies.[22] As I suggest in Chapter 1, Toni Morrison's work on race and classic American writers offers one possible path in that direction.

CHAPTER I

Reading Slavery and Race in "Classic" American Literature

During the 1980s and 1990s, Henry Louis Gates Jr., Houston Baker, Frances Foster, Paul Gilroy, William Andrews, Carla Peterson, and a number of other critics helped to bring slavery and race to the forefront of American literary studies. Toni Morrison's "Unspeakable Things Unspoken: The Afro-American Presence in American Literature" (1989) was especially influential. In that essay, she laid the groundwork for a new way of reading canonical white authors, arguing that slavery and race were haunting presences in their writings. This chapter pays homage to Morrison's critical vision while raising questions about her notion of haunting.

In his influential *Main Currents in American Thought* (1927), the progressive critic Vernon L. Parrington explored the impact of the debate on slavery on major writers of the nineteenth century, devoting full chapters to the antislavery writings of William Lloyd Garrison, John Greenleaf Whittier, and Harriet Beecher Stowe, and even discussing the proslavery writings of Nathaniel Beverley Tucker, John Pendleton Kennedy, and John C. Calhoun.[1] But by the mid-twentieth century, slavery as a topic for critical inquiry had for the most part vanished from American literary studies. Perhaps Americanists working during the heyday of the New Criticism didn't want to taint the literary with the political, or perhaps Americanists committed to the consensus politics of the Cold War era didn't want to address an appalling aspect of the nation's history. Whatever the reason, the major critics who helped to shape the field of American literary studies had little to say about slavery. The word "slavery" does not even appear in the index of such foundational works as F. O. Matthiessen's *American Renaissance* (1941), R. W. B. Lewis's *The American Adam: Innocence, Tragedy, and Tradition in the Nineteenth Century* (1955), and Richard Chase's *The American Novel and Its Tradition* (1957).

The Civil Rights Movement brought fresh attention to the study of slavery and American literature, along with the recovery of such writers as

Frederick Douglass, Stowe, and William Wells Brown. Still, it wasn't immediately clear that antislavery writers were worthy of being read alongside such canonical writers as Emerson, Melville, and Whitman. In the most popular American literary anthology of the 1970s, Cleanth Brooks and R. W. B. Lewis's *American Literature: The Makers and the Making* (1973), for instance, Douglass and other "political" writers were relegated to the margins in the anthology's strangely titled section "Literature of the Nonliterary World."[2] Well into the 1980s, African American writers in particular continued to be regarded as having little relation to the great tradition of "classic" American literature. The same could be said for white antislavery writers, including Stowe. Given the field's reluctance to wrestle with slavery as Parrington had wrestled with the topic during the 1920s, there was a need for a provocateur who could generate fresh critical perspectives. That is precisely the burden that Toni Morrison took up in "Unspeakable Things Unspoken: The Afro-American Presence in American Literature" (1989) and *Playing in the Dark: Whiteness and the Literary Imagination* (1992). Influenced by race theorists such as Henry Louis Gates Jr., Morrison's reflections on slavery and race in American literary history helped to inspire much new work on these interrelated topics, to some extent dismantling the idea of distinct and hermetic black and white literary traditions. Morrison's critical intervention was highly salutary, but she encouraged a way of reading the classic white writers of the nineteenth century that is in need of reconsideration.

Morrison's central insight is that race, or blackness, is a haunting presence and fundamental constituent of canonical American writings of the nineteenth century. In "Unspeakable Things Unspoken," she focuses on textual silences and evasions in white-authored literary texts as symptomatic of what she calls "the nineteenth-century flight from blackness." She argues, on the one hand, that "the presence of Afro-Americans has shaped the choices, the language, the structure – the meaning of so much American literature," and, on the other, that there is scant evidence of this engagement on the surface of most classic American texts of the nineteenth century. While Richard Chase and others had used melodramatic terms to describe American literary romance (or fiction) as engaged with a metaphysics of blackness (evil), Morrison asks of the form: "Where, I wonder, in these romances is the shadow of the presence from which the text has fled?" Similarly, she asks of both the nineteenth-century American authors who putatively fled the black presence and the critics who reproduced their flight: "What intellectual feats had to be performed by the author or his critic to erase me from a society seething with my presence?" In *Playing in the Dark*, Morrison talks more pointedly about slavery itself, arguing that "Black slavery enriched the country's creative possibilities. For in that construction of blackness *and* enslavement could be found not only the not-free but also, with the dramatic polarity created by skin color, the projection of the not-me." Ideas about freedom, in other words, gained their currency precisely because of the practice of slavery. Even such dominant themes in canonical American literature as "individualism, masculinity, social engagement versus historical isolation; acute and ambiguous moral problematics; [and] the thematics of innocence coupled with an obsession with figurations of death and hell," Morrison contends, took shape in relation to that which cannot be seen with any great clarity in the works themselves: "a dark, abiding, ... Africanist presence."[3]

But did slavery as a social practice and subject for debate truly "haunt" American literature, or was it right there out in the open as a primary concern of nineteenth-century American literary culture? Well before Toni Morrison's critical interventions, Vincent Freimarck and Bernard Rosenthal published a landmark anthology on the subject, *Race and the American Romantics* (1971), which offered a selection of writings on slavery by James Fenimore Cooper, William Cullen Bryant, Poe, Hawthorne, Melville, Thoreau, Whittier, James Russell Lowell, and Whitman. From Freimarck and Rosenthal's perspective, the problem with these classic writers wasn't evasion or repression as much as bad politics. Freimarck and Rosenthal lament that "writers such as Melville, Hawthorne, Whitman, and Poe, to name the most conspicuous examples, declined to use their literary art as a polemical instrument against slavery." Working on the assumption that these writers *should* have acted as polemicists, the editors speculate (or pronounce) on why they failed to do so: "The explanation, unpleasant as it will prove to those who prefer their Romantics on the side of the angels, is that, at best, in a surprising number of cases no passionate antipathy against slavery existed among the American Romantics. At worst, they were racists."[4] Such sweeping claims bring with them the risks of reductionism. Arguably, some of these writers were racialist, which is different from being racist. Or it may be that Melville and others resisted polemics so that they could address slavery and race in the complex ways of a literary artist. Recognizing that connections between aesthetics and politics are not always straightforward, Morrison makes the case for capacious reading practices that are not simply about rendering political and moral judgments. She states, for example, that her "deliberations are not about a particular author's attitudes towards race" or about authors' political positions, but instead about how the artistic strengths of a number of classic American writers can be understood in relation to the presence of slavery in the culture.[5]

In the remaining pages of this chapter, which will focus on four canonical works – Cooper's *The Last of the Mohicans* (1826), Poe's *The Narrative of Arthur Gordon Pym* (1838), Melville's *Benito Cereno* (1855), and Hawthorne's *The House of the Seven Gables* (1851) – I want to engage Morrison's approach to classic American writers of the nineteenth century with the help of what the critical theorists Stephen Best and Sharon Marcus have termed "surface reading." As opposed to "symptomatic reading," which they describe as "an interpretive method that argues that the most interesting aspect of a text is what it represses" (such as what Morrison calls the haunting presence of slavery and race), they advocate a reading practice that pays attention to verbal surfaces, "what is evident, perceptible, apprehensible in texts; what is neither hidden nor hiding." Though their approach might sound like an under-graduate's dream vision of literary analysis – no more interpretation! no more critical theory! (because everything can be discerned on the surface) – there is a sophisticated argument about reading at work here that has significant implications for taking account of slavery in nineteenth-century American literary texts. In the strongest possible terms, Best and Marcus insist on the importance of reading what's on the page – verbally and formally – instead of trying to figure out what a text represses or is haunted by. They take as their starting point that texts have their own agency and knowledge, that texts, as they put it, "can reveal their own truths because texts mediate themselves." Moreover, they maintain that critics are not necessarily more free or insightful than the writers they are examining. Thus they resist the sort of morally judgmental criticism exemplified by Freimarck and Rosenthal and many other race and slavery critics to follow. Their embrace of "surface reading" means "accepting texts, deferring to them instead of mastering or using them as objects." To be sure, their championing of surface reading has not been without controversy. What does it mean to focus on surfaces, and what exactly is a "surface"? Are textual meanings always found on "surfaces," as Best and Marcus suggest? And should we abandon ideological criticism? While I share Best and Marcus's interest in close reading, I remain suspicious of surface reading as a new master paradigm for American literary studies. Still, as I hope to elaborate, such an approach, which complements what Best and Marcus might term Morrison's "depth model of truth," can help to illuminate even further the centrality of slavery and race to classic writings of the nineteenth century.[6] Nineteenth-century American writers may have been even more knowing and canny about these topics than Morrison and others have hitherto acknowledged.

Consider the frontier novels of James Fenimore Cooper. It is well known that Cooper spoke out against slavery during the 1820s and 1830s, remarking even in his conservative tract *The American Democrat* (1838) that it is "an impolitic and vicious institution" that threatens to lead to a "war of extermination" between the races. Like Thomas Jefferson in *Notes on the State of Virginia* (1785), who worried over blacks' desires for the "extirpation" of the whites who had enslaved them, Cooper's concern about the potential for such violence conveys his recognition of blacks' essential humanity.[7] Given Cooper's critical remarks on slavery in both his earlier nonfiction work, *Notions of the Americans* (1828) and *The American Democrat*, and given the importance of slavery to the debates on the Missouri Compromise of 1821, one would imagine that slavery would have an important place in his writings about the frontier. In the manner of Toni Morrison, Ezra Tawil suggests that slavery is "a significant absence – what we might call an eloquent silence," in the frontier romances of the period, including Cooper's; and he ingeniously argues that Cooper and other frontier writers of the time "offered a powerful way of transcoding the crisis of antebellum slavery into fictional narratives of frontier violence." Thus Cooper and his contemporaries could engage "the same issues central to the slavery debate," such as conflicts over property and matters of "racial descent," without seeming to be addressing slavery, even as slavery remained one of the driving forces behind their writing.[8]

And yet slavery is right on the surface of the most canonical novel of the Leatherstocking series, *The Last of the Mohicans* (1826), where there is no transcoding at all. In a key scene at the center of a novel set right around 1760, the Virginian Duncan Heyward declares to the Scotsman Colonel Munro his interest in marrying Munro's younger daughter, Alice. He makes this declaration at the embattled Fort Henry in the northern region of New York, which at the time of the marriage discussion is surrounded both by French troops under Montcalm's command and Iroquois Indians loyal to Magua. There is something highly improbable and theatrical about the conversation, though its geopolitical significance, taking place as it does during the French and Indian War, soon becomes apparent. Dismayed that Heyward is not interested in marrying Cora, his older daughter, Munro provides a genealogical history of both daughters, which dramatically brings slavery in the Americas to the forefront of the novel. Munro tells Duncan that after his initial marriage plans were thwarted by his beloved's father, who was concerned about his lack of wealth, Munro "departed the country" as a military man in the service of the king. His subsequent remarks are worth quoting in full:

> "[D]uty called me to the islands of West Indies. There it was my lot to form a connexion with one who in time became my wife, and the mother of Cora.

She was the daughter of a gentleman of those isles, by a lady, whose misfortune it was, if you will, ... to be descended, remotely, from that unfortunate class, who are so basely enslaved to administer to the wants of a luxurious people! Ay, sir, that is a curse entailed on Scotland, by her unnatural union with a foreign and trading people."[9]

This is a rich moment in *The Last of the Mohicans* and the larger Leatherstocking series. Through Munro's personal history, Cooper makes clear that the contention between Great Britain and France central to the novel's depiction of warfare in New York is part of a larger contention in the Americas between these two great European powers. (France, too, had colonies in the West Indies.) He also makes clear how pervasive slavery is in the Americas, while using the Scotsman Munro, who resents England's grab for empire, to speak out against its practice ("basely enslaved"). Munro's critique is bold and prescient, anticipating one of the main antislavery arguments of the Republican Party during the 1850s – that slavery, by undermining free labor, creates a luxurious aristocratic class.[10]

In his later *American Democrat*, Cooper addresses what he believes are the problems of racial "amalgamation," but in his most famous novel he creates a character who challenges the racism of his time. Concerned that Haywood prefers his younger daughter, Alice, because she is "white" (the daughter of his later marriage to his faithful true love), Munro pointedly asks the Southerner Heyward if he "scorn[s] to mingle the blood of the Heywards, with one so degraded – lovely and virtuous though she be?" Heyward responds, "Heaven protect me from a prejudice so unworthy of my reason," while at the same time thinking that, yes, he does feel some revulsion toward the woman of color, "as if it had been engrafted in his nature." The exchange somewhat contradictorily challenges racism while suggesting that an attraction to a person of one's own color or race is "natural." But Cooper's larger insight here is that given the practice of slavery in the Americas, the idea of racial purity (or the idea of the existence of people without a "cross") might best be taken as a fiction. Munro's account of an interracial Americas thus exposes the naïveté of the hero Natty Bumppo's famous and oft-stated assertion that he is a man whose whiteness (he seems to know for certain) is "without a cross."[11] (I will have more to say about Natty Bumppo and race in my discussion of *The Deerslayer* [1841] in Chapter 2.)

The presentation of slavery and race at this climactic moment in *The Last of the Mohicans* has important ramifications for thinking about European colonialism in the Americas. In *Mohicans*, the North American Indians are linked to the blacks of the West Indies through their shared subjugation to European powers. Cooper underscores those linkages by presenting two of the central Indian characters of the novel – Magua and Uncas – as attracted to the "black" Cora and by depicting the mostly sympathetic Munro as willing to discipline those under his authority in the way of a slave master. Magua describes how he was cruelly flogged by Munro after succumbing to the alcohol that the British had encouraged him to drink. He asks Munro's two daughters (who at the time are his prisoners): "[I]s it justice to make evil, and then punish for it!" He then tells his captives what happened when he was discovered drunk: "The Huron chief was tied up before all the pale-faced warriors, and whipped like a dog." This whipping produces "marks on the back of the Huron chief" similar to the marks left on the backs of flagellated slaves. Though the narrator later refers to Magua's "fancied wrongs," Magua's critique of the British colonizers is consistent with Natty's Indian friend Chingachgook's similar critique of how the Dutch colonizers (known as slave traders) "gave my people the fire-water."[12] True, there is some transcoding of slavery in the Leatherstocking novels, but overall, and in ways that are meant to be troubling, slavery and colonialism are presented as entwined and absolutely central to the nation's history and future development.

In *The Last of the Mohicans*, both Magua and Chingachgook express their anger at the white fathers. In Edgar Allan Poe's *The Narrative of Arthur Gordon Pym* (1838), characters express their anger at white fathers from the beginning to the end of the novel. In this context, it is odd that many critics regard *Pym* as proslavery, though perhaps not so odd if we accept the view, championed by the critic John Carlos Rowe, that Poe was "a proslavery Southerner" whose racist proslavery politics "should be reassessed as such in whatever approach we take to his life and writings."[13] To be sure, it is not difficult to find racist imagery in Poe's writings, though as Freimarck and Rosenthal observed decades ago, it's also not difficult to find racist imagery in the works of numerous other classic writers of the period. My concern, then, is that an over-determined conception of Poe as proslavery and racist will inevitably lead to what the critical theorists Best and Marcus term "symptomatic" readings, analyses that find exactly what they're seeking and avoid interpretive challenges posed by the literary text itself. In *Pym*, Poe, rather than upholding ideals of white supremacy, shows what happens to those who accept its a priori assumptions: they are revealed as bad readers.

The Narrative of Arthur Gordon Pym gains considerable force from its engagement with racial and slavery discourses of the time, but Poe hardly develops a proslavery allegory. As Maurice Lee observes, Pym himself can be thought of as a "fugitive slave."[14] The novel begins with Pym sneaking off twice against his family's wishes to take to sea, and making a particular point of defying his grandfather. Pym's friend Augustus rebels against his father, the captain of a whaler, by hiding Pym in the ship's hold. If slavery is about maintaining hierarchal and paternal authority, *Pym* seems invested in what Poe regularly portrays as the all-too-human desire to rebel against all forms of authority – the desire that Poe in his essays and fiction calls "perversity." The murderously mutinous crew on Augustus's father's ship, the *Grampus*, enacts in extreme Pym's and especially Augustus's own rebellious rage against the (white) fathers. Invoking the Nat Turner slave rebellion of 1831, Poe makes the leader of the mutiny the ship's black cook, who is described as "a perfect demon."[15] Unlike Nat Turner, however, who had others kill for him, the cook uses an axe to dispatch his victims. Poe may have put the black cook at the center of the rebellion in order to tap into the racial anxieties and reactionism spawned by the Turner conspiracy. But what emerges from all of the rebellions in the novel is a vision, again not unlike Jefferson's in *Notes on the State of Virginia*, of how asymmetric power relations (such as slavery) breed rage that can lead to frightening social violence. In its brutality and racial dynamics, the mutiny on the *Grampus* anticipates the novel's later rebellion by the black polar islanders called the Tsalalians against the crew of the British ship the *Jane Guy*. But whereas the rebellion on board the *Grampus* can be understood as the culmination of the rebellion against patriarchal authority initiated by the young white men of the novel's opening chapters, Poe presents the Tsalalian rebellion in the context of the white colonialism and domination over racial others central to the slave culture of the time. And he does this right on the surface of his fictional narrative.

With the late introduction of the *Jane Guy* of Liverpool, historically a center of England's slave trade, Poe supplies a good deal of information about Britain's global imperialism, providing the dates when the British "discovered" and took control of various islands in the Americas. Consistent with such a presentation, shortly after the *Jane Guy* arrives at Tsalal, the ship's captain Guy proposes to establish an enterprise using the Tsalalian islanders, whose "complexion [is] a jet black," to harvest the tasty sea slug *biche de mer* "in the hope of making a profitable speculation." The whites of the *Jane Guy* thus immediately seek to take bodily and economic control over the blacks on an island whose rocky ledges bear "a strong resemblance to cotton." Is the eventual Tsalalian rebellion against such presumptuous authority a proslavery warning about the need for vigilance over "savage" blacks, or yet another story, in a novel replete with such stories, about people choosing to resist patriarchal authority? Not only is the latter interpretation more in the spirit of the novel, but Poe enhances what can already read like an antislavery allegory by emphasizing how the whites of the *Jane Guy* woefully misjudge the blacks over whom they presume to take control. Quite simply, the whites who believe that the Tsalalians are happy to serve their interests are bad readers, not unlike proslavery Southerners who argue that blacks are happy as slaves.

By keeping the point of view fixed on the whites' perspectives, Poe exposes those who are surprised by the eventual Tsalalian plot as bad readers, too. Poe never presumes to get inside the Tsalalians' heads, but instead depicts the black islanders as acting to preserve themselves by luring the white crew into a ravine and then crushing them with the rocks that had initially been compared to cotton. Pym at this apocalyptic moment confesses to his own failure at reading the Tsalalians, remarking on his surprising realization that the "apparent kindness" of the black islanders (clearly a ruse) was "the result of a deeply-laid plan for our destruction, and that the islanders for whom we entertained such inordinate feelings of esteem were among the most barbarous, subtle, and bloodthirsty wretches that ever contaminated the face of the globe."[16] That "esteem" is completely paternalistic; and among the many ironies of this passage is the echo of Pym's earlier description of himself and the survivors of the *Grampus* choosing to slaughter and drink the blood of a fellow crew member in order to survive. Clearly, the most bloodthirsty characters in the novel are white.

In *The Narrative of Arthur Gordon Pym*, then, Poe draws the reader into the white racist colonialist point of view only to reveal its blind spots. The reader ends up learning either what the character Pym suggests – that the islanders are demonic – or what Pym is not quite willing to acknowledge: that the Tsalalians are like himself. The racism that is so central to the practice of slavery is what keeps Pym from seeing, and Poe's willingness to represent such blindness, and even to thematize that blindness as part of the reading process, helps to make *Pym* a sophisticated meditation on slavery rather than a proslavery tract posing as a fiction. Some read the enigmatic "Note" at the end of the novel, with its descriptions of chasms that seem to speak a language of binary opposition – "To be shady," "To be white" – as Poe's effort to offer a scriptural justification of slavery, particularly with the appearance in the novel's final paragraphs of an enigmatic "white figure" whose skin "was the perfect whiteness of snow."[17] But Poe offers little help on how to read these images. What we're left with is an emphasis on color polarities and conflict. Poe's representation of slavery and race in *Pym* has surprising similarities with Melville's *Benito Cereno*. Rather than being "haunted" by slavery and race, as Morrison suggests, Poe engages these topics head on.

Ever since the publication of Carolyn Karcher's *Shadow over the Promised Land: Slavery, Race, and Violence in Melville's America* (1980), Melville has been understood as an antislavery writer who challenged whites' antiblack racism. Indeed, Karcher presents Melville as one of the great antislavery voices of the nineteenth century. While I don't dispute the claim that antislavery thinking is important to Melville's writing, the fact is that Melville in his own time was not known as an antislavery writer. In part this has to do with the difficulty of his writing, which, in the manner of Emily Dickinson's poetry, often tells its truths slant. Though there are moments when Melville's antislavery sentiments are expressed relatively straightforwardly – such as his unambiguous denunciation of slavery in Vivenza (a version of the United States) in his allegorical novel *Mardi* (1849) and his criticism of the slave trade in the Liverpool section of *Redburn* (1850) – he more typically addresses slavery and race indirectly. In *Moby-Dick* (1851), published a year after the passage of the Compromise of 1850's Fugitive Slave Act, which required all Americans, North and South, to return runaway slaves to their masters, Melville chronicles a ship on a path to destruction. Is the *Pequod*, with its racially diverse crew members, Melville's figure for the American ship of state? Is Captain Ahab, the man obsessed with a white whale, an allegorical stand-in for Daniel Webster, the architect of the Fugitive Slave Law and the man obsessed with Union? When Ishmael asks in chapter 1 of the novel, "Who aint a slave?," is Melville indicating that his novel is fundamentally engaged with the problem of slavery in America? Or are the evocations of debates on slavery and race in American culture deployed in the service of Melville's larger philosophical meditations? The historian Greg Grandin remarks that Melville "tended to treat bondage as a metaphysical problem and freedom as an idea best suited to some inner realm of personal sovereignty," and thus could be elliptical and evasive about the actual politics of antislavery.[18] As Freimarck and Rosenthal lament, and as others have celebrated, Melville did not write antislavery polemics. But in his 1855 *Benito Cereno*, set for the most part off the coast of Chile in 1799, Melville focused directly on slavery in the Americas in a novella that, as is true for all of his work, is not without interpretive challenges or larger philosophical ambitions.

Even more than in Poe's *Pym*, there are tensions between surfaces and depths in *Benito Cereno*, which is to say that Melville's complex novella raises questions about the surface reading championed by Best and Marcus as well as the depth model championed by Morrison. In *Benito Cereno* we read about a white American sea captain who, like the whites in *Pym*, seems unable to conceive of blacks rebelling against white authority. Because he mainly responds to surfaces, Captain Delano of Massachusetts, who encounters the Spanish slave ship the *San Dominick* in Chilean sea waters, is unable to see that Babo and his fellow blacks have taken over the ship and are re-staging slavery as a way of maintaining their control. Unlike in Poe's *Pym*, however, which also deals with forms of cultural blindness, Melville does not work with a first-person narrator: he works with a third-person narrator who sometimes seems privy to Delano's thoughts, and sometimes not. And that narrator, from beginning to end, traffics in racial stereotypes that are not always easily linked to Delano. The narrator asserts, for example, that "the negro ... mak[es] the most pleasing body servant in the world; ... less a servant than a devoted companion"; that there is great "beauty" in the master-slave relationship; and, most famously, when Babo, the leader of the slave revolt, puts a razor to Delano's throat in order to keep him quiet, that "[t]here is something in the negro which, in a peculiar way, fits him for avocations about one's person. Most negroes are natural valets and hairdressers; taking to the comb and brush congenially as to the castanets." Given the narrator's use of such stereotypes, and given that the novella concludes with a friendly conversation between the two white sea captains after Delano puts down the slave revolt and restores order on the *San Dominick* – in other words, given that Melville with his slippery narrator offers his readers virtually no clear guidance on how to read the novella – it is not surprising that *Benito Cereno* had absolutely no impact on the antislavery movement. Readers of antislavery writings of the time were accustomed to the strongly articulated voices of Garrison, Douglass, Stowe, and many others, but here the meanings emerge from that which is "voiceless": the head of the executed Babo "fixed on a pole in the Plaza" of Lima, Peru.[19] That haunting final image of Babo's black head thus begs the question: is this a novella haunted by blackness?

I think not, and Morrison in her major writings on race and classic American writing would appear to agree, for Melville is the nineteenth-century American writer whom she presents as having interpretive perspectives on American culture and narrative most like her own. In the January 7, 2014, issue of the *Nation*, Morrison remarks on Melville: "I always sensed Melville's deliberate misdirections: that he was telling some other story underneath the obvious one. So it was not hard to suspect his manipulation of the reader as well as his tendency to hide/display deeper revelations underneath the surface narrative."[20] There is something just a bit contradictory about both hiding and displaying beneath the surface, but this contradictoriness nicely speaks to the tensions between surfaces and depths in *Benito Cereno*, a novella that deliberately *deploys* tropes of black haunting by developing a link between the "voiceless" black head at the end of the novella and Melville's own submerged narrative presence. In this way Melville subtly and quietly presses his most canny readers to read from the point of view of Babo. Rereading the novella from Babo's perspective, we find that Delano's near-blindness to what's clearly before his eyes has a comic dimension, and that Babo's effort to gain freedom for the slaves through aesthetics (staging a play) artfully manages to "disguise the truth" as Melville himself disguises the truth. The deposition states that "the negro Babo was the plotter from first to last"; but of course in terms of narrative practice, Melville has been the plotter from first and last.[21] In this respect, it is not the novella that is haunted by the black presence but the many readers of Melville's novella who are unable to find their way past the anxious perspective of Delano and choose surfaces over depths. With its demanding, dynamic interplay between surfaces and depths, *Benito Cereno* remains one of the most challenging and disorienting literary works on slavery by a classic American writer.

While Melville's critical engagements with the discourses and practices of slavery have come to be widely recognized and celebrated, Hawthorne has not fared so well. The major Americanist critics of the mid-twentieth century generally built on Melville's praise for Hawthorne in his 1850 "Hawthorne and His Mosses," taking special note of Melville's remarks on "the power of blackness" in Hawthorne's fiction. Connecting "blackness" not to race but to Calvinism, which is probably what Melville meant by that word in his essay, Hawthorne scholars initially focused on antinomies of whiteness and blackness in what they regarded as melodramatic romances set in worlds elsewhere. Indeed, in the wake of Chase's influential *The American Novel and Its Tradition*, Hawthorne emerged in these ahistorical terms as the American romancer par excellence. More recent critics have been less taken with a romance tradition that seems to avoid one of the great moral issues of the antebellum period, and have criticized Hawthorne for his literary escapism. They have also raised questions about his allegiance to a Democratic Party that fought to sustain the practice of slavery.[22] Though Hawthorne denounced slavery in his 1852 campaign biography of Franklin Pierce, terming it one of the world's "evils," that biography helped to elect a man who had no interest in abolition or emancipation. During the Civil War Hawthorne conveyed his skepticism about Abraham Lincoln in "Chiefly about War-Matters," published in the

July 1862 *Atlantic Monthly*, and alienated his antislavery Massachusetts neighbors by dedicating his 1864 nonfictional book, *Our Old Home*, to Franklin Pierce. (See Chapter 8, below, for more on Hawthorne and slavery.) Still, in "Chiefly about War-Matters" Hawthorne declared that slavery had a "monstrous birth" on the *Mayflower*, and some recent critics have argued that Hawthorne engaged this monstrousness in his major fiction. Leland S. Person and Jay Grossman, for instance, note that tropes of race, miscegenation, and slavery inform *The Scarlet Letter* and that Hawthorne (as Person suggests) depicts Hester Prynne herself in the context of discourses about slave mothering.[23] In all of his major romances, Hawthorne invokes master-slave relationships when portraying mesmerists or any character who manages to hold sway over another. It is significant that *The Scarlet Letter*'s Chillingworth, *The House of the Seven Gables*'s Maules and Pyncheons, and *The Blithedale Romance*'s Westervelt and Hollingsworth are all depicted as slave masters of sorts who rule over what Hawthorne in *The House of the Seven Gables* and *Blithedale* calls their "bond-slave[s]."[24] To be sure, Hawthorne's use of slavery imagery is to a large extent metaphorical. But in *Gables* slavery is both metaphorical and actual, and in the "Alice Pyncheon" chapter of that novel, Hawthorne produced one of the great antislavery stories of the 1850s.

The antislavery thrust of the "Alice Pyncheon" chapter does not have to be recovered through a complex hermeneutics; it is right there on the surface. Within the fictional frame of the novel, the chapter consists of a historical tale, written by Holgrave, that the aspiring author now reads aloud to Phoebe. A Hawthornean storyteller, Holgrave looks back to the eighteenth century to tell the story of the violation and death of Alice Pyncheon (Phoebe's distant ancestor) by the vengeance-seeking Matthew Maule (Holgrave's distant ancestor and the grandson of the executed Matthew Maule). Complicit in Alice's death is her father, Gervayse Pyncheon (another of Phoebe's distant ancestors and the boy who in the novel's opening chapter discovers the dead Colonel Pyncheon). Summoned by Gervayse, Matthew Maule is met at the door of the House of the Seven Gables by what's termed the house's "black servant," known as Black Scipio, who calls Gervayse "Massa."[25] But this is a black servant in pre-abolition Massachusetts who in all likelihood is a slave. Matthew is angered at being greeted by a black man, and Scipio takes such pride in his position as house slave that he acts patronizingly toward a white man, a laborer, whom he regards as his inferior. Perhaps aware of the tensions that existed between white laborers and African Americans during the 1840s and 1850s, Hawthorne shows how slavery diminishes both men while undermining any possibility of interracial class solidarity.[26] Not surprisingly, Matthew Maule is on his own when he turns on the master.

Before he does, however, Hawthorne's storyteller discloses that Gervayse Pyncheon has slaves in his house in addition to Black Scipio, thus calling attention to Salem's long historical participation in the slave trade. Viewing Gervayse's House of the Seven Gables from the outside, in the manner of a casual observer, the narrator describes how slaves pass back and forth behind the windows of one of the town's most prominent houses: "Now and then, ... the shining, sable face of a slave, might be seen bustling across the windows, in the lower part of the house." Within this context of master-slave relations, Gervayse, the aristocrat, asks the working-class Matthew Maule for help in locating a secret place in his house that might be holding an Indian deed granting the Pyncheons a large tract of land. Maule agrees to help Gervayse Pyncheon if he will give him access to his daughter, Alice Pyncheon, whose admiring look Maule mistakenly interprets as arrogant disdain. Possessing an "Evil Eye," and skilled in mesmerism, Maule takes revenge against the greedy slave master and his innocent daughter by hypnotizing the daughter, Alice, and making her into a kind of slave. When he displays the formerly proud Alice to Gervayse as under his control, Hawthorne is clear about the nature of this new relationship. Holgrave explains: "while Alice Pyncheon lived, she was Maule's slave, in a bondage more humiliating, a thousand-fold, than that which binds its chain around the body."[27]

Though Hawthorne could be accused of diminishing the actual humiliations (and pain and suffering) of chattel slavery by describing a free white woman as a slave, he begins the chapter with a portrait of a prideful house slave, describes actual slaves under Gervayse Pyncheon's control, and concludes with Matthew Maule treating Alice so cruelly, as a servant and slave, that she dies of pneumonia. There is nothing pretty about any of the forms of slavery depicted in this chapter. Holgrave's story, which is shaped for the sleepy antebellum reader/auditor Phoebe, points to the pathologies of the master-slave relationship, and depicts the temptations of power and the humiliations of slavery in ways that are as compelling as anything in Cooper, Melville, and Poe. But the chapter does still more. By bringing slavery into *Gables* as both a social practice and metaphor, the chapter shows that slavery wasn't limited to the South and that antislavery discourse wasn't limited to the practice of chattel slavery. During the 1840s and 1850s, antislavery was part of a larger reformist project in which temperance, feminism, and antislavery often went hand in hand. Hawthorne's next novel, *The Blithedale Romance* (1852), drew on these interrelated discourses and movements. Published the same year as Harriet Beecher Stowe's *Uncle Tom's Cabin*, the most popular antislavery novel of the century, which also links temperance and antipatriarchal sentiments to its antislavery politics, *Blithedale* depicts patriarchal mesmerists attempting to make "bond-slaves" of women in a world in which men are depicted as drunk on alcohol and power. The novel merits fresh reconsideration as a text that both extends the antislavery thematics of *House* and complements the antislavery thematics of *Uncle Tom's Cabin*.

In short, when we approach works by Cooper, Poe, Hawthorne, and Melville as engaged with slavery and race, we find shared concerns among these canonical writers that are not usually acknowledged. Informed by an awareness of the discourses and practices of slavery, their works are not easily reduced to political statements. Deferring to these texts (i.e., choosing to *read* them rather than reductively labeling or judging them) helps to reveal writers who thought about slavery historically and diasporically and in a range of cultural contexts. The writers I've focused on are hardly alone in representing slavery in nineteenth-century American literature. Margaret Fuller developed analogies between patriarchal husbands and slave traders in her landmark *Woman in the Nineteenth Century* (1845), linking those who champion women's rights to those who are "the champions of the enslaved African." At around the same time, Ralph Waldo Emerson first wrote directly against slavery in his 1844 "Emancipation in the British West Indies," but throughout his career, as Morrison observes, he conceived of freedom in relation to slavery. Thoreau similarly thought about interrelationships between slavery and freedom, advising his readers in *Walden* (1854) that there was nothing worse than being "the slave-driver of yourself." That same year, in "Slavery in Massachusetts" (1854), he compared Massachusetts under the Fugitive Slave Law to Milton's "hell." In his 1855 "Song of Myself," Whitman presumptuously, or boldly, depending on your perspective, imagined himself as the "hounded slave" who is beaten "violently over the head with whip-stocks." "Agonies are one of my changes of garments," he writes.[28] And of course Stowe, Douglass, William Wells Brown, Frances Harper, Lydia Maria Child, and a host of other American writers often wrote self-consciously as antislavery writers and found thousands of responsive readers. Twenty years after the abolition of slavery, when Mark Twain chronicled Huck's travels with the fugitive slave Jim in his classic *Huckleberry Finn* (1885), he provided a sort of précis, or summa, of the writing that had come before him. The controversial ending of *Huck Finn*, in which it becomes clear that Huck and Tom have been scheming to liberate an already freed slave, ultimately works to suggest that the freed blacks of the post-Civil War era still need to be liberated.[29] For good reason, then, as Morrison discusses at the conclusion of "Unspeakable Things Unspoken," race and the aftermath of slavery would remain crucial constituents of American literature long after the publication of the classic works of the nineteenth century. From W. E. B. Du Bois to Ralph Waldo Ellison, and beyond, American writers would continue to press their readers to see what is right before their eyes.

CHAPTER 2

Temporality, Race, and Empire in Cooper's The Deerslayer

The Beginning of the End

In the five novels of his Leatherstocking series (1823–41), Cooper engages the long history of empire in the Americas by focusing on the competition between European nations to take possession of the North American continent. To some extent, then, Cooper portrays the United States as a nation among nations even before the nation comes into being, setting three of those novels in the pre-Revolutionary period and all of them in relation to the frontier, the very space that Charles E. Maier argues has historically worked to produce empire through violence.[1] This chapter takes as its starting point the striking fact that the last novel in the Leatherstocking series, The Deerslayer *(1841), is chronologically its first and thus in effect revises a series that began in 1823. Literary and cultural historians have argued that US empire unfolded and developed over time, built on a foundation of white racial superiority that helped to give rise to, among other things, Andrew Jackson's Indian removal policy. By contrast, the Leatherstocking series moves back and forth in time, depicting empires in conflict while raising questions about racial essentialism, or what Natty Bumppo calls racial "gifts." Again and again, Indians emerge in these novels as prescient critics of the white colonizers. Their communities may be threatened, but that has more to do with the violence that attends empire building than with teleological notions of racial destiny. In this reading of the Leatherstocking series, particularly its concluding novel, Cooper emerges as a more complex theorist of race, nation, and empire than most critics have allowed.*

The Deerslayer (1841) both begins and ends the five novels of Cooper's Leatherstocking series (1823–41). In terms of the chronological temporality of the novels, *The Deerslayer* is the first, set in the early 1740s, when Natty Bumppo is in his mid-twenties, and *The Prairie* (1827) is the last, culminating in Natty's death over sixty years later at the time of the Louisiana Purchase. But in terms of Cooper's actual composition of the series, *The Deerslayer* comes last. The first, *The Pioneers* (1823), portrays Natty during the 1790s at the New York settlement of Templeton (Cooper's fictionalized version of Cooperstown); *The Last of the Mohicans* (1826) moves Natty back in time to 1757 during the height of the Seven Years' War; and then, after projecting Natty forward to the early 1800s in *The Prairie*, Cooper moves him back in time again to the Seven Years' War in *The Pathfinder* (1840), which is set a few years after *The Last of the Mohicans*. Finally, Cooper moves two decades further back, setting *The Deerslayer* in the still naturally pristine forests of what would soon be known as upstate New York. D. H. Lawrence declared that Cooper's five Leatherstocking novels constitute a "lovely myth" of America, steadily chronicling Natty's life "from old age to golden youth."[2] But, in fact, over the approximately twenty-year composition period of the series, Cooper jumped forward and backward in a jagged, uneven fashion very different from the steady regression evoked by Lawrence.[3] Still, the ending of the Leatherstocking series does take us to the beginning, and that beginning, I will be arguing in this chapter, provides a clarifying and revisionary ending to the series. My reading of *The Deerslayer* addresses the complicated temporality of the Leatherstocking series in relation to the chronology of its composition history, raising questions about the less complicated temporality informing current critical discussions of Cooper as a writer who allegedly used the series to champion white US empire.

Assertions of Cooper's implication in US empire building tend to deploy overdetermined critical strategies of temporal juxtaposition and homology that take as a given that literary history and the history of expansionism can best be understood, not as a complicated zigzag within a deep and uneven time frame, but as a simple (and symbiotic) chronological unfolding. Although Cooper throughout his career was fascinated by echoes, repetitions, progress, and regression, and although the culture itself was marked by "heterogeneous temporal modes,"[4] there has been a flattening of temporal thinking in most considerations of the Leatherstocking series. As a number of critics have elaborated, Cooper wrote the series during a period in which the future of the Indians in the United States was being debated by white political leaders (the 1820s), Indian Removal was adopted as law (1830), and the Cherokees of Georgia were pushed west on the infamous Trail of Tears (1838–39), a forced march that led to the deaths of thousands of the Cherokees, especially women and children. For some critics, the simple juxtaposition of historical atrocity and novel writing is enough to indict Cooper. Joshua David Bellin ominously notes that "Cooper's *Last of the Mohicans* appeared two years after James Monroe presented a formal plan of Indian removal to Congress and four years before Andrew Jackson signed act into law," with the clear implication that Cooper's novel lent support to those efforts simply by virtue of the temporal overlap. Philip Fisher similarly builds a case against Cooper through overlap, remarking that "Cooper writes *The Deerslayer* in 1840 at the moment of the conclusion of Jacksonian Indian Removal" – as if this fact makes *The Deerslayer* complicit in what Fisher terms "the inevitable extermination of the American Indian." (Fisher never considers that a novel concluding with whites' massacre of Indian women and children might be raising questions about a providentially inscribed "inevitable extinction.") In a study focusing on the first three novels of the Leatherstocking series, Theresa Strouth Gaul asserts that there was "collusion between literary policy and national polity during the period immediately preceding the passage of the Indian Removal act of 1830." However, the only evidence Gaul offers for collusion between Cooper and the makers of public policy is once again temporal overlap, as she focuses on suggestive homologies (structural resemblances) between juridical and literary "modes of race representation" in the Supreme Court's 1823 ruling on *Johnson v. McIntosh*, which dispossessed Indians of land, and Cooper's 1823 *The Pioneers*.[5]

Reading through such political interpretations of *The Pioneers, The Last of the Mohicans*, and the other novels of the Leatherstocking series, one might be surprised to learn that Cooper did not work for the US government's Bureau of Indian Affairs and that he had virtually nothing to say about the Jacksonian policy of Indian removal. I have been unable to find anyone writing during the 1823–41 period (critic or political leader) who draws connections between the Leatherstocking novels and Indian removal. In fact, most commentators on the series complained that Cooper's portrayals of Indians were too positive.[6] And yet, over the past two decades, it has become a tenet of US literary studies that Cooper's Leatherstocking series supported and enabled Indian removal, gloried in an emerging white US empire, and trafficked in essentialist notions of race.[7] My point isn't that Cooper was a progressive reformer who actively worked for Indian rights, but that the connections that most commentators insist upon between cultural context and Cooper's novels have become rigidified to the point where we are virtually unable to see conflict and critique in the Leatherstocking series. It is almost as if we need Cooper forever fixed as our "demon of the continent"[8] so we don't have to read him anymore. I want to suggest that within the constraints of his somewhat typically nineteenth-century vision of the Indians, Cooper raises significant questions about Indian policy and, in a larger sense, about the nature of white empire on the North American continent. At the very least, there is much in the Leatherstocking series that voices clear opposition to whites' racist violence against the Indians.

Cooper is nowhere clearer in his critique of white racist violence and the course of empire in the region that would become the northern United States than in the concluding novel of the Leatherstocking series, the 1841 *The Deerslayer*. This last-written but chronologically first novel of the series can be taken as Cooper's critical commentary on the entire Leatherstocking project. Reading the four earlier novels through the lens of *The Deerslayer* can be a transformative experience, as Cooper in this novel revises and more clearly articulates his vision of race and empire in the Americas, leaving readers with a feeling of revulsion at the "rise" of a white empire based on untenable notions of racial differences and violence. In *The Deerslayer*, binaries between good and bad Indians, and Indians and whites, are exposed as fictions, and Indians and women emerge as the most prescient critics of the violence identified with colonizing Euro-Americans. In this, his most feminist novel, Cooper builds to an antipatriarchal and antiracist critique of a nascent US empire. That critique fundamentally alters our reading of the earlier novels and of the Leatherstocking series itself.[9]

Arguably, it is precisely because *The Deerslayer* represents an act of authorial (re)interpretation of the Leatherstocking series that Cooper in 1841, and again in 1850, made an effort to enjoin those new to the series to read *The Deerslayer* first. In a letter of January 31, 1841, to his publisher Richard Bentley, Cooper declares that "[t]he order of the books, as regards time, will be, this book [*The Deerslayer*], Mohicans, Pathfinder, Pioneers, Prairie"; and in his prefaces to *The Deerslayer* and the Leatherstocking series, he underscores the importance of reading the novels in that order. He writes in the 1841 preface to *The Deerslayer* that this is "the last in execution, though the first in the order of perusal"; and he remarks in the 1850 preface to the five novels of the series that "taking the life of the Leather-Stocking as a guide, 'The Deerslayer' should have been the opening book." He is most insistent on the order in which the novels should be read in the 1850 preface to *The Deerslayer*: "'The Deerslayer' is properly the first in the order of reading, though the last in that of publication."[10]

There are complicated issues of temporality here, for readers remain free to read the novels in any order they choose. Moreover, as Geoffrey Rans points out in his excellent study of the Leatherstocking series, there are also fascinating temporal issues raised by reading the novels in their order of publication, for each earlier novel, he argues, is immanent in the novel to come. *The Last of the Mohicans*, for instance, published shortly after *The Pioneers*, contains within its scene of 1757 what we know from *The Pioneers* will happen by the 1790s. Thus, to take an obvious example, Natty and

Chingachgook cannot be killed in *The Last of the Mohicans* because we already know they will live into the 1790s. Given Rans's emphasis on compositional temporalities, *The Pioneers* (the first published novel) remains key to his interpretation of the series: "Whatever attraction the sequence read in chronological order possesses, *The Pioneers* is the controlling determinant simply because as the first written it prescribes certain unalterable conditions."[11] True, *The Pioneers* establishes unalterable conditions of plot, but, given the importance of unresolved conflict to all of the novels, there remains the alterable space of social, cultural, and historical ideologies. The series presents an unfolding, often highly conflicted, conversation on race and empire, and Cooper's late comments on the series suggest that he wants us to begin that conversation with *The Deerslayer*. In this way, oddly enough, Cooper seeks to alter readers' understanding of the conversation to come in the four novels written before the last one.

Much of the talk and action in the Leatherstocking series focuses on the "rise" of a white US empire in North America, and in *The Deerslayer*, as in all of the novels, Cooper's approach to this topic is profoundly historical. Inspired by D. H. Lawrence's mythic reading of the novel, H. Daniel Peck asserts that *The Deerslayer* is set in "a time *before* history," and William P. Kelly similarly proclaims that the novel is set at a moment of "timelessness consistent with the force of myth."[12] And yet Cooper explicitly states that the novel is set "between the years 1740 and 1745" (16), not too long after the end of "a time of peace between England and France" (146).[13] This is the historical moment that we know will culminate in the Seven Years' War, which Cooper will take up (or, depending on one's temporal point of view, has already taken up) in *The Last of the Mohicans* and *The Pathfinder*, and it is a time of historical conflict that is absolutely crucial to an understanding of US history in a global context. As historian Thomas Bender notes, "The struggle between England and France ... for the riches of empire was played out on a global scale between 1689 and 1815." Gregory H. Nobles reminds us that within that same time frame, from around 1689 to 1783, "[t]he struggle for control of North America embroiled European governments and their American colonists in a series of wide-scale wars."[14] In the coda-like conclusion of *The Deerslayer*, which jumps forward fifteen years, Cooper situates the action in relation to *The Last of the Mohicans* and *The Pathfinder* through a proleptic limning of Natty and Chingachgook's role in the ongoing wars between England and France as depicted in previously published novels: "A peace had intervened, and it was on the eve of another and still more important war, when he [Natty Bumppo] and his constant friend, Chingachgook, were hastening to the forts to join their allies [the British]."[15] The conclusion thus underscores the importance of the contention for empire in the entire series. *The Deerslayer* focuses on one distinct moment in the global and hemispheric war for empire, and in many respects offers "prefatory" guidance on how we might understand that war in the already written Leatherstocking novels that follow.

Key to the contention for empire depicted in *The Deerslayer* is, to borrow Philip Fisher's term, a "hard fact": both the French and the English have offered bounties for scalps of their enemies (Indians and whites).[16] For many critics, the overarching suggestion of the five Leatherstocking novels is that "civilized" whites are different from "savage" Indians, and that within the progressive design of the series, whites should therefore naturally ascend to power while the Indians, lamentably, should "vanish."[17] But Cooper's presentation of Europeans' promotion of scalping in the chronologically first novel of the series raises questions about such differences, and even about Natty's oft-stated claim, here and elsewhere in the series, that scalping constitutes one of the Indian's racial "gifts."

In a disturbing scene in *The Last of the Mohicans*, for instance, Chingachgook scalps a friendly French sentry, and Natty defends the action because it is an Indian who does the scalping: "'Twould have been a cruel and an unhuman act for a white-skin; but 'tis the gift and natur of an Indian."[18] Critics have generally regarded Natty's interpretation of that moment as Cooper's. Consider how John P. McWilliams uses the depiction of scalping in the 1826 *Mohicans* to shape an interpretation of the 1841 *Deerslayer*. He writes (correctly, I think) that the "entire narrative of *The Deerslayer* rests upon two laws enacted by the colonial authorities. The French army in Canada has passed a law paying bounty for the scalps of all Englishmen and Delawares. The English army along the Hudson has passed a law paying bounty for the scalps of all Frenchmen and Hurons." But he also asserts that "[t]he white Christians have sunk to legalizing Indian codes of vengeance." The scalping laws do play a crucial role in the action of *The Deerslayer*, but have the white Christians really "sunk" (or merely continuing their brutal policies), and is scalping truly central to "Indian codes of vengeance"? Moreover, are Indians really more "vengeful" than whites? McWilliams further argues that "the frontiersman becomes an Indian, while the Indian resembles an honorable white."[19] This is precisely how Natty understands such reversals in *The Deerslayer*, but the question remains as to whether Natty's views are portrayed uncritically by Cooper. In short, despite Natty's remarks, we need to ask if there are essential differences between whites and Indians, if Indians more "naturally" turn to scalping and vengeance, and if whites acting cruelly and sadistically have turned against their "gifts." McWilliams's reading of racial gifts in *Mohicans* works with Natty-inflected notions that may have had a greater force in the novels published during the 1820s, but which Cooper by 1841, particularly in a scene in which Indians scalp *only* because of the white bounty, comes to suggest are fictions. Through his repeated injunctions that we should be reading *The Deerslayer* first, Cooper undertakes a temporal revision of the presentation of race or "gifts" in the earlier novels.

Before turning to race, a few words on the plot of *The Deerslayer*, a novel that Mark Twain singled out for its unintentionally comic improbabilities.[20] In this, the longest novel of the Leatherstocking series, Natty Bumppo seeks to help his friend, the Delaware Chingachgook, to rescue his beloved Wah-ta!-Wah, or Hist-oh!-Hist (usually called Hist), who had been kidnapped by a renegade Delaware into a Huron (Iroquois) tribe residing by Glimmerglass (Cooper's fictionalized name for New York's Otsego Lake). At the novel's opening, Natty accompanies Henry March, known as Hurry Harry, who is in love with Judith Hutter, one of the two "daughters" of Thomas Hutter, a former pirate who basically claims Glimmerglass and the immediately surrounding lands as his property. There are ambiguities about whether Hutter is actually the father of Judith and her sister, the feeble-minded Hetty (it turns out that he's not); and there are rumors that the beautiful and boldly assertive Judith had earlier been seduced by a British army officer. Hutter has recently "buried" his wife in Glimmerglass, and one suspects that a buried family history will eventually come to surface. Crucial to the unfolding action is the historical fact that the English and French are competing to gain dominion over the North American continent. That larger geopolitical conflict between European powers remains the essential backdrop to Natty's and Chingachgook's efforts to liberate Hist from the Hurons, and the Hurons' own efforts to fight off the whites (especially Hurry and Hutter) who want their scalps for the reward money. There are repeated scenes of captivity and escape. Cooper details Judith's growing love for Natty and her increasing revulsion at Hurry, and clearly the author has a soft spot for Hetty, whose mental slowness doesn't stop her from evincing a Christian love for the Iroquois. Viewed in relation to the Leatherstocking series, *The Deerslayer* has a vital role in depicting what many regard as a mythic aspect of the series: Natty's emergence as a killer.[21] In a great early chapter, Cooper shows how Natty comes to kill his first Indian – an act of self-defense in which Natty lovingly comforts the man that circumstances suggest he was forced to shoot. By killing another human being, the Deerslayer in this last novel becomes the Hawkeye of the works that chronologically follow. But despite scenes of intense action amidst the sublime beauty of the wilderness and Glimmerglass, the bulk of the novel consists of conversations on topics central to the Leatherstocking series – religion, war, marriage, law, the seeming course of history, and race.

Race, of course, is essential to Natty's conception of himself in all five novels of the series, for the man who has spent years with the Delaware Indians regularly finds it necessary to assert his identity as a pure white. But in *The Deerslayer*, Natty is not the only character affirming the importance of whiteness. Dana D. Nelson describes Hurry Harry as "the spokesperson for racial purity," and in this respect he has to some extent taken over this function from Natty, who in *The Last of the Mohicans* in particular repeatedly asserts versions of "I am genuine white" with "no cross in my veins."[22] In *The Deerslayer*, Cooper presents Natty's race thinking much more critically, for Natty's insistence on his pure whiteness becomes inextricably linked with Hurry's virulent and violent racism. As the narrator remarks, "Hurry was one of those theorists who believed in the inferiority of all of the human race, who were not white."[23] Hurry baldly lays out his vision of racial hierarchy: "White is the highest colour, and therefore the best man; black comes next, and is put to live in the neighborhood of the white man . . .; and red comes last, which shows that those that made 'em never expected an Indian to be accounted as more than half human" (49–50). Hurry's racial views are repeatedly enlisted as justifications for his violence, for he regards all Indians as "animals, with nothing human about 'em" (60). Whereas Natty declares that it is "onlawful to take the life of man, except in open and ginerous warfare" (22), Hurry and Hutter view the frontier as in a perpetual state of war that perpetually legitimates whites' violence against the Indians, a vision that obscures the historical specificity of their actions. As Hutter asserts in general terms, without a glimmer of recognition of the larger context of white imperial aggression: "We . . . must do to our enemies as our enemies would do to us" (91).

Given that whites have instituted the scalping bounties, and given that Hurry Harry and Hutter are presented as violent racists who are willing to kill Indian women and children for pay, how seriously are we meant to take Natty's repeated assertions of racial difference, or what Natty calls "nat'ral gifts" (34)? The idea of grounding "gifts" or racial characteristics in nature would suggest an ideology that emphasizes biology over culture, and an ideology, at least as elaborated by Natty in *The Last of the Mohicans* and *The Deerslayer*, which is in many ways consistent with the romantic racialism circulating in the antebellum United States. As Alexander Kinmont and other romantic racialists of the period argued in their lectures and writings, different blood contributes to different behaviors among different races, and those differences, viewed in Natty Bumppo fashion as "gifts" derived from blood, are not necessarily bad. For instance, both Kinmont and Harriet Beecher Stowe saw blacks as natural Christians because of the way their blood supposedly made them more domestic and attached to the land. Praising blacks as "naturally and originally distinct" from less religious whites, Kinmont wrote in his 1839 *Twelve Lectures on the Natural History of Man* that it was all for the good that "each peculiar race of men should occupy those limits, which have been assigned" by what he terms "an express law of nature."[24] In *The Last of the Mohicans* and other Leatherstocking novels, there are suggestions that Indians' "gifts" for life in the wilderness make them unsuitable for a rising civilization and that they should therefore "occupy those limits" of the ever-vanishing forests. But in *The Deerslayer* the appeal to biology (or blood) soon comes to seem incoherent, merely serving the interests of racists who appear anything but civilized. That incoherence has much to do with Cooper's sly importing of the racial terms of the 1830s and early 1840s into a novel of the 1740s that in crucial respects would also raise questions about racial hierarchies in Cooper's own historical moment.

Again, the matter of bounty is key to the novel's troubling of the concept of racial gifts. Natty initially speaks about racial gifts in relation to a providentially ordered nature, stating that "it's sinful to withstand nat'ral gifts" (34). But in his response to the British and French offers of bounties for scalps, Natty, while insisting that his own racial gifts will keep him from scalping, begins to loosen his hold on such appeals to nature, becoming a critic of white culture from the perspective of the Indians: "Even the Indians, themselves, cry shame on it [white scalping for pay], seeing it's ag'in a white man's gifts. . . . I will maintain that tradition, and use, and colour, and laws, make such a difference in races as to amount to gifts" (50). Looking forward (or backward) to *The Pioneers*, which builds to Natty's resistance to Judge Temple's laws, Natty makes the radical declaration that laws running "ag'in the laws of God . . . ought not to be obeyed" (51), a declaration that in *The Deerslayer* links him with the Indians. At the very least, he insists that he will refrain from scalping, even as he is implicated with Hurry as a defender of Hutter's dwelling, boat, and putative daughters. He asserts that he will be "clinging to colour to the last, even though the King's Majesty, his governors, and all his councils, both at home and in the colonies, forget from what they come, and where they hope to go" (125). According to this critique, both the French and English have gone "red" by turning against their natural gifts. But this last novel in the series hardly naturalizes or supports such stereotypical thinking. It is worth observing, for instance, that the narrator regularly belittles "Deerslayer's innocent vanity on the subject of colour" (123), remarking rather bluntly that Natty's ideas of "gifts" are ultimately based on "prejudice": "This tyrant of the human mind . . . had made some impression on even the just propensities of this individual" (49). The narrator's critique of Natty's concept of racial gifts becomes even more pronounced over the course of the novel, as does Natty's confusion on his favorite topic. By focusing on Natty's confusion about ideas that can be linked both to the 1740s and to the romantic racialism of the antebellum period, Cooper destabilizes notions of race, which the novel (and overall series) suggests were always unstable in the culture anyway.[25]

Relatively early in *The Deerslayer*, Natty announces that "Revenge is an Injin gift, and forgiveness a white man's" (89). But over the next several hundred pages, whites are extraordinarily vengeful and Indians regularly display an ability to forgive. After Hutter and Hurry are ransomed from the Hurons for chess pieces in the form of elephants, the narrator notes that the white men's "humility partook of the rancor of revenge" (254). Hurry's vengeful feelings lead to the random killing of an Indian woman, which I discuss in more detail below. Hutter is eventually scalped by the Hurons, but he had already been mortally wounded by the chief Rivenoak, who in the novel kills only in self-defense, and Cooper makes clear that Hutter is scalped not because scalping is an Indian gift but because the Hurons needed "the usual trophy" (355) – a scalp – in order to be paid by the French. Hurry's response to the scalping is to castigate Natty for trying to stop him and Hutter from killing for profit: "I heartily wish old Hutter and I had scalped every creatur' in their camp" (404).

Faced with such overwhelming evidence that whites can be just as vengeful and cruel as Indians – which is to say, faced with evidence that stereotypes about white/Indian differences simply do not work – Natty is forced to rethink his concept of racial gifts. Although Natty in *The Deerslayer* initially conceives of such gifts in relation to biology (or blood), he becomes increasingly uncertain on the subject.[26] By the end of the novel, Natty, who has seen whites exhibiting vengeance in "savage" ways and who has wrestled with the historical reality that the English and French have been promoting scalping, offers one final disquisition on "gifts" in which he mainly reflects on the highly determinative role of culture over biology. He elaborates his views to Hetty and Judith in the manner of a schoolmaster who has finally come to understand the subject he has been teaching: "A natur'," he explains, "is the creatur' itself; its wishes, wants, idees, and feelin's, as all are born in him. . . . Now, gifts come of sarcumstances. Thus, if you put a man in a town, he gets town gifts; in a settlement, settlement gifts; in a forest, gifts of the woods.... Still, the creatur' is the same at the bottom; just as a man who is clad in regimentals is the same as the man that is clad in skins" (439). Here is a fundamental rejection of the romantic racialism of the early to mid-nineteenth century and a rejection, as well, of the racialism that at times seems to inform the Leatherstocking series. The collapsing of men in regimentals with men in skins also raises questions about conventional progressive readings of the series, pointing us toward the darker Thomas Cole-like cyclical vision implicit in the images of the mounds in *The Prairie* as burial sites of former civilizations.[27]

To underscore my argument about the revisionary temporality of the Leatherstocking series: here we have Natty's "final" reflections on "gifts" in the final novel of the series, but in a novel that, when read in the chronological order Cooper advises, actually initiates the series' debate on "gifts" and race. One could say that Natty changes his views later in the chronological time of the series, or even simplifies his views (which is what we might argue if Cooper wrote the Leatherstocking novels in chronological order over chronological time); or, as I am suggesting, one could say that Natty's reflections on "gifts" in this final novel work to revise our understanding of the discussions to come in the four earlier novels. Viewed in this light, one of Cooper's great contributions as a historical novelist to a philosophy of history is the a-chronological temporal revision-ism of the Leatherstocking series, which unfixes connections between time and space in order to emphasize repetition over progress, even as he shows that such temporal revisionism allows for the possibility of new knowledge and cultural change both in the past and in the future.

Nowhere is the revisionary force of Natty's rethinking more apparent than in the way he connects his new ideas about gifts to a revised view of heaven. Again, what's interesting here in terms of temporality is the way that Natty rethinks notions in an 1841 novel (set in the early 1740s) that had initially been elaborated in an 1826 novel (set in 1757). At the conclusion of *The Last of the Mohicans*, the Delaware young women's mourning song about Uncas and Cora dwelling together in heaven disturbs Natty. The narrator writes: "But when they spoke of the future prospects of Cora and Uncas, he shook his head, like one who knew the error of their simple creed, and resuming his reclining attitude, he maintained it until the ceremony – if that might be called a ceremony, in which feeling was so deeply imbued – was finished. Happily for the self-command of Heyward and Munro, they knew not the meaning of the wild sounds they heard."[28]

The narrator seems to be aligned with Natty in rejecting the notion of an interracial heaven, though there are ambiguities. We cannot be absolutely certain about why Natty shakes his head, and the use of the word "Happily" perhaps means to highlight the prejudices of both Cora's admirer and her father, rather than to convey solidarity with such prejudices. That Natty at the close of *Mohicans* is depicted as holding hands with Chingachgook and vowing to remain by his side in the wilderness also would appear to be at odds with his views. Would Natty think it a good thing to be separated from Chingachgook in heaven?

Apparently not, for in *The Deerslayer* Natty has a change of mind on the subject. In the same discussion of "gifts" and "natur'" that comes late in the novel, he also talks to Hetty and Judith about heaven: "The Delaware, here, and Hist, believe in happy hunting grounds, and have idees befitting their notions and gifts, as red skins, but we who are of white blood hold altogether to a different opinion" (436). In certain respects, Natty at this moment seems to share the beliefs of his older self in the earlier *Mohicans*. But then years before facing the conundrum of the earlier-published but chronologically-later *Mohicans*, he has an insight into how he might remain with Chingachgook even after death do they part: "Still, I rather conclude our heaven is their land of spirits, and that the path which leads to it will be travelled by all colours alike. 'Tis onpossible for the wicked to enter on it, I will allow, but fri'nds can scarce be separated, though they are not of the same race on 'arth" (436). Viewed from this perspective, the Delaware women at the end of *The Last of the Mohicans* get things right. Having reformulated his views while speaking to Hetty and Judith, Natty then conveys the happy news to Chingachgook and, as in *The Last of the Mohicans*, they "warmly" (457) hold hands. Cooper gives the last word on the subject to Chingachgook himself: "The Delawares believe that good men and brave warriors will hunt together in the same pleasant woods" (456).

Despite Chingachgook's emphasis on men, *The Deerslayer* suggests that women like Hetty and Hist will also be part of a racially inclusive heaven. That the "fallen" Judith is depicted as a victim of seduction makes her a good candidate as well. But to move from heaven back to earth: Cooper's troubling of the notion of "gifts" has important consequences for how we might think about the rise of white empire. Given that Natty never quite achieves clarity on the matter of race, it is not surprising that the women characters of *The Deerslayer* emerge as the most prescient critics of Anglo-American empire in particular, which throughout the novel works its will through racism and patriarchal violation. Cooper's valuing of the critical perspectives of Judith, Hetty, and Hist is made clear not only in the text itself but in his January 31, 1841, letter to his publisher, when he suggests as possible titles for his novel "Judith and Esther; or, the Girls of Glimmerglass"; or "Wah!-Ta-Wah!, or, Hist!-Oh!-Hist!"[29] Hurry and Hutter's violence, as I have been emphasizing, is regularly directed at Indian women and children. As Hutter proclaims about the bounty: "If there's women, there's children, and big and little have scalps; the Colony pays for all alike" (87). Hurry goes on to justify their plans to scalp Native women and children as an act of revenge, and it is Judith, not Natty, who poses the most compelling challenge to his world view: "is it religion to say that one *bad* turn deserves another" (87). Her frustration and anger build over the course of the novel. As she remarks shortly after the two men go in pursuit of scalps: "I get warm, when I think of all the wrong that men do" (137). The religious Hetty poses a similar challenge to the violence of Hurry and Hutter, and the English more generally, through sentimental appeals to the heart and Bible, and Cooper honors the moral clarity of her vision. Still, he leaves it to Judith and Hist to articulate the sharpest critiques of white imperial culture. In certain respects, then, they emerge as Cooper's best guides to reading the dominant themes of the Leatherstocking series.

Hist's role as a critic of the violence, racism, and hypocrisy undergirding white empire (that is, as a critic of the course of empire depicted in the series when read in the chronological order of plot) is especially important. Throughout the novel, she counsels and instructs the feeble-minded but noble Hetty about the realities of their conflict-ridden world. Early on, for example, when Hurry and Hutter are being held by the Iroquois, Hetty is allowed to visit because the Indians admire her spirituality and honesty. In the spirit of honesty, she asks Hist to tell the Iroquois the truth of the matter about why the white men had been stalking the Indians: "Tell them, first, that father and Hurry came here with an intention to take as many scalps as they could, for the wicked governor and the province have offered money for scalps, whether of warriors, or women, men or children" (190). Hetty's phrasing suggests that Hurry and Hutter cannot be understood apart from the imperial conflicts devastating the Indians; her recognition of white violence also threatens to undermine her confidence in the goodness of white Christians. Hetty thus stumbles as she attempts to teach Hist about the value of the Bible, as both Hist and the Iroquois chief Rivenoak point to the limits, indeed the evils, of those who use the Bible to legitimate conquest. Rivenoak wonders why Bible-reading whites, who are "ordered to *give* double to him that asks only for one thing," decide instead to "*take* double from the poor Indian who ask for *no* thing" (194). When Hetty starts weeping from confusion, confiding that "I *know* that all I have read from the book is true, and yet it woud'n't seem so, would it, by the conduct of those to whom the book was given," it is left to Hist to make sense of such contradictions. After expressing a caustic rage that a Bible calling for love "is the law by which my white brethren professes to live" (194), Hist attempts to comfort Hetty with her own form of racial egalitarianism: "Why you so trouble? You no make he book, if he be wrong, and you no make he pale face if he wicked. There wicked red man, and wicked white man – no colour all good – no colour all wicked" (195). These are some of the most profound words uttered in all of *The Deerslayer*.

Still, as the novel develops, it can seem that wickedness falls mainly on the side of the white colonizers, and that it is Hetty, Hist, and Judith who call white men to account. Shortly after Hutter is scalped by Indians who want the reward money, both Hetty and Judith take note of the poetic justice. As Judith pointedly remarks to Hurry: "His skin and hair have been torn from his head to gain money from the governor of Canada, as you would have torn theirs from the heads of the Hurons, to gain money from the governor of York" (362). Though Hutter is killed by the Hurons, it is Hurry who commits the most despicable act of the novel, wantonly killing an Indian woman in revenge for having been held prisoner. Shortly after being ransomed from captivity, Hurry returns with a gun, demonstrating that revenge knows no color, and shoots randomly into the Indian settlement. Cooper describes the scene: "The crack of a rifle succeeded, and then followed the roll of the echo along the eastern mountains. Almost at the same moment, a piercing female cry arose in the air in a prolonged shriek. The awful stillness that succeeded was, if possible, more appalling than the fierce and sudden interruption of the deep silence of midnight" (317). When *The Deerslayer* is read as the first of the Leatherstocking series, this "act of unthinking cruelty" (321), as the narrator terms it, undergirds all of the novels to come, and it is an act that, at the very least, makes it difficult to read the series as about the "natural" ascent of white men to power in the North American continent. This is the first of two major assaults by white men on the Iroquois, both of which result in the killing of women, and the wantonness and cruelty of the assaults help to illuminate the Indian anger that we see in the chronologically succeeding novels. The woman's scream and subsequent silence are haunting, and the description of her dying (she had been shot shortly after meeting with her lover) only adds to our sense of outrage: "[S]he was in the agonies of death, while the blood that trickled from her bared bosom betrayed the nature of the injury she had received" (317–18). Her body tells the story of violation, and while Natty can barely say a word, it is Hist who once again mounts the most telling challenge to

Hurry's evil action: "What for you shoot? ... How you feel, your wife killed? ... Why you so wicked, great pale-face?" (322).

The novel builds to a horrific scene of violence, indeed, of wickedness, which vindicates both Hist's and Judith's critiques of English colonial forces. The critic Eric Cheyfitz, basing his reading of the Leatherstocking series on *The Pioneers*, the first novel published in the series, writes that "the 'good' Indians must fight on the side of the 'good guys,' who, in Cooper's story of the development of the United States, which is the overriding story of the Tales, are necessarily the English and their descendants."[30] But in *The Deerslayer*, the revisionary first novel of the series, distinctions between "good" and "bad" Indian, Delaware and Iroquois, have broken down. The Iroquois chief Rivenoak is one of the most exemplary Indian characters in all of Cooper's fiction, a democratic leader who has risen to power in his tribe "purely by the force of talents, [and] sagacity" (489), while it is the Delaware Briarthorn, who kidnapped Hist and for a while manages to pass as Iroquois, who contributes to the novel's overall violence. More important with respect to Cheyfitz's argument, while the Iroquois and Delaware are presented as exemplars of democratic practice – "it is well known that little which could be called monarchical, or despotic entered into the politics of the North American tribes" (489) – the English, who serve the King, emerge as monarchical and self-satisfied killers (in the manner of Hurry Harry), thus raising all sorts of questions about the Leatherstocking Tales' "overriding story."[31]

In the novel's final dramatic scene, the red-faced British Captain Warley, who has been presented as Judith's probable seducer and whose redness links him with stereotypes of Indian savagery, arrives at Glimmerglass as the "rescuer" of Natty and his compatriots, guided by the racist, hate-filled Hurry. Warley's English troops, Hurry, and Natty himself subsequently participate in a battle that involves the indiscriminate killing, by the troops' phallicized bayonets, of Indian women and children. There is nothing heroic or admirable about white killers wearing "the scarlet of the King's livery" (521). Natty uses his gun to kill his enemies, but mostly the final battle is about the bayonet: "[T]he shrieks, groans, and denunciations that usually accompany the use of the bayonet followed. That terrible and deadly weapon was glutted in vengeance. The scene that succeeded was one of those, of which so many have occurred in our own times, in which neither age nor sex forms an exemption to the lot of a savage warfare" (522). The reference to "our own times" points to outrages in Cooper's contemporary moment, suggesting (against the grain of those who see Cooper as complicit in Jacksonian removal policies) that he may well have been troubled by reports of the deaths of Indian women and children on the Trail of Tears. In his account of the aftermath of the massacre, Cooper is scathing in his portrayal of Warley. Like Hurry, this "hard featured, red faced, man" (524) betrays no concern about the deaths of the Indians. Hetty dies from a bullet wound (the Hurons or perhaps a British soldier fire the inadvertent shot), and she is joined in death by the numerous Huron women and children who have been stabbed by the British: "The Sumach, all the elderly women, and some of the Huron girls, had fallen by a bayonet" (526).

In a novel that has at its center women's outrage at Hurry's wanton killing of an Indian woman, Cooper is unambiguously critical of English brutality, which can be viewed as on the continuum of the white violence that leads to the "rise" of the US nation in the Leatherstocking novels to come. If there is a hero in the concluding section of *The Deerslayer*, it is Rivenoak, who maintains his self-command to the very end: "That he mourned the loss of his tribe, is certain; still he did it in a manner that best became a warrior and a chief" (526). Cooper is often criticized for supposedly confusing the possibility of extinction with extermination, but there is no ambiguity here. Rivenoak's tribe has been decimated by the bayonets of troops linked to a British seducer. Judith's outraged declaration the day after the massacre resonates as a feminist critique that aligns her with Hist's outrage at Hurry and his murderous compatriots, and in certain ways announces an end to the Leatherstocking series: "I wish never to hear of marks, or rifles, or soldiers, or *men*, again" (530; Cooper's emphasis).

But we hear just a bit more about men in *The Deerslayer*'s unsettling concluding chapters. Natty, who has accepted Judith's gift of Killdeer (the magnificent rifle found in Hutter's trunk) and is now Hawkeye and not Deerslayer, proclaims that he will be joining forces with Warley and his successors in order to keep the French from the land claimed by England. Cooper's vision is apparently Whiggish or progressive, as he depicts both this battle and the Seven Years' War to come (previewed in the final chapter's jump forward to the 1750s) as essential to the emergence of the US nation and a burgeoning American empire. And yet his representation of such a historical trajectory is not without conflict or reservations. It is accurate to say with Philip Fisher that over the course of the novel Natty has become a killer;[32] but it would also be accurate to say that from beginning to end Cooper seems at a distance from this killer. When Natty, after accepting Judith's gift of Killdeer, declares that he will now "become King of the Woods" (390), it is difficult not to cringe at his use of the language of empire. While Natty looks forward to a continent cleared of the French and their Indian allies, Cooper at the conclusion of the novel offers an image of inevitable cyclical decline, remarking about post-massacre Glimmerglass that the beautiful lake will always be there while humans come and go. Even the "frightful event of the preceding evening," Cooper remarks, "had left no impression on the placid sheet" (523). But the "placid sheet" covers numerous dead bodies, as do the mounds in *The Prairies*, which Cooper here "anticipates" and enriches through his imaging of Glimmerglass itself as a burial ground. The eternal natural beauty of Glimmerglass is re-invoked in the closing semi-hopeful sentences of the novel: "We live in a world of transgressions and selfishness, and no pictures that represent us otherwise can be true, though, happily, for human nature, gleamings of that pure spirit in whose likeness man has been fashioned, are to be seen relieving its deformities, and mitigating if not excusing its crimes" (548). How apt that the final word of the Leatherstocking series is "crimes."

With his emphasis on crimes, Cooper provides new ways of thinking about what is implicit in the earlier-published Leatherstocking novels that chronologically follow *The Deerslayer*. The death of Chingachgook in *The Pioneers*, Tamenund's and Magua's sharp critiques of the English in *The Last of the Mohicans*, the mounds of *The Prairies*, and the violence of the French and the Indians in both *The Last of the Mohicans* and *The Pathfinder* all resonate very differently in light of the revisionary implications of the final novel of the series, which really does point to the end. It is difficult, for instance, to make significant distinctions between the Iroquois' slaughtering of English women and children at the midpoint of *The Last of the Mohicans* and the English troops' slaughtering of Iroquois women and children at the conclusion of *The Deerslayer*. If anything, that violence asks readers to regard the Iroquois' violence in *The Last of the Mohicans* as having been prompted by the earlier crimes of the English invaders' "lawless empire" (45).

Near the end of his life, as he was preparing the 1850 prefaces which would urge readers to begin the Leatherstocking series by reading *The Deerslayer*, Cooper became close friends with George Copway, an Ojibwa Indian also known as Kah-ge-ga-gah-bowh, whose autobiography, *The Life, History, and Travels of Kah-ge-ga-gah-bowh (George Copway)* (1847), republished as *The Life, Letters, and Speeches of Kah-ge-ga-gah-bowh, or G. Copway* (1850), went into multiple editions and became a best seller. Copway was a Methodist convert who in the late 1840s emerged as an influential writer on Indian affairs, arguing in particular against federal efforts to relocate (or remove) the Ojibwa from Michigan and Wisconsin to Minnesota. While lecturing in

New York against removal, he met Cooper, and the two became friends. Although Americanists tend to regard Cooper as a writer whose Leatherstocking novels lent ideological support for Indian removal, Copway saw him as a writer whose works spoke to Indian grievances and ennobled rather than belittled Indians. In all likelihood Copway had read *The Deerslayer*, and if so, it is not surprising that he would see Cooper as that rare white writer who gave voice to Indians' resistance to white empire. After spending time with Cooper at Cooperstown, Copway wrote him in 1850: "Of all the writers of our dear native land, you have done more justice to our down trodden race than any other author. . . . By your books the noble traits of the savage have been presented in their true light." In a letter of June 1851, Copway wrote Cooper asking for a contribution to a new journal, *Copway's American Indian*. That journal, he told Cooper, would be "a channel of information for the American people and to the Indian Race of all such things which will tend to give [both] a better idea of each other." Cooper contributed a letter to the first of twelve issues published between July 10 and September 27, 1851, and Copway subsequently published an appreciative essay on Cooper in the July 19 issue and then an admiring obituary (six days after Cooper's death) in the issue of September 20. Cooper's letter to Copway of June 17, 1851, shows why Copway was such an admirer and friend. "Certainly I should take great interest in the success of a journal like that you have mentioned," Cooper writes. "The red man has a high claim to have his cause defended, and I trust you will be able to do much in his behalf." Though he says that sickness will make it difficult for him to offer a substantial contribution, Cooper concludes his letter by remarking on their friendship: "I hope you may find leisure to make your promised visit and that we may expect the pleasure of seeing you again at my house."[33]

A Cooper who believes that the "cause" of the Indians should be "defended"; a Cooper who works closely with an Indian activist; a Cooper who regards Indians as alive and well in the United States and not on the verge of extinction; a Cooper who numbers among his friends at the close of his life an Ojibwa Indian – this is not the Cooper of current American literary studies. It is time that we reread the Leatherstocking novels by beginning with the end.

CHAPTER 3

Fifth of July
Nathaniel Paul and the Circulatory Routes of Black Nationalism

The African American Baptist minister Nathaniel Paul (1793–1839) was an influential leader in his own time, but he remains mostly forgotten today. Recovering his career as an antislavery and antiracist reformer brings into focus a number of issues in nineteenth-century African American literary and cultural studies: the transnational dimension of black nationalism; the importance of circulation (of bodies and texts) to the development of that nationalism; and the leadership role of black Americans in the antislavery struggle. Paul laid the groundwork for figures like Martin Delany, Frederick Douglass, and William Wells Brown, and deserves to be better known.

The opening decades of the nineteenth century were a hopeful time for African Americans in the Northern states. Strong black communities emerged in Philadelphia, New York, and other cities, and black leaders became increasingly vocal in calling for emancipation.[1] Following the New York legislature's relatively late decision to abolish slavery in the state, effective July 4, 1827, New York's African American leaders began to imagine the possibility of blacks achieving equal status with whites as enfranchised citizens. Among those buoyed by the prospects of emancipation, according to an article in *Freedom's Journal*, the first African American newspaper, were the free blacks of Albany, New York. At a formal "meeting of the people of colour, of the city of Albany, held at the African meeting-house, March 27, 1827, for the purpose of taking into consideration the expediency of celebrating the abolition of slavery in the state of New-York, which is to take place on the 4th day of July, 1827," Nathaniel Paul, the charismatic and highly respected pastor of the First African Baptist Church in Albany, delivered a "short but pertinent address" instructing New York's blacks on "a just sense of their own rights and the duties which they owe to the community." Paul also offered a resolution that was resoundingly adopted by the group: "Resolved, That whereas slavery by the laws of this state is ABOLISHED on the 4th of July next, we deem it a duty to express our gratitude to Almighty God and our public benefactors, by publicly celebrating the same." Though grateful for emancipation, Paul was hardly naive about the difficulties facing African Americans in a white supremacist culture. Thus he championed the group's more ironically conceived resolution as well, which pointed to the limits of New York's emancipation act in a nation in which slavery remained the law of the land: "Resolved, That whereas the 4th day of July is the day that the National Independence of this country is recognized by white citizens, we deem it proper to celebrate the 5th."[2]

This chapter traces the career of the somewhat obscure but highly influential Nathaniel Paul, focusing on what I term the circulatory routes of his black (trans)nationalism. Paul was regularly in motion, and, at the peak of his career as a writer, lecturer, and activist, he was working for antislavery reform and black elevation in three different countries. Born in New Hampshire in 1793, Paul attended the interracial Free Will Academy in Hollis, New Hampshire, which trained Baptist ministers. He moved to Boston in 1805 or 1806 to join his older brother, Thomas Paul (1773–1831), the founder and leader of the First African Baptist Church in Boston. In 1814, Nathaniel married Elizabeth Lamsno of Hollis, New Hampshire, and six years later, after their four-year-old son died from influenza, the couple moved to Albany. There, Paul became pastor of the city's First African Baptist Church, and by the mid-1820s he had become a highly regarded leader of the black community. But rather than remain in Albany to work for blacks' rights in the United States, Paul moved to Canada in 1830 to join the newly formed black community at Wilberforce. He then made a notably successful fundraising tour in Britain from 1832 to 1836, before eventually returning to Albany. Unlike Frederick Douglass, who consistently worked for black elevation and freedom in the United States, Paul for approximately six years aligned himself with an alternative black community, which he apparently believed had the potential to develop a black nationality, if not in the United States, then in Canada. Paul thus anticipated the antislavery and antiracist work of such figures as William Wells Brown and Martin Delany, who, while beginning their antislavery careers in the manner of Douglass (focusing on black uplift in the United States), at various times supported the development of separatist black communities in Canada, the southern Americas, and Africa as part of their commitment to a diasporic black nationalism.[3]

Sterling Stuckey has usefully defined black nationalism in the United States as a consciousness among African Americans "of a shared experience of oppression at the hands of white people" and as a program that "emphasized the need for black people to rely primarily on themselves in vital areas of life."[4] As Stuckey and others have observed, black nationalism could embrace a range of sometimes competing and conflicting options – such as black uplift and emigrationism – and had to be constructed and reconstructed in relation to different exigencies and contexts. One large context that has received considerable attention over the past two decades is what Paul Gilroy terms "the black Atlantic." In his influential study, Gilroy urges cultural historians to consider the black experience in relation to the diasporic figure of "ships in motion across the spaces between Europe, America, Africa, and the Caribbean," an approach that brings into focus "the circulation of ideas and activists as well as the movement of key cultural and political artefacts." Adopting such a circulatory perspective on "themes of nationality, exile, and cultural affiliation," he suggests, also helps to "accentuate the inescapable fragmentation and differentiation of the black subject."[5] There is certainly motion, fragmentation, and differentiation in the circulatory routes of Nathaniel Paul, whose evolving politics at times can appear to move beyond the category of the nation. But ultimately what holds his career together is the metaphor of the Fifth of July, which speaks to the differentiation and fragmentation of the African American subject, while at the same time implying the potential for civic participation and wholeness. Emerging from a black oppositional politics, the Fifth of July as a rhetorical figure holds US nationalism to its ideological promises, even as it skews US nationalism. Suggestively postnational, the Fifth of July also raises questions about location, for the figure suggests that the black nationalist project is not limited to the United States, but is sometimes inside and sometimes outside, or even beside (as with Canada), as a form of critical parataxis. For Paul, Fifth of July thinking allowed him to creatively construct a politics of black nationalism that evolved in response to new challenges and situations. But because the Fourth of July remained the implicit foundational term of his Fifth of July politics, he never entirely relinquished his hopes for a transformed (or redeemed) US nationalism that was just, equitable, and racially inclusive.

Paul's hopes for such a transformative redemption were powerfully enunciated in his eloquent Fifth of July speech, *An Address, Delivered on the Celebration of the Abolition of Slavery, in the State of New-York, July 5, 1827*, which he presented to a gathering of African Americans in Albany. Anticipating Douglass's famous Fifth of July speech, "What to the Slave Is the Fourth of July?" (1852), Paul addresses head on what he refers to as "the medley of contradictions which stain the national character." Locating the contradictions in the nation's failure to honor the egalitarian ideals of its founding documents, Paul declares to his auditors: "[P]aradoxical as it may appear to those acquainted with the constitution of the government, *or who have read the bold declaration of this nation's independence*; yet it is a fact that can neither be denied or controverted, that in the United States of America, at the expiration of fifty years after its becoming a free and independent nation, there are no less than fifteen hundred thousand human beings still in a state of unconditional vasalage [sic]." That continued bondage exposes the hypocrisy of Fourth of July celebrations. But despite the persistence of slavery in the new republic, Paul, speaking at the optative moment of 1827, sees great possibilities for the nation's free blacks, and so he devotes much of his speech to encouraging African Americans to assume responsibility for their own self-elevation. Sharing the views of many other black leaders of the time, Paul insists that the best possible refutation of whites' antiblack racism would be for the free blacks to demonstrate their ability to rise in Northern market culture. Thus he places a considerable burden on the shoulders of New York's African Americans: "This day commences a new era in our history; . . . new duties devolve upon us; duties, which if properly attended to, cannot fail to improve our moral condition, and elevate us to a rank of respectable standing with the community; or if neglected, we fall at once into the abyss of contemptible wretchedness."[6]

But even as Paul makes the case for black elevation, he remains acutely aware that white racist practices present huge barriers to black progress in the United States. He also knows that slavery and racism have made US blacks into what Delany would call "a nation within a nation."[7] In declaring, for example, that he and his auditors "will tell the good story" of the abolition of slavery in New York "to our children and to our children's children, down to the latest posterity," Paul establishes from the outset of his speech that blacks constitute an ethnic community that has different experiences from whites, in large part because blacks have been forcibly brought to the Americas as slaves. And he does not simply blame US whites for the problem of slavery. One of the more fascinating aspects of Paul's 1827 speech is his patriotic willingness, in the tradition of Jefferson's Declaration of Independence, to indict England for introducing slavery to North America: "It was before the sons of Columbia felt the yoke of their oppressors, and rose in their strength to put it off that this land became contaminated with slavery. . . . It was by the permission of the British parliament, that the human species first became an article of merchandize among them." While Paul believes that Britain bears at least some responsibility for the existence of slavery in the United States, he notes that many of the principal abolitionists of the past thirty years have been British, praising "the immortal Clarkson" and "the immortal Wilberforce" for devoting themselves "to the holy purpose of rescuing a continent [Africa] from rapine and murder."[8] (Paul would meet both Thomas Clarkson and William Wilberforce during his British tour of the 1830s.) Paul thus brings to the forefront of his mostly US nationalistic address the transatlantic context that, as Gilroy and others have argued, works against the concept of the autonomous or exceptionalist nation-state.

Africa, too, has an important place in Paul's Fifth of July speech. It is crucial to note that Paul gave his speech approximately ten years after the formation of the American Colonization Society (ACS), a white "philanthropic" organization – championed by Henry Clay, Lyman Beecher, and other "moderate" whites – which claimed that the "natural" place for blacks was Africa. The goal of the ACS was to ship the free blacks back to their putative homeland in Africa, specifically to the ACS's colony of Liberia, and in this way make the United States into an all-white nation. Most African Americans of the period vigorously opposed the ACS, though John Russwurm, the editor of *Freedom's Journal*, eventually came to support Liberian colonization. In his Fifth of July speech, Paul seems somewhat conflicted about Africa. Insisting that blacks deserve US citizenship, he nonetheless depicts blacks as different from whites, not only because of their shared experience of slavery and racism in the United States, but also because of their genealogical connection to Africa. In a particularly compelling moment, Paul describes blacks being taken from "the shores of Africa" and suffering the horrors of the Middle Passage: "I view them casting the last and longing look towards the land which gave them birth, until at length the ponderous anchor is weighed . . .; I behold those who have been so unfortunate as to survive the passage, emerging from their loathsome prison, and landing amidst the noisy rattling of the massy [sic] fetters which confine them." For Paul, the question remains as to why a benevolent God would allow such an awful practice to occur, and he concludes that God wanted to "bring good out of evil" by exposing blacks to western Christianity and science. He proclaims: "the glorious light of science is spreading from east to west, and Afric's sons are catching the glance of its beams as it passes; its enlightening rays scatter the mists of moral darkness and ignorance." According to Paul, the ultimate result of this historical movement will be the redemption of "Afric's sons" and of Africa itself, which will one day "take her place among the other nations of the earth."[9]

A lecture that begins as a call for black uplift in the United States thus quickly enlarges to offer a diasporic vision of the redemption of Africa and then the advent of a revolutionary moment in which the black slaves themselves fight to bring about the end of slavery. Paul imagines this emancipatory moment less in US than in hemispheric terms. According to Paul, "the recent revolution in South America, the catastrophe and exchange of power in the Isle of Hayti, the restless disposition of both master and slave in the southern states, the constitution of our government" all point to the eventuality that slavery will "be forever annihilated from the earth." Paul may link African Americans to Haitian revolutionism, South American revolutionism, and a redeemed Africa, but by asserting near the end of his speech the Biblical notion that "God . . . has made of one blood, all nations of men," he celebrates egalitarian ideals from a monogenetic, religious point of view in ways that trouble racial and national borders. That said, he remains hopeful about blacks' prospects in the United States, despite making the self-consciously political decision to celebrate "the day in which the cause of justice and humanity have triumphed over tyranny and oppression," not on the Fourth of July, but on the Fifth.[10]

Paul is less hopeful two years later in his 1829 Sixth of July speech, *An Address, Delivered at Troy, on the Celebration of the Abolition of Slavery, in the State of New York, July 6, 1829. – Second Anniversary.* Though he continues to appeal to US nationalism, he laments what now seem to him the nearly insurmountable obstacles in the way of black elevation in the foreseeable future. As he explains, "[A]lthough the shackles of slavery are broken, and we are no longer under bondage; yet many circumstances have combined to render our condition in many things, far behind our more highly favored [white] countrymen." Despite the promises of the 1827 emancipation, he states, white racists have worked in insidious ways to maintain the status quo. But again, despairing as he is in his Sixth of July address, Paul holds onto the July Fourth ideals which implicitly inform both his Fifth and now Sixth of July speeches. Still committed to bringing about black elevation in the United States, he tones down the vision of African redemption that had such an important place in his 1827 address, characterizing the ACS's project of ridding the United States of its black population "as utterly chimerical and absurd." Convinced that the ACS agenda makes it all the more urgent for blacks to insist upon the legitimacy of their rights to US citizenship, he invokes the deeds of blacks who fought in the American Revolution, declaring in no uncertain terms: "We claim this as *our country*, as the land of our nativity, and to achieve its independence, our fathers faced her enemies on the field of battle, and contended even unto death." (William C. Nell would make a similar argument for black citizenship in *The Colored Patriots of the American Revolution* [1855].) Although Paul seems less hopeful about African Americans' immediate prospects, he concludes his 1829 Sixth of July address with a vision of racism vanishing from the United States at "some more distant period," a time when "prejudices, however long their standing or deeply rooted, will be eradicated, and distinctions shall be known no more."[11]

Paul must have imagined such a quixotic moment occurring at a *very* distant period, for less than a year after delivering this speech, he decided to abandon his pastorate in Albany and move to the agrarian black community of Wilberforce in Upper Canada. Named in honor of the great British abolitionist, the community of Wilberforce, near what is now Lucan, Ontario, was established in late 1829 or early 1830 in response to an 1829 decision by Cincinnati's legislators to enforce the state's Black Codes of 1804 and 1807, which among other things required blacks to display their freedom papers and post bond when entering the state. Cincinnati's approximately three thousand African Americans resisted the enforcement of these laws by rioting and making plans for a mass exodus to Canada. Serving as the principal agents of the ultimately small group that emigrated to Canada were Israel Lewis and Thomas Cresap, who initially contracted to purchase four thousand acres from the Canada Land Company for $6,000. When it became clear that they could not raise that kind of money, they purchased eight hundred acres for their proposed black community with the help of donations from Quakers in Indiana and Ohio. Lewis then went on a recruitment mission in New York State, and managed to enlist the black abolitionist grocer Austin Steward (1793–1865), Nathaniel Paul, and another of Paul's brothers, Benjamin Paul (?–1836), a Baptist minister in New York City. By July 1831 the community had established a board of managers, with Steward serving as chairman, and had approximately two hundred participants.[12]

Despite the disillusionment evident in his 1829 speech, it is difficult to say why Paul chose to transplant himself to Canada. A possible personal reason for the move was that he wanted a change of scene after the death of his wife in 1828. Was he also renouncing the United States? Though it is true that some blacks emigrated to Canada as an act of renunciation, for many others a move to Canada signaled a continued commitment to the promises of US nationalism. The hope was that the development of prospering free-black communities on the Northern borders of the United States would demonstrate to US whites what blacks could achieve when not fettered by racism or slavery. To be sure, some of those participating in Wilberforce conceived of their group as a Canadian community and felt warmly toward a nation that seemed considerably less racist than the United States, but Wilberforce never developed much of a distinctive identity. Its principal leaders retained ties with the US abolitionist movement and chose to present Wilberforce to such notable white abolitionists as Benjamin Lundy and William Garrison as prima facie evidence of the possibilities for black uplift in the United States. Paul probably chose to participate in Wilberforce precisely because he regarded the community as having the potential to improve the condition of African Americans and thus of fulfilling the vision of his 1827 Fifth of July address. Though he may have been an enthusiastic participant at the start, his extant writings reveal little evidence of an attachment to Wilberforce or Canada. In fact, what is striking about Paul's participation in Wilberforce is how briefly he lived there and how quickly he developed a new sense of identity as a transatlantic reformer in England.

That new identity was in some ways forced upon Paul. Because Wilberforce had virtually no capital, the board of managers decided, as Austin Steward remarked in his 1857 memoir, *Twenty-Two Years a Slave, and Forty Years a Freeman*, to commission "two agents for the purpose of soliciting aid for the erection of houses for worship, and for the maintenance of schools in the colony."[13] Israel Lewis was authorized to seek support in the United States, while Paul was tapped for Great Britain. What ensued was not a pretty story, as conflicts arose among the principal leaders that eventually led to the collapse of the community around 1837. Although Paul's mission to Great Britain was closely tied to his identity as a member of the Wilberforce community, that identity very quickly was transmuted into what could be termed a transatlantic or "black Atlantic" identity which, oddly enough, was both highly racialized and deracialized. Like Douglass during the mid-1840s, Paul experienced in England a heightened sense of identity and purpose as a black man, while at the same time discovering what he believed was an Enlightenment world of racial egalitarianism in which color seemed not to matter. Embracing a dualistic (black/postracial) transatlantic identity, Paul did some of his most significant and impassioned cultural work.

Though the documentary record consists mainly of newspaper accounts, we can nevertheless do a reasonably good job of reconstructing the shape and significance of Paul's British tour. As described in the September 17, 1831, issue of Garrison's antislavery newspaper, the *Liberator*, Paul's mission to England was initially related to the goal of raising funds for the Wilberforce colony. In an article titled "Colony in Upper Canada," the anonymous writer reports that the "Rev. Nathaniel Paul, agent of the Wilberforce Settlement in Canada, and formerly pastor of the African Baptist Church in this city, arrived here [Albany] on

Wednesday, the 10th August, bringing with him letters of introduction, and other credentials authorizing him to visit Great Britain, to solicit such aid as may be conducive to the prosperity and future welfare of that infant settlement." But even before Paul set sail for England on December 31, 1831, the reportage in the *Liberator* suggests that something more was at stake in his transatlantic voyage than simply soliciting funds for Wilberforce. In a front-page article in the January 14, 1832, *Liberator*, "R." (most likely the black abolitionist Charles Remond) refers to Paul's goal of obtaining "funds in aid of this little Colony [Wilberforce]" as merely the "ostensible purpose" of his voyage to England, and concludes with a poem pointing to a significantly larger mission. In a key stanza, R. writes:

> And when you arrive on Albion's shores,
>   May you with holy fervor trace
> The unjust treatment of our foes,
>   Who spurn, exile, our helpless race.[14]

Clearly, R. regards Paul as taking on the responsibility of representing the "race" and specifically of describing blacks' sufferings in the United States.

The record shows that Paul quickly subordinated his Wilberforce assignment to what he, too, came to regard as his larger role of working for the emancipation of US blacks. As Paul informs Garrison in a letter of July 3, 1832, which was included in an August 1832 article in the *Liberator* titled "Rev. Nathaniel Paul," shortly after his arrival he took the measure of his British audiences and realized that "the people of this country are alive to the cause of abolition." Paul then excitedly reports on the first material result of his speaking efforts: "What would you think, sir, of seeing a petition *a half mile long*, and containing more than ONE HUNDRED THOUSAND NAMES, sent to the Congress of the United States? Surely you would think that, ere long, slavery must be abolished in this country."[15]

As is evident from this report, Paul was enormously successful as a speaker. Moreover, he quickly came to understand that while circulating on the lecture circuit, he could also circulate in print in both Britain and the United States as an author of letters and as a speaker whose lectures garnered an enormous amount of publicity. But it was mainly his success as a speaker that made him such an influential black abolitionist in his own time and beyond, paving the way for Remond, Douglass, William Wells Brown, and many other African Americans who participated in the British antislavery lecture circuit. Right from the start of Paul's tour, white British and US abolitionists discovered that antislavery arguments made an especially strong impact on white audiences when coming from a black person, someone who could speak from first-hand experience about the ravages of racism and slavery, and someone whose intelligence and moral authority made a mockery of proslavery assertions of black inferiority and dependency. As the secretary of a local antislavery society in Edinburgh wrote to the British abolitionist George Thompson on one of Paul's triumphal speaking engagements: "I never saw one more kindly treated by all parties. The color of his skin was an excellent introduction to him, something surely that will surprise Brother Jonathan. I never saw the feeling of sympathy for the manner in which the free blacks in America are treated, so powerfully brought forth. Here there is no prejudice about the color of a man's skin. The darker it is, the more likely is he to receive kind attention and support."[16] Aware that Paul had a special relationship with British abolitionist audiences, the leading abolitionists of the time sought to share the stage with the dark-skinned Paul, who inevitably found himself discussing colonization and abolition at the expense of Wilberforce.

Increasingly central to Paul's antislavery lectures in England was a concerted effort to expose the mendacity of the ACS. Paul was forced to go on the offensive with his anti-ACS position, for right around the time of his arrival in England, the ACS's Philadelphia-based agent Elliott Cresson began a speaking tour on behalf of the group, entreating concerned Britons to help the cause of African Americans by donating funds to ship them to Liberia. During 1832 Paul collaborated with the British abolitionists Captain Charles Stuart and James Cropper in an increasingly successful effort to undermine Cresson's campaign, and in 1833 Paul was joined on the antislavery lecture circuit by Garrison himself. Historian Manisha Sinha remarks that "Paul's and Garrison's British lecture tour was the first triumph of interracial immediatism," and she emphasizes that, despite his recent publication of the anti-ACS *Thoughts on African Colonization* (1832), "Garrison followed in [Paul's] black footsteps." Typically Garrison is regarded as the white abolitionist leader who sought to control his black speakers, but in this instance he learned from Paul. And it was clear that Paul, more than Garrison, was running the show. As Garrison biographer Henry Mayer reports, Paul developed two large arguments that he would sound again and again in his speeches of 1833: "He would tell meetings . . . of the overwhelming opposition to colonization among American blacks, and he would defend his fellow citizen Garrison from Cresson's smears that he was a mere pamphleteer who lacked standing in the United States because he had served a jail term on a libel charge."[17]

In his attacks on the ACS, Paul challenged racialist notions that blacks "naturally" belong in Africa, and, perhaps more importantly, regularly sounded the black nationalist themes of his Fifth of July address, insisting again and again on African Americans' rights to citizenship in the United States. Thus Wilberforce had to be presented, in effect, as a means to an end: as a voluntary black community (wholly unlike the ACS's comparatively involuntary colony of Liberia) that shouldn't distract from the larger goal of improving blacks' condition in the United States. In a letter printed in the April 1833 *Liberator*, Paul describes the speeches he has been delivering of late: "I have been engaged, for several months past, in traveling through the country and delivering lectures upon ... the importance of promoting the cause of education and religion generally among the colored people. My lectures have been numerously attended by from two to three thousand people, the Halls and Chapels have been overflown, and hundreds have not been able to obtain admittance." He goes on to describe his meeting with the great abolitionist Thomas Clarkson and his breakfasting "with the venerable WILBERFORCE." As for the Wilberforce mission itself: "I do not hold out the delusive idea that the whole of the colored people are going to Canada; but have invariably said, that in spite of all that will ever remove there, or to any other part of the world they will continue to increase in America."[18]

Two major extant speeches by Paul provide a good sense of topics he addressed while making the case for emancipation and blacks' rights to US citizenship. At a July 1833 meeting of over two thousand abolitionists at London's Exeter Hall, Paul, who shared the stage with Garrison, George Thompson, Daniel O'Connell, and other prominent abolitionists, began his speech by celebrating Garrison. At the heart of Paul's speech, however, which mostly concerned itself with ridiculing the politics and methods of the ACS, were scathing Fifth of July remarks on the contradictory practice of slavery in the young republic, attacks that were no doubt greatly enjoyed by his British auditors. Paul sarcastically declares: "Perhaps it is not generally known that in the United States of America – the land of freedom and equality – the laws are so exceedingly liberal that they give to man the liberty of purchasing as many negroes as he can find means to pay for ... and also the liberty to sell them again." And in his resounding attack on the ACS, he repeatedly invokes "American" ideals of "freedom and equality" to challenge the ACS's claim that Africa was the "natural" place for blacks. According to Paul, the ACS has closed its eyes to blacks' crucial place in the founding and development of the US nation, and thus "undertakes to expel from their native country hundreds of thousands of unoffending and inoffensive individuals, who, in time of war, have gone forth into the field of battle, and have contended for the liberties of that country." In this respect, the ACS, like the

Southern slave power, seeks "to rob the colored men in that country of every right, civil, political or religious, to which they are entitled by the American Declaration of Independence."[19]

Soon after delivering his successful Exeter Hall speech, Paul again pressed his argument against the ACS in his forceful "Compensation for Slaves," which was printed in the August 31, 1833, *Liberator* and first delivered as a speech to British abolitionist audiences. As a speaker and writer, Paul was continuing to circulate both in Britain and the United States. In the lecture/essay, Paul attacks an ACS proposal to compensate Southern slaveholders for freeing their slaves, arguing that such a compensation plan would be akin to paying a thief for the return of stolen property. In the manner of his Fifth of July address, he also invokes the Declaration to expose the moral shortcomings of both the ACS project and those citizens of the US nation who are willing to give such a society its financial and moral support.

But there is a significant difference in his invocation of the Declaration of Independence in "Compensation for Slaves," for he presents it less as a founding document of the United States than as a powerful expression of ideas about human rights shared by enlightened men and women throughout the world. In short, he presents the Declaration as but one of many late eighteenth-century statements on human equality, with the implication that Jefferson's document needs to be reconceived in an international Enlightenment context as a contribution to emerging notions on both sides of the Atlantic about the evils of the despotic, uncivilized, and antiquated practice of slavery. Inspired by Britain's momentous West Indian Emancipation Act of 1833, Paul refers to "the immediate and universal emancipation of the slaves, in all the British Islands in the Gulf of Mexico" as "one of the most cheering and important events for the happiness of mankind, which has happened since the Declaration of Independence." Linking the Declaration to global revolutionary movements, and not just to the ideological origins of the United States, Paul builds his speech to a climactic mandate that, as with the writings of Thomas Paine, can be regarded in national, transnational, and postnational terms: "BE FREE!"[20]

Paul's liberatory mandate here and in other of his lectures and essays of the mid-1830s also had a transracial (or postracial) dimension that can be traced back to his Exeter Hall speech of 1833. Though he rhetorically foregrounded in that speech what could be termed a politics of color authenticity – "the complexion that I wear ... shall speak in my behalf" – he had by this time become attracted to a transnational notion of a humanist community that could see beyond color. Thus, even as he speaks

as a black, he identifies as one of the great evils of the ACS that its leaders
and members think only in terms of color, desiring to ship the free blacks
from the United States simply "[b]ecause the God of heaven has given
them a different complexion from themselves." Opposed to African colonization, which arguably also had ideological sources in the discourses of
what Gilroy terms "the Enlightenment Project," Paul, in this and other of
his post-1827 speeches and writings, takes care to downplay any genealogical, racial, or cultural attraction he might feel to Africa, speaking only of
his pity for what he terms "the sad condition which that country [sic] is in,"
while championing the importance of an enlightened leadership that will
lead Africa from "vilest superstition" to "civilization and Christianity."
Such a vision of an enlightened, nonracist group of leaders was no doubt
inspired by his amazement at what he regarded as an absence of color
prejudice in England. In his April 1833 letter to the *Liberator*, for example,
he states, "Here, if I go to church, I am not pointed to the 'negro seat' in the
gallery; but any gentleman opens his pew door for my reception."[21] Paul's
response to a perceived lack of prejudice was not to embrace British nationalism but rather to celebrate a transnational community of enlightened,
educated, humane "gentlemen," especially as represented by such international reformers as Clarkson, Wilberforce, Garrison, Thompson, and
O'Connell. On a personal level, Paul's ability to see beyond the nation-
state and race was demonstrated when he married Anne Aday (ca. 1791–?), a
white English woman and fellow abolitionist, sometime in 1833.

For Steward and the Wilberforce board, however, Paul's move toward
what could be termed a cosmopolitan abolitionism, particularly as
emblematized by his marriage to a British white woman, pointed to the
limits of Paul's color-blind transnationalism. From their perspective, Paul
was allowing his mission to be co-opted by whites who had little sympathy
for the project that had sent him to England in the first place. But to
understand the full context of Steward's disillusionment with Paul, we
need to return to 1831, for it was at that time that Steward and the
Wilberforce Board of Managers, shortly after authorizing Israel Lewis to
solicit funds in the United States, came to regard their US agent as a thief.
Convinced that Lewis was taking funds intended for Wilberforce for his
own personal gain, the board dismissed him in late 1831. In response, Lewis,
who retained the support of Paul's brother Benjamin, threatened to sue the
board for defamation of character, and he continued collecting money for
what he now called his own Wilberforce Colonization Company. In 1833,
the *Liberator* began to print regular notices, signed by Wilberforce's board
and the prominent white abolitionist Arthur Tappan, warning subscribers

against giving their Wilberforce donations to Lewis, whom they presented as a con man attempting "to gull the public out of money for individual purposes."[22] The *Liberator*'s warnings led to Lewis's disgrace, and he soon vanished from sight. As far as fundraising was concerned, the community's hopes lay with Nathaniel Paul. These hopes were expressed in a declaration from the Wilberforce board printed in the July 16, 1836, *Liberator*: "That although we have not received One Hundred Dollars from said LEWIS, yet when we shall have received the funds collected by our Agent, REV. NATH'L. PAUL, in England, for us, we will refund, as far as our abilities will allow, and our friends may require, the money contributed for our *supposed benefit*, by them in the States."[23]

Increasingly impatient for Paul's return, Steward and the Wilberforce board sent the Canadian Henry Nell to England with the mission of bringing Paul back to Wilberforce; but Nell himself became enamored of England and decided to remain there. In *Twenty-Two Years a Slave*, Steward denounces Nell as even "less worthy of confidence than the agent [Paul]," and states (incorrectly) that Paul returned to New York in the fall of 1834 and was unwilling to come to Wilberforce until the spring of 1835. In fact, as the 1836 notice of the board's desire for Paul's return suggests, Paul continued his successful British tour through 1835 and early 1836. The December 19, 1835, *Liberator* printed a resoundingly positive assessment of Paul's ongoing accomplishments while overseas: "Mr. Paul's statements contributed most materially to accomplish the glorious measure of slave emancipation in the British dominions in the opinion of every friend to the abolition party in England.... The name of the American Paul is rendered dear to every friend of humanity in Great Britain, and his memory is enshrined in the grateful remembrance of the emancipated race whose fetters he has assisted to unloose."[24] Significantly, this anonymous writer says nothing about Paul's Wilberforce connection, assessing his value in relation to Great Britain and the even larger anti-slavery community consisting of "every friend of humanity."

In *Twenty-Two Years a Slave*, Steward presents Paul as a veritable money-making machine who "was making money too easily, to like to be interrupted."[25] But Paul eventually did return to Wilberforce, arriving in the spring of 1836, most likely in response to the news that his brother Benjamin had recently died. Upon his return, Paul, to Steward's considerable outrage, claimed that the Wilberforce Board of Managers owed *him* money and not the other way around. As he explained to the board, while abroad he had collected over $8,000 for Wilberforce, but his expenses during this same period were over $7,000, and because the salary he and the board had agreed on was $50 a month, the board owed him approximately $1,000. In his autobiography, Steward concedes that, according to their contractual agreement, the group did indeed owe Paul money, though he states that as a man of honor and as someone concerned about Wilberforce, Paul at the very least should have repaid the initial $700 he was loaned to make the British trip. Also, Steward is clearly skeptical of Paul's claim, which he made to the board, that he loaned Garrison $200 for his return trip to the United States and that the board should assume that expense as well. (In an appendix to *Twenty-Two Years a Slave*, Steward prints a June 1856 letter from Garrison denying that the loan ever took place, but Garrison's memory was faulty; two decades earlier, in a letter of December 17, 1835, to fellow abolitionist Lewis Tappan, Garrison states that Paul lent him the money "so that I could return home without begging."[26])

Asserting that "as far as the monied interest of the colony was concerned, [Paul's] mission was an entire failure," Steward allows that Paul may have accomplished some good during his British tour: "It is said that he continually addressed crowded and deeply interested audiences, and that many after hearing him, firmly resolved to exert themselves, until every chain was broken and every bondman freed beneath the waving banner of the British Lion." Despite some of the positive things he has to say about Paul, Steward emphasizes the overall failure of Paul's mission by focusing on – indeed scapegoating – Paul's British white wife as the reason for Paul's neglect of Wilberforce. In his autobiography, Steward immediately follows his description of Paul's failure to bring back money for Wilberforce by asking how he managed to take care of an aristocratic white wife, implying that he must have done so with funds he collected for the community: "[H]is expenses had been considerable; besides, he had fallen in love during his stay in England, with a white woman, and I suppose it must have required both time and money to woo and win so fine and fair an English lady." Though there is little extant information on Paul's wife, there is every indication that she was a committed abolitionist who, in linking herself to a relatively poor black man, had made financial and social sacrifices. Nevertheless, Steward presses his case against Paul through a highly unflattering description of Paul's wife in all of her supposedly aristocratic, narcissistic glory: "[W]e were immediately ushered into the presence of Mrs. Nathaniel Paul, whom we found in an inner apartment, made by drawn curtains, carpeted in an expensive style, where she was seated like a queen in state, – with a veil floating from her head to the floor; a gold chain encircling her neck, and attached to a gold watch in her girdle; her fingers and person were sparkling with costly jewelry." What makes this description particularly unfair and unseemly is that Steward is describing her in the process of consoling the recently bereaved wife of Benjamin Paul. Steward's scapegoating persists into his account of Nathaniel Paul returning to Albany and dying in poverty, illness, and obscurity. Steward blames Paul's wife for his downfall: "I have been told that his domestic life was far from a peaceable or happy one, and that in poverty, sorrow, and affliction, he lingered on a long time, till death at last closed the scene."[27]

Paul died in 1839, but hardly in obscurity. When he returned to Albany in 1836, accompanied by his wife, he became pastor of the Union Street Baptist Church and continued his antislavery preaching. African American newspapers of the period present a picture of a vital clerical leader who was highly respected for his antislavery and antiracist politics. In a lecture of February 1838, delivered to the Albany Anti-Slavery Society and reprinted in the March 14, 1838, issue of *The Friend of Man* (Utica, NY), Paul showed that he remained acutely aware of the problem of color prejudice in the United States and that, rather than abandoning black people, as Steward implies, he retained a Fifth of July black nationalist politics that continued to admonish the nation for failing to honor its founding ideals. In this February 1838 lecture, Paul attacks slavery and the slave masters, but he also focuses on the racism that remains pervasive among abolitionists, warning of "the kind of abolitionist who hated slavery, 'especially that which is 1,000 or 1,500 miles off,' but who hated even more 'a man who wears a colored skin.'" In all likelihood Paul delivered this speech in partial response to the condemnations of his interracial marriage that he received (implicitly and explicitly) from white and black abolitionists when he returned to the United States. Evidence of the persistence of Paul's political activism can also be found in a June 1839 issue of *The Colored American*, the most influential African American newspaper of the time, which announced, in light of Paul's gravely ill condition, "a subscription meeting at Albany which would feature the last public appearance of the popular figure, Nathaniel Paul, pastor of the Union Street Baptist Church."[28] Even as he struggled with the illness that would take his life later that year, Paul was making plans to attend this gathering of black editors, writers, and readers.[29]

Swayed by Steward's negative assessment of Paul in his autobiography, the historian Robin W. Winks concludes, "If Lewis was a felon, Paul was a fool."[30] Steward presents Paul as particularly foolish in marriage, with the suggestion that such foolishness reveals Paul's selfishness, dishonesty, and disloyalty to his race. But in focusing on Paul's white wife, Steward ultimately displays his inability to understand the transnational and postracial dimensions of Paul's black nationalism as it developed in England. Hardly a fool, Paul realized while in England that there were much larger matters to address than Wilberforce, and in forging his identity during that period as a transatlantic abolitionist, he helped to define the role of the black abolitionist in Britain from the 1830s to the time of the Civil War. Though Paul came to embrace an Enlightenment humanist politics of universal emancipation, he never stopped trying to improve the lot of African Americans, and his improvisatory, transatlantic politics of antislavery paved the way for figures as diverse as Wells Brown, and Delany – both of whom crossed national borders and experimented with emigrationist options while retaining an allegiance to a Fifth of July vision of a flawed but potentially redeemable United States. Paul's career may therefore be taken as both exemplary and paradigmatic, reminding us of the conceptual fluidity of race and nation in the careers of a number of representative African American male leaders. Not the least significant aspect of Paul's career is that he was a first-rate speaker and writer; his 1827 Fifth of July speech and his 1833 "Compensation for Slaves" merit a place in the canon of African American writings. Attending to Paul's writings and circulatory routes helps us to see more clearly the complex rhetorical and cultural work integral to the creatively resilient black nationalism of the nineteenth century.

CHAPTER 4

American Studies in an Age of Extinction
Poe, Hawthorne, Katrina

Climate change has become increasingly important to transnational American literary studies. The global warming triggered by the massive infusion of carbon dioxide and methane into the atmosphere has no respect for national borders and presses us to think about the nation in a planetary context. I wrote the initial draft of this chapter in the immediate wake of Hurricane Katrina. Although Katrina is discussed only in the final short section, my sense of Katrina as a sign of worse things to come informs the entire essay, which is haunted by the prospect of human extinction. What impact should such a prospect have on our work as Americanists? To begin to answer such a question, I turn to Poe and Hawthorne, who wrote some of their best short fiction when concerns about human extinction were rampant. Their reflections on extinction in several of their tales address tensions between the local and the global in ways that can help us to think more self-consciously about similar tensions in our own critical work.

Concerns that life on the planet may be coming to an end are pervasive and help to define our present moment. Anxieties about nuclear annihilation were everywhere in the 1950s and 1960s, and those anxieties remain with us today. But there are now added fears about apocalyptic terrorist plots, mutating killer viruses, and sundry other dark scenarios, such as computers one day turning against their creators and genetic engineering leading to unforeseen disasters. For many decades now, there have also been heightened concerns in Protestant evangelical culture about the imminence of the end. Hal Lindsey's *The Late, Great Planet Earth* (1970), the best-selling book of the 1970s, discerned in the unfolding events of the Middle East and elsewhere signs of the approach of the Antichrist, and such fears (or, actually, desires to be present during the Last Days) came to inform the phenomenally popular "Left Behind" books and movies.[1] But of late it is human-induced climate change that has generated the greatest concerns about the possibility that the planet will soon be unable to support life, human and otherwise. The World Conservation Union's 2007 report listed 16,306 species on the verge of extinction, and several months after the release of that report, the United Nations' Intergovernmental Panel on Climate Change warned that carbon emissions' growth must end by the year 2015 in order to avoid "widespread extinction of species, a slowing of the global currents, decreased food production, loss of 30 percent of global wetlands, flooding for millions of people and higher deaths from heat waves." The year 2015 came and went, and the news about human damage to the planet and widespread extinctions has only gotten worse. Recent studies suggest that sea levels are rising even more dramatically than initially predicted, with the possibility that cities like Miami will be under water by 2050. In her recent best-selling book, *The Sixth Extinction*, Elizabeth Kolbert reports that scientists now predict "that one-third of all reef-building corals, a third of all fresh-water mollusks, a third of sharks and rays, a quarter of all mammals, a fifth of all reptiles, and a sixth of all birds are headed toward oblivion." Indeed, two recent NASA studies suggest that, without a relatively quick reduction of carbon output to near zero, the world will soon run out of potable water.[2] And that, truly, would be the end.

Visions of the end have a long tradition in American culture. In his classic *Redeemer Nation: The Idea of America's Millennial Role* (1968), Ernest Tuveson discusses two distinct modes of end-of-the-world thinking in the United States: millennialist and millenarian. The dominant mode is millennialist, or postmillennialist, a belief that the US nation itself will help to bring forth the triumph of Christian principles, culminating in a thousand-year reign of Christ with His saints. Such a reign would, in effect, lead to the end of the world as we know it by creating heaven on earth from sea to shining sea. This is a fundamentally nationalist vision of sacred history undergirded by the notion of US exceptionalism. By contrast, the millenarian, or premillennialist, has virtually no use for the nation and rejects the progressive historical vision of a steady march to a thousand-year reign. For the millenarian, the end will come through apocalyptic destruction orchestrated by Christ (figured as a Jehovah avenger) who would subsequently take the saints to a better world elsewhere.[3] National identities and boundaries, like most everything in the fallen world, are irrelevant to such a spiritual vision.

The millenarian generally thinks outside of time and nation; the millennialist is firmly located within time and nation. At the risk of some critical reductionism, we could say that American studies scholarship as traditionally practiced is (post)millennialist. Whether we're talking about the field-defining scholarship of Leo Marx and others of his generation or the revisionary scholarship of Paul Lauter, American studies has generally been concerned with examining the nation over time, with the hope of helping to bring about the "millennial" triumph of such valued principles as democratic equality and justice for all. But for the competing, more recent school of American studies scholarship, such as the "New Americanists" represented in Donald E. Pease and Robyn Wiegman's influential *The Futures of American Studies* (2002), there is much skepticism about the value of the nation-state as a critical frame, and a rejection of traditional chronological or progressive notions of history. Practicing a form of critical millenarianism, these revisionary critics seek to liberate the field from the constraints of time and nation through temporal displacements and transnational reorientations which, as Pease and Wiegman put it, "construct multiple pasts and imagine disparate futures out of ... nonsynchronous historical materials."[4] A significant influence on this new critical millenarianism is Walter Benjamin, whose "Theses on the Philosophy of History" (1940) envisioned the emergence of a liberatory "Messianic time," not as the culmination of an orderly progressive movement but rather as a revolutionary irruption, a "Judgment Day," that would reconfigure conceptions of time and space through a "cessation of happening." Pease and Wiegman echo such messianism when they write of the "utopian possibilities" inhering in "alternative futures," proclaiming that future-oriented projects forged in temporal realignments promise to "release the field's most creative aspects."[5] What they and the contributors to their volume fail to confront is the possibility that one of those futures might be extinction.

This chapter addresses the critical challenge of contemplating the "cessation of happening" and, like Pease and Wiegman, finds inspiration in Benjamin's notion of "the beginning of knowledge" that can emerge from what he terms a "state of emergency." But rather than imagining the post–Judgment Day or the postrevolutionary introduction of what Benjamin calls "a new calendar,"[6] I will be considering the end of calendars – the end of humankind – by focusing on the mid-nineteenth century, when end-of-the-world thinking permeated US popular culture and was addressed by Poe and Hawthorne. As Pease and Wiegman might have predicted, these antebellum writers, in fact, did experience a release of creative energy when contemplating the future, however dire their visions of the future might have been. In this respect, their contemplations have renewed relevance for American studies in an age of extinction. Before turning to Poe, Hawthorne, and their contemporaries, however, I want to offer a few additional remarks on end-of-the-world thinking in our own time.

To some extent, such thinking has become a form of entertainment that avoids questions of critical consciousness. Recent movies such as *I Am Legend* (2007), *WALL-E* (2008), *The Road* (2009), *The Book of Eli* (2010), *Contagion* (2011), and *World War Z* (2013) make apocalypse into a divertingly fun hundred minutes or so. Entertainment is also crucial to Elizabeth Kolbert's *The Sixth Extinction* (2014), which takes readers on a guided tour of the planet in order to address a topic, "mass extinction," in ways that Kolbert says right up front make for "fascinating" entertainment. Anticipating and perhaps helping to guide the way for the market success of Kolbert's and other writers' works on the possibility of human extinction was Alan Weisman's *The World without Us* (2007), an international best-seller that announces at the outset that "[h]uman extinction is a fait accompli," and then takes the reader on a science-based tour of a post-apocalyptic world without humans. As Weisman makes clear in disarmingly jaunty prose, the immediate consequence of humans' disappearance from the world is that nature will stage a comeback: "On the day after humans disappear, nature takes over and immediately begins cleaning house – or houses, that is. Cleans them right off the face of the Earth. They all go." Because Weisman mainly explores the impact that a revivified nature would have on human detritus over time (and vice versa), he avoids the question of what sort of critical or artistic work one might do at a moment in history when we are contemplating such an end (beyond writing or reading a best-seller on the subject). Through the global vision of his study, he encourages readers to rethink the primacy of the nation, given that human planetary damage crosses national boundaries. In this respect, he makes an implied argument relevant to American studies scholarship about the importance of transnational thinking at a time of environmental crisis. But that is about as far as he goes in addressing questions of critical consciousness. The millenarianism that informs his study is intended to instruct and entertain, which is perhaps why his book found such a wide readership and even inspired popular film "documentaries" on the subject. It is worth mentioning, however, that during his tour of the post-human world, Weisman points out that, contrary to popular belief, paper can do just as well as plastic in surviving the ravages of time. As one of his experts reports: "That's why we have 3,000-year-old papyrus scrolls from Egypt. We pull perfectly readable newspapers out of landfills from the 1930s. They'll be down there for 10,000 years."[7] Here Weisman at least offers the consolation to scholars in an age of extinction that whatever sort of critical work we manage to get into print will perhaps survive for millennia, even if there are no readers.

A considerably more thoughtful meditation on human extinction can be found in Jack Miles's "Global Requiem: The Apocalyptic Moment in Religion," an essay published at the start of the twenty-first century, when there was an increasing awareness, as Miles reports, that "the rate of extinction [of species] is estimated at one every five minutes." Miles makes the logical leap from species extinction to human extinction, stating that "time after time extinction has followed on the loss of habitat when the species at risk was not able to adapt." The extinctions that occur approximately every five minutes wreak havoc on the human habitat, which leads Miles to accuse humankind of "species suicide." One of the main purposes of his essay is to prompt people to take action to save their world and themselves. But his darker suggestion is that inertia and human stupidity will ultimately reign and that it is not too soon to begin contemplating the end. In his own contemplations, Miles insists on the importance of asking "what the consequences for religion and for the arts, especially literature, will be if and when we conclude that the effort to produce a sustainable society has definitely failed?" He suggests that a new religion and a new art could arise from a consciousness of the end, but he's not sure what that new religion and art would look like or whether they would lead to any significant rethinking of the nation. Because the diminishment of resources may only exacerbate international conflict, thereby refueling nationalism, he concludes that the "prospects for a religion [or art, or critical consciousness] that would subordinate national interests to species survival cannot be called good."[8] In this formulation, American studies in an age of extinction may persist as American studies as we know it.

Then again, it may not. Ironically, in his rather gloomy essay, Miles as a critical millenarian evinces a surprising optimism about the possibilities for enlarging rather than closing down how we might think about doing critical work. Published in a volume addressing the place of religion in US cultural studies, Miles's essay ultimately turns against the fatalism that typically attends the contemplation of the end of humankind, suggesting how such contemplation can inspire and reinvigorate critical thinking. Despite the essay's publication in a volume focused on US cultural studies, Miles also departs from both traditional and revisionary forms of American studies scholarship, which tend to engage national ideologies from a variety of perspectives. In his view, the most important end-of-the-world thinking will adopt new forms and perspectives existing apart from the nation and other forms of local attachment. But Miles leaves his reader on a precipice, for he is ultimately unable to imagine the shape that those new forms and perspectives would take.

In order to address some of the end-of-the-world questions about art, religion, and nation that Miles raises, I want now to loop back to the American 1830s and 1840s, when a surprisingly large number of people believed that they were approaching the end. As historian Whitney R. Cross notes, "[W]ell over fifty thousand people in the United States became convinced that time would run out in 1844, while a million or more of their fellows were skeptically expectant."[9] Specifically, thousands of people thought that human history would come to an end on March 21, 1843, then March 21, 1844, and, finally, October 22, 1844. The inspiration behind such thinking was William Miller (1782–1849), a farmer and itinerant preacher from Low Hampton, New York, who claimed that Scripture presented irrefutable evidence that Christ planned to return to the world in order to destroy it. In his numerous sermons delivered to upwards of a half million people during the 1830s and early 1840s, Miller spoke of a final holocaust, a purging conflagration, that would rid the world of humans and all other forms of life. After the apocalypse, he said, the righteous would be resurrected into a new world, Christ's Kingdom, which may or may not have a material existence (Miller was never clear about that).[10] Many of those known as Millerites sold their property and gave up their jobs in anticipation of the final day. When they awoke on October 23, 1844, to discover that the world remained intact, they were understandably confused. Some joined the Shakers; others collaborated to form the Seventh-Day Adventists; and others simply struggled along in the temporal world, trying to make ends meet.

Miller was a product of what historians have dubbed the Second Great Awakening, the upsurge of evangelical fervor in the United States in the opening decades of the nineteenth century. The majority of the evangelicals and their followers shared a postmillennial optimism, discerning in the Book of Daniel, St. John's Book of Revelation, and other prophetic texts of the Old and New Testament unambiguous evidence that Christ would return to the world for a glorious spiritual reign with His saints. That reign, they believed, would be ushered in by the converts, who would help to bring about a thousand years of social and religious perfection, whereupon God would descend in all of His glory, wipe out the sinners, end the world as we know it, and reunite with His saints. US postmillennialists thus had a progressive vision of history in which the saints recurrently defeated the forces of evil, bringing about an ever-greater spiritual perfection in the nation and throughout the world that would hasten the arrival of Christ. This postmillennial vision may appear to be postnational, as well, but in early national and antebellum US culture, nationalism and millennialism often went hand in hand. As Jan Stieverman observes, "[T]he convergence of (post-)millennialism and nationalism ... [was] one of the major organizing principles of an emerging collective identity in nineteenth-century America." By the 1840s, the postmillennial religious vision of the Second Great Awakening had been thoroughly absorbed into nationalist ideologies, to the point that many of those espousing the continental expansionism known as Manifest Destiny had become convinced that the United States was the New Israel ushering in the millennium.[11]

But not all US millennialists of the pre-Civil War period were US nationalists. Miller was among a sizable group of millennially inclined Americans who rejected notions of temporal progress and spiritual redemption through human effort. They also silently rejected US nationalism. These premillennialists, or millenarians, were antiprogressives, convinced that humans could accomplish nothing meaningful in the world other than turning to God. For these particular religious thinkers, there was no hope for social perfection; instead, everywhere they looked they saw human frailty and evil. Thus, instead of believing in the possibility of a thousand-year reign of the saints ushering in Christ, they imagined a vengeful God simply descending one day to obliterate the world, eventually resurrecting those He chose to save in some sort of heavenly place. Miller and his tens of thousands of followers in the northeast region and elsewhere were convinced that that day was just about at hand.[12]

Miller elaborated his end-times views in his lectures, which he collected as a volume, *Evidence from Scripture and History of the Second Coming of Christ, about the Year 1843*, published in Troy, New York, in 1838, and republished in Boston in 1842. As a premillennialist, Miller focused on Judgment Day. For Miller, death and destruction (the Last Days) are all that humankind has to look forward to: "I say I can find nothing in the word of God to warrant me to believe that we ought to look for or expect a happier period than we now enjoy, until he [sic] who has promised to come, shall come the second time without sin until salvation, and cleanse us, the world, and make all things new." As is clear from this passage, Miller's prognostications are based on his reading of the Bible ("the word of God"), especially the prophecies of Isaiah, Daniel, and John, which he regards as crucial indicators of the imminence of what he terms "the judgment of the great day." That judgment, or "day of vengeance," he says, will bring utter devastation, sparing only "the wise," which is to say, the regenerate saints. Miller remains unclear about the location of the post-judgment world, positing that the reign of the saints "will be on earth" or "in the air." What he is clear about is the timing, which he understands in terms of simple schemas of chronology. In one of many numerico-typological readings that he develops from his close attention to Scripture, Miller proclaims that Biblical "days" have to be read metaphorically as "years," and he adduces as a starting point for his countdown a passage in Daniel 8 on the 2,300 days (which he reads as years) before God offers humans sanctuary. He asks the key question – "When did the 2300 years begin?" – and provides this answer: "Let us begin in where the angel told us, from the going forth of the decree to build the walls of Jerusalem in troublous times, 457 years before Christ; take 457 from 2300, and it will leave A.D. 1843." As even Miller himself seems to acknowledge, all of this may be a stretch, but he points out to his readers that the truth (or lack of truth) of his vision will soon become evident: "If I have erred in my exposition of the prophecies, the time being so near at hand will expose my folly."[13]

In the manner of some end-of-the-world millennialists, Miller works with clear chronologies that move in linear fashion from specific prophe-cies (type) to the day of fulfillment (antitype), which is imagined as bringing an end to time as we know it. Because there would appear to be no jags or ruptures in his vision, he differs somewhat from those premil-lennialists who emphasize the surprising irruption of apocalypse. He is more typically premillennialist in presenting his prophecies as lacking in nationalist exceptionalism and notions of worldly progress. Thus such key events as the American Revolution and the War of 1812 have no place in his chronological schema. Again and again he appeals across national borders to the wise, saintly, and potentially regenerate among "ye inhabitants of the earth." Miller's global perspective becomes clear in the closing page of his volume, when he asks rhetorically: "Will God punish nations, and not individuals? That cannot be, for nations are composed of individuals, and God is just, for he hath appointed a day in which he will judge the world in righteousness."[14]

As a millenarian, then, Miller offers a postnational or transnational vision, encompassing a spiritual history of humankind that is disconnected from US nationalism. But because he cannot release his hold on Biblical prophecy as the key to making sense of the universe, Miller never looks beyond "extinction" to new ways of thinking about time and space, or, to put this somewhat differently, he never uses the prospect of extinction to imagine new ways of understanding the world. But what happens to end-time thinking when untethered to the Bible? And how can such thinking affect our own critical perspectives on time, space, and nation? Poe's and Hawthorne's Miller-inspired tales open up possibilities by anticipating some of the questions about a new critical millenarianism that Jack Miles addressed in 2001.

Approximately one year after the appearance of Miller's widely publicized lectures, Poe published a Millerite-inspired end-of-the-world tale, "The Conversation of Eiros and Charmion," in the December 1839 issue of *Burton's Gentleman's Magazine.* He republished the tale in his 1840 *Tales of the Grotesque and Arabesque* and (with the revised title "The Destruction of the World") 1845 *Tales.* Like Miller, he imagines the destruction of the world as an apocalyptic event that has little to do with nation. Though Poe follows Miller and other premillennialists in imagining some sort of life beyond the end of calendar time, indeed beyond the end of the world, he departs from Miller in disconnecting the final cataclysm from scriptural prophecy. The emphasis of Poe's story is ultimately on the question of how we might think about human history and culture, and the planet itself, when confronting the imminence of extinction without the comforts of Biblical hermeneutics. Arguably, Poe finds something of even greater value in his end-of-the-world imaginings than a Millerite spiritual cleansing: a reconception of time and space, somewhat on the order of a Benjaminian state of emergency, which has the liberating potential of producing new knowledge from previously unimagined vantage points.[15]

The tale is framed as a conversation between two angelic spirits, Eiros and Charmion (the names of Cleopatra's servants in Shakespeare's *Antony and Cleopatra* and Dryden's *All For Love*), who now exist in "Aidenn," a place that critics have traditionally identified as a type of "heaven" but which the spirit Eiros identifies more complexly as "the speculative Future merged in the august and certain Present."[16] Right from the start, there is a collapse of present and future, with a Benjaminian sense that the collapse has reoriented the present as "the 'time of the now,'"[17] as opposed to a time linked to particular national or scriptural histories. There is also a sense, drawn from Miller and other pre- and postmillennialists, that the end of the world as described by Eiros and Charmion has brought about what Miller terms a "reign ... in the immortal state,"[18] though clearly a reign without Christ.

Charmion initiates the conversation between the two immortals by referring to humankind's "last hour," asserting that it would be best to "converse of familiar things, in the old familiar language of the world which has so fearfully perished." Of course the narratological truth of the matter is that if the spirits were to speak in a new, unfamiliar language,

Poe's readers would be unable to understand the conversation, which is clearly being staged for eavesdroppers. Once Charmion initiates the conversation, Eiros basically takes over, with the final two-thirds of the sketch consisting of Eiros's monologue on how the world has come to an end. Because it is the specter of the world's imminent end that inspires new thinking, it would be useful to jump to the end of the tale itself, which, like "The Fall of the House of Usher" (also first published in *Burton's* in 1839), merges the end of the world described in the fiction with the end of the fiction itself. In a moment that also bears some resemblance to the apocalyptic conclusion of *The Narrative of Arthur Gordon Pym* (1838), Eiros tells Charmion near the end of the sketch what s/he already knows about the end of the world:

> "For a moment there was a wild lurid light alone, visiting and penetrating all things. Then – let us bow down, Charmion, before the excessive majesty of the great God! – then, there came a shouting and pervading sound, as if from the mouth itself of HIM; while the whole incumbent mass of ether in which we existed, burst at once into a species of intense flames, for whose surpassing brilliancy and all-fervid heat even the angels in the high Heaven of pure knowledge have no name. Thus ended all."[19]

An apocalypse brought about by flames beyond description eerily anticipates our own concerns about nuclear annihilation and global warming, even as Poe draws on the rhetoric of Miller and other millennialists (including the eighteenth-century postmillennialist Jonathan Edwards) who typically warn of a retributive Jehovah subjecting sinners to the flames of hell. Crucial to the modernistic feel of "The Conversation of Eiros and Charmion," however, is that the Jehovah figure – "HIM" – remains vague, and the cessation of happening is not simply about retribution. It is about post-apocalyptic knowledge, a "pure knowledge" which, because of the unprecedented occasion of the end, has no name. But, as in other fiction by Poe, it is the very fact that all has "ended" that allows for the possibility of meaning. Poe writes in his aesthetic manifesto "The Philosophy of Composition" (1846): "It is only with the *dénouement* constantly in view that we can give a plot its indispensable air of consequence."[20] Given that the denouement here is extinction (the story suggests that no humans remain on Earth, and that no Earth remains), Poe has the opportunity to use his conversing spirits to address the matter of how the knowledge of impending human extinction changes everything (just before the end).

As we learn from Eiros, that which eventually brings about the end is a comet. In a critique of mere Earth-bound thinking, Eiros scoffs at those scriptural prognosticators whose end-of-the-world messages are guided by "fear-enkindled ... biblical prophecies," remarking that their various predictions are ultimately limited, "having reference to the orb of the earth alone." Whether or not they are swayed by such prophecies, the masses fail to consider Earth in relation to the larger solar system, and thus for a long while remain in denial about the distinct possibility, recognized by just "two or three astronomers of secondary note," that, because of the distant comet, the world will soon be no more. Even those whom Eiros terms the "learned" regard the dangers as only about "probable alterations in climate," although as these people consider the new evidence of climate change, they become increasingly convinced that such change would be catastrophic. As Eiros recalls, climate change soon becomes the main focus of human concerns: "It could not be denied that our atmosphere was radically affected; the conformation of this atmosphere and the possible modifications to which it might be subjected, were now the topics of discussion." Scientists begin to worry that a steady loss of nitrogen in the climate will lead to an oxygen-based "combustion irresistible, all-devouring, omni-prevalent, immediate." And yet before too long the same scientists realize that such combustion wouldn't even matter, for the speeding comet is on a direct path to Earth.[21]

The knowledge of imminent extinction is ultimately what inspires urgent new efforts to know. As Eiros reports to Charmion (but more insistently to the reader, who would not know all of this), the knowledge of a new telos – the imminent end of everything – brings about a revolution in conventional thought, something like a messianic moment but without a messiah and without any sort of use-value beyond the attainment of "perfected knowledge." Eiros remarks on the comet itself: "We could no longer apply to the strange orb any *accustomed* thoughts. Its *historical* attributes had disappeared" (emphasis in the text). With the recognition of the imminent end of history comes a reorientation of time and space, a revolutionary reconceptualization that resembles Benjamin's imaginings of the heightened immediacy of the present "shot through with chips of Messianic time."[22] What Eiros says about the comet appears to be true about all phenomena under observation in the final days: sedimented thought falls by the wayside as "*Truth* arose in the purity of her strength." Such is Poe's artful indirection that the nature of that "*Truth*," as in Miles's essay, remains vague, though it is precisely that vagueness which heightens the urgency of pursuing some sort of "perfected knowledge" outside of the conventionally historical or national. In the midst of what Eiros describes as the "frenzy of mankind," people across the planet "felt an unusual elasticity of frame and vivacity of mind." Like the millenarian Miller, Poe's angelic spirits are unconcerned about nations, just as the comet itself takes no account of nations. Instead, the comet becomes "the consummation of Fate."[23] That consummation is precisely what is described at the tale's end, where there is a blending of fate and God for that brief knowledge-infused duration between the moment the danger has been identified and annihilation.

Arguably the large point of Poe's story, with its materialist account of the discovery of a new comet, is that there are good reasons to regard any age as a possible age of extinction, and that the contemplation of the end is therefore incumbent upon all serious thinkers. For this reason, the end-of-the-world "Conversation" is not a tragic story. In the tale, Poe insists that critical thought in an age of extinction, rather than closing down avenues of investigation, inevitably opens them up, rejuvenating a tired and sleepy age that has far too long functioned with "the old familiar language of the world." Eiros's initial remark on how the two angels exist in "the speculative Future merged in the august and certain Present" speaks both to the fictional fate of the angelic characters and to the reconceived temporal consciousness that Poe seeks to evoke through his Miller-inspired tale: a present infused with meaning as a result of the abrupt recognition of a future without a future. Such a perspective, however vaguely or suggestively, liberates the present from the constraints of time, from both the additive and progressive. And, as one might expect from Poe, who was suspicious of US literary nationalism, the new perspective has nothing to do with nation.[24] Still, the tale enacts a certain nostalgia for "the old familiar language of the world," for without that language Poe would be unable to evoke apocalypse. And without readers in the old familiar world, his vision would be lacking in urgency.

In 1843, a year after the Boston publication of Miller's *Evidence from Scripture and History*, Hawthorne published two Millerite-inspired sketches that place an even greater emphasis on the tension between the familiar and the millenarian.[25] These sketches emerged from Hawthorne's own short-lived commitment to postmillennial reform, as exemplified by his seven-month stay in 1841 at the socialist reform community Brook Farm, in West Roxbury, Massachusetts, which he would later take as the subject of *The Blithedale Romance* (1852). Hawthorne is generally regarded as a social conservative, but during the 1830s and 1840s he was a Jacksonian democrat outraged by aristocratic privilege, and for a while he was genuinely inspired by the reformers in the Boston-Concord circle who were convinced they could help to create a better United States. Although

Hawthorne was initially enthusiastic about Brook Farm's prospects, by late 1841 he had come to believe that the reformers themselves needed reforming. From this perspective, the premillennialist vision of the Millerites, with its images of destruction *preceding* actual human reform, spoke to his disillusionment with the postmillennial notion that Americans could fashion their own redeemed nation. And yet, for much of his career Hawthorne retained his interest in what could be termed millennial reform, raising questions about social inequality in many of his fictional works and on several occasions voicing his objections to slavery. Hawthorne's conflicted views on reform are at the center of the first of his two Miller-inspired sketches of 1843, "The Hall of Fantasy."

In the sketch, set in an undisclosed future, the narrator provides the reader with a tour of the reformers scattered throughout the Hall of Fantasy, a sort of "public Exchange" with white marble floors, pillars, and an impressive dome. The reformers are presented as "dreamers" touched by a "contagious" form of "madness," but also as serious people driven by genuine (and admirable) desires for social change. Thus the narrator states that even a "conservative," perhaps not unlike the sketch's author, "could hardly have helped throbbing in sympathy with the spirit that pervaded these innumerable theorists." After describing various reformers who believe they can "cast off the whole tissue of ancient custom, like a tattered garment," the narrator leads the reader to the unlikely figure of "Father Miller himself," described as "an elderly man of plain, honest, trustworthy aspect," who with "the sincerest faith in his own doctrine . . . announced that the destruction of the world was close at hand." The narrator subsequently underscores the stark differences between the post-millennialist and the premillennialist: "They [the secular-postmillennial social reformers] look for the earthly perfection of mankind, and are forming schemes, which imply that the immortal spirit will be connected with a physical nature, for innumerable ages of futurity. On the other hand, here comes good Father Miller, and, with one puff of his relentless theory, scatters all their dreams like so many withered leaves upon the blast."[26] The questions raised by the sketch's grouping of optimistic worldly reformers with the premillennialist Miller are in some respects similar to the questions raised by our own historical moment: What should people do if the end of the world is "close at hand"? How might they think, act, teach, or write under the pressure of such an awareness?

Hawthorne brings these big questions into focus when he grants Miller his donné and imagines the coming of the end. Like Miller and Poe, he envisions the world going up in flames. The force of the sketch thus lies in the conjectural imagining of apocalypse. But Hawthorne offers no post-apocalyptic commentary from angels, no insight or spiritual "solution" to what the narrator terms the "riddle" of life. Instead, he simply worries over the challenge of gaining larger meaning from the imminence of cataclysmic destruction. As the narrator confesses to the reader, should the world be "burnt to-morrow morning, I am at a loss to know what purpose will have been accomplished, or how the universe will be wiser or better for our existence and destruction." Poe aggressively challenges the reader to rise to the occasion of imagining new ways of thinking; Hawthorne remains "at a loss" and allows for a retreat into a nostalgic recovery of the conventional. At the sketch's end, he depicts parents who are desirous that "their new-born infant should not be defrauded of his life-time" by "the consummation, prophesied by Father Miller." Domestic ideals thus prevail over end-of-the-world imaginings. Still, in an intriguing moment, Hawthorne implicitly addresses the fate of writing in an age of extinction, presenting us with a "youthful poet" who, in response to Miller's prophecies, glumly "murmured, because there would be no posterity to recognize the inspiration of his song."[27] The tale suggests that if one is writing for posterity in an age of extinction, some adjustments may be in order (though Hawthorne offers no hints as to what those adjustments might be).

Hawthorne directly addresses connections between writing and posterity in a subsequent sketch, "The New Adam and Eve," also published in 1843. If in "The Hall of Fantasy" Hawthorne momentarily entertains Miller's end-of-the-world prophesy, only to take refuge in conventional notions of domesticity, here he bases an entire story around Miller's prognostications. Right from the start, the narrator of "The New Adam and Eve" asks the reader to imagine that Miller is correct: "[L]et us conceive good Father Miller's interpretation of the prophecies to have proved true. The Day of Doom has burst upon the globe, and swept away the whole race of men. From cities and fields, sea-shore and midland mountain region, vast continents, and even the remotest islands of the ocean – each living thing is gone." Taking the end of the world as the tale's pretext and point of departure, Hawthorne anticipates Alan Weisman's *The World without Us* by leading the reader on a tour of the marks that humans have left on the world. The narrator surveys the initially humanless scene: "No breath of a created being disturbs this earthly atmosphere. But the abodes of man, and all that he has accomplished, the foot-prints of his wanderings, and the results of his toil, the visible symbols of his intellectual cultivation and moral progress – in short, everything physical that can give evidence of his present position – shall remain untouched by the hand of destiny." In *The World without Us,* Weisman guides his reader through that post-human world as he imagines it with the help of his wide scientific reading. Hawthorne, on the other hand, offers his readers a "half-sportive and half-thoughtful" tour of the postextinction world with the help of a new Adam and Eve, who view what remains of that previous human world through their innocent and constantly bewildered eyes. There is a Thoreauvian feel to Hawthorne's sketch, as he depicts his new Adam and Eve baffled by Parisian fashion, prisons, courts, banks, jewelers' shops, alcoholic beverages, and the detritus of nineteenth-century life – in short, what the new Adam terms "heaps of rubbish of one kind or another." As a Jacksonian democrat, Hawthorne is especially intent on using the innocence of his new Adam and Eve to highlight, from the point of view of their incomprehension, the evidence of class inequities, which they see just about everywhere they look. Because they lack the verbal gifts and historical consciousness that would enable them to articulate the meaning of what they encounter, the narrator does that work for them in rhetorical fashion: "When will they comprehend the great and miserable fact, – the evidences of which appeal to their senses everywhere, – that one portion of earth's lost inhabitants was rolling in luxury, while the multitude was toiling for scanty food?"[28]

Notably, the narrator's critique of social inequality focuses on the "earth" and not the nation. And yet Hawthorne's readers would have recognized, through the description of Adam and Eve's wanderings, that the story examines humans' "foot-prints" in Boston and nearby areas. The localness of the sketch becomes especially clear when the new Adam and Eve journey "into the suburbs of the city" and "stand on a grassy brow of a hill, at the foot of a granite obelisk." When the new Adam regards the obelisk as "a visible prayer," the narrator can't resist identifying it as the monument "on far-famed Bunker Hill." At this point Hawthorne has the opportunity to recuperate the national through the invocation of American Revolutionary ideals. Instead, he uses the occasion to meditate on war apart from nationalist ideologies, anticipating (and perhaps influencing) Melville's equally satirical account of the Bunker Hill Monument in the preface to *Israel Potter* (1855; see Chapter 7, below). Using the prospect of the end of the world to demythify a battle that had come to be celebrated as a founding moment of the new nation, the narrator remarks (in the same year that the monument was completed and dedicated): "Could they guess that the green sward on which they stand so peacefully, was once strewn with human corpses and purple with their blood, it would equally amaze them, that one generation of men should

perpetuate such carnage, and that a subsequent generation should triumphantly commemorate it."[29] The fact of the extinction of all humans prior
to the new Adam and Eve thus allows the narrator to think in Benjaminian
fashion about war apart from the ideological imperatives of particular
national histories or particular temporal frames. War becomes simply
war, with no clear beginning, middle, or end, and no clear sense of
purpose. After all, a key consequence of human extinction is that historical
narrative, too, becomes extinct, a relic of the past. In "The Hall of
Fantasy," the murmuring poet imagines a time when his poems can no
longer be fathomed because there is no longer a posterity; thus he chooses
simply to follow his inspiration. To some extent the narrator of "The New
Adam and Eve" takes a similar path by adopting a historical perspective
that has little to do with nationalistic ideologies. Nevertheless, like the
poet, he is concerned about posterity. His critical millenarianism does not
quite achieve the boldness of Poe's.

Consistent with Hawthorne's interest in posterity, near the end of the
sketch the narrator describes the new Adam and Eve's journey to "the rich
library of Harvard University," the penultimate stopping point of these
indefatigable wanderers. There they are confronted by innumerable mysterious objects lined up on shelves – books from the past that have come to have
no meaning. Written at a moment when thousands of Americans were
considering the possibility of extinction, the sketch itself, we might say,
reflects on its own eventual lack of readers or meaning. And more: Given
that Harvard Library has volumes from the past and present, the sketch raises
questions about the historical traditions of literature, the monumentalization
of certain types of literature, and the creation of the institution of the library.
As the perplexed Adam puzzles over the "mystic characters" and "unintelli-
gible thought" contained in the volumes, the scene is rich with tension. He
feels the pull of the volumes, which attract him with such force that the
narrator intervenes to express his own desire that Adam abandon his interpretive efforts and return to the natural world: "Oh Adam, it is too soon, too
soon by at least five thousand years, to put on spectacles, and busy yourself in
the alcoves of a library!" Within the fictional frame of the sketch, Eve does
the work for the narrator, coaxing Adam outside. By resisting the temptations of "the mysterious perils of the library," Adam and Eve keep alive the
millennial possibility that out of catastrophe will emerge new works of art
with "a melody never yet heard on earth."[30]

The new Adam and Eve make one final stop before they sleep, journeying to Cambridge's Mount Auburn Cemetery, where they find a "Child, in
whitest marble." As in "The Hall of Fantasy," Hawthorne concludes his

post-apocalyptic tale with an appeal to domesticity. But what follows is perhaps the eeriest evocation of family in nineteenth-century literature, as the marble monument of course memorializes a dead child. Thus when Adam says to Eve, "Let us sleep, as this lovely little figure is sleeping,"[31] we are left with Adam and Eve joining that "adopted" dead child in an act presaging their own inevitable end. In this respect, Hawthorne's sketch suggests that even if his is not an age of extinction, death (extinction) will continue to remain the final stop on every individual's worldly journey.

Much more than Poe, then, Hawthorne's contemplations on extinction draw on the local and familiar – the Bunker Hill Monument, Harvard Library, Mount Auburn Cemetery, and tropes of the family central to nineteenth-century domestic ideology. But despite their differences, both writers use their fictions about the world's end to challenge progressive concepts of history and to dissent from the nationalist exceptionalism that Miller also had little use for. Even with all of its attendant horrors, catastrophe has the potential to be liberating, particularly in the way that it can reframe the present. Pease and Wiegman remark in their introduction to *The Futures of American Studies* that the temporal realignments and reimaginings they call for must beware "the self-satisfactions of presentism" (ironically, the very charge that critics have leveled against the so-called New Americanists).[32] But what Poe, Hawthorne, and other end-of-the-world writers reveal is that contemplations about the end work to heighten attention to the present in ways that can free critical thought from the conventional and historical. In this sense their apocalyptic fictions move from mere presentism (an engagement with Miller's millenarianism) to a more spiritual, even messianic notion of what Poe terms "the august and certain Present" as reconfigured by the "speculative Future" of no future at all. Thinking about temporality in such a way can push us to regard the critical work that we do at our own precarious moment as part of a new beginning, even if it is the beginning of the end.

* * *

I conclude this reflection on American studies in an age of extinction with a Poe- and Hawthorne-inflected consideration of efforts to grapple with a catastrophe in our own time, the 2005 Hurricane Katrina and its aftermath. In two interrelated essays on the topic, Wai Chee Dimock proposes that the most effective frame for talking about Katrina is the planetary, particularly the dynamics of climate change which have little respect for borders, boundaries, and conceptions of national sovereignty. As she remarks about Katrina in the larger context of the planet:

Violent storms, floods, soil erosion, loss of wetlands – these are problems we associate with New Orleans and the Gulf of Mexico. It should not come as too much of a surprise, though, to see them also played out, thousands of miles away, in the Arctic Ocean, because there is no dividing line separating these two bodies of water. This single, crisscrossing, and already-damaged hydrology makes it clear that climate, geology, and human and nonhuman life are all complexly intertwined, part of the same fluid continuum.

Taking account of the ongoing work of MIT's Department of Earth, Atmospheric, and Planetary Sciences, Dimock accordingly calls for "the study of the planet as an integral unit," and imagines a reconceived American studies that would move beyond the artificial boundaries of local and national histories to develop "as a body of knowledge aggregated on a different scale, with connecting threads running through other dimensions of the planet." In a formulation that seems greatly indebted to the rhetoric of extinction, and in the tradition of Poe's vision of catastrophe in "The Conversation of Eiros and Charmion," she elaborates on her notion of the planetary: "The 'planetary' emerges here as the bearer of a scale indifferent to human institutions and indifferent to the human species itself." Dimock's insistence on such indifference seems intended to underscore that humans may not be around all that much longer, that in the larger scheme of things "the human species itself" isn't all that special. With her attention to scale, her work can also be read in relation to recent hemispheric approaches that consider Katrina in the context of the Gulf of Mexico and other histories of trans-American catastrophes.[33]

While Dimock has enlarged our vision of American studies by offering a planetary frame for Katrina, Spike Lee's HBO documentary *When the Levees Broke: A Requiem in Four Acts* (2006) compels us to look as closely as possible, often from street and house level, at the day-by-day unfolding of the catastrophe in relation to what could be termed nation-time. For Lee, the sufferings in New Orleans had much to do with the failure of local and national government, such as the long history of neglecting the levees and ignoring the urban poor. In a companion text, *Teaching The Levees: A Curriculum for Democratic Dialogue and Civic Engagement*, published by The Rockefeller Foundation in 2007, the editors include several "Hurricane Katrina Timelines" that deploy old-fashioned chronology as a powerful explanatory framework. Whereas Dimock links Katrina to climate change, with the possibilities of even greater catastrophes to come, Lee and his collaborators remind us that by the time Katrina hit New Orleans, it had become a category-1 or -2 hurricane. Their point is that the disaster would have occurred even if carbon emissions had been curbed years ago, extinction were less of a prospect, and category-5 storms were a rarity. Lee's four-hour film moves back and forth between New Orleans's present and past, for the most part ignoring larger planetary and hemispheric contexts, in order to show that national policies based on racial and class hierarchies had much to do with the suffering that he so powerfully records. More recently, Christopher Lloyd has noted about Katrina that "as the floodwaters receded, the old racial demarcations of the city were brought into stark relief." Accordingly, he warns that an emphasis on the transnational or planetary over the local risks closing our eyes to the structural inequities that contributed to the storm's human costs.[34] Viewed from the vantage point of, say, Google Earth, there is much in New Orleans that we simply cannot see. Lee's and Lloyd's street-level views offer us something very different from a satellite.

The local, national, hemispheric, and global/planetary have all come into play in the best work on Katrina, which has helped to reinvigorate the field of American studies by pushing critics to think anew about geographical and temporal frames, perhaps in preparation for what we all suspect will be the greater catastrophes to come.[35] Had he been around in 2005, William Miller may have joyfully proclaimed that the flooding in New Orleans was foretold in The Revelation of St. John, which prophesies that among the apocalyptic events preceding Christ's Second Coming will be a "second vial . . . poured out 'upon the sea'" (Rev. 16.3). Even if one doesn't share such a Biblically-based millennial notion of apocalypse, it is difficult at the current moment not to contemplate catastrophic possibilities of the end. In an age of extinction, practitioners of American studies may well find themselves adopting a Benjaminian phenomenology of "a present which is not a transition, but in which time stands still and has come to a stop,"[36] a perspective that is not so very different from the "elasticity of frame and vivacity of mind" that Poe's Eiros describes taking hold just before the destruction of the planet. But as Hawthorne suggests in both "The Hall of Fantasy" and "The New Adam and Eve," it is not so easy, or even wise, to toss aside the familiar; and Poe, too, gestures to the familiar in order to push his readers toward something new. What I am suggesting here, through my attention to Poe and Hawthorne in particular, is the potential for productive exchanges between the millennialist, nation-based tradition of American studies and a postnational critical millenarianism. Such a dialectical approach, difficult as it might be to chart out with any sort of methodological precision, may offer the best possible hope for helping us to see where the meanings are before we are no more.

CHAPTER 5

The Slave Narrative and the Revolutionary Tradition of African American Autobiography

Slave narratives are much read, taught, and analyzed, but they remain a problematic genre, or perhaps don't constitute a genre at all. Some critics even claim that slave narratives are so intimately tied to white editors and abolitionist organizations that it would be a mistake to regard them as having distinctive authors and autobiographical stories. This chapter argues that, like all autobiographies, slave narratives make use of conventions that have the potential to energize and not just delimit autobiographical writing. In the spirit of Toni Morrison, the chapter examines connections between white and black writing, focusing in particular on the relationship of slave narratives (or antebellum black autobiographies) to the classic tradition of American autobiography as represented by Benjamin Franklin. In addition to being in conversation with Franklin, slave narratives are often in conversation with each other. These conversations are central to what I am calling the revolutionary tradition of African American autobiography.

Is the slave narrative a subspecies or subgenre of autobiography? That is one of the large questions posed by John Sekora in his seminal "Black Message/White Envelope" (1987), a study of the crucial role that white abolitionists played in publishing, and indeed helping to shape, the antebellum slave narrative. Asserting that the slave narrative usually presents an account of a life "mandated by persons other than the subject" and that the "black message" of the slave narrative therefore inevitably comes "sealed within a white envelope," Sekora regards slave narratives as the products of a racist cultural process in which "white sponsors compel a black author to approve, to authorize, white institutional power." That process, he says, necessitates the relative silencing of black voices. Moreover, because the slave narrative, according to Sekora, emphasizes not the "individualized Afro-American life, but rather the concrete detail of lives spent under slavery," he insists that it cannot do what autobiography typically does: creatively work with language and narrative to portray an individual self.

Given his skepticism about black narrators' active role in fashioning the texts that just about always bear their names, Sekora's response to his rhetorically posed question about the status of the slave narrative as autobiography comes as no surprise: "[T]he separately published [slave] narratives are thus not a subspecies of autobiography." In reaching this conclusion, Sekora aligns himself with James Olney, who elaborates a similar argument in "'I Was Born': Slave Narratives, Their Status as Autobiography and Literature" (1984), which analyzes the formal components structuring a number of slave narratives: the opening announcement of the slave's birth without a known birthday or clear sense of parentage; the accounts of separations from family members; the portrayals of brutal masters and overseers; the attainment of literacy, often by trickery; and the eventual escape to the North. Maintaining that, with the exception of Frederick Douglass's 1845 *Narrative*, virtually no slave narrative manages to "rise above the level of the preformed, imposed and accepted conventional," Olney, too, denies the slave narrative the status of autobiographical art.[1]

But these influential negative assessments of the slave narrative as auto-biography raise more questions than they answer. For instance, is it true that "classic" white-authored autobiography exists apart from the conventional? After all, many autobiographers of the eighteenth and nineteenth centuries rather traditionally describe the course of a life history running from childhood to the defining moments of adulthood that helped to occasion the autobiography in the first place. In some respects, there is nothing more conventional than Benjamin Franklin's autobiography, which can be read as a secularized updating of the Puritan John Bunyan's spiritual autobiography, *The Pilgrim's Progress* (1684). Moreover, can it really be said that white autobiographers, as opposed to the black narrators of the slave narrative, truly stand apart from the mediating forces of their culture? One could easily make the opposite argument, that precisely because white autobiographers are located more comfortably within their culture, they can assume such mediating forces as a given, and thus remain relatively oblivious to racial and class hierarchies. In this respect, however artful or socio-critical they may seem, white autobiographies, much more than the slave narrative, can work to shore up and sustain the dominant culture. Benjamin Franklin, for instance, whose influence on the development of the slave narrative was consider-able, presents himself in the second part of his autobiography as respond-ing to Benjamin Vaughan's request to provide the postrevolutionary generation with a model "for the forming of future great men; and . . . improving the features of private character, and consequently of aiding all

happiness both public and domestic."[2] Accordingly, unlike in the autobiography's first part, his calls for virtue and social order can be taken as
relatively traditional, even coercive, efforts at "improving" the status quo.

Vaughan made his request to Franklin in a letter that Franklin included as
a preface to the autobiography's second part. Because of the formal similarity
of the Vaughan letter to the letters, prefaces, and authenticating appendices
that typically frame the slave narrative, the letter raises questions of agency
that are also relevant to considerations of the slave narrative in an American
autobiographical tradition. Most would agree that, despite the prefatory
letter, Franklin retained agency as an autobiographer, for the simple reason
that he had the option of using the Vaughan letter for his own purposes. The
black narrators of the slave narrative typically did not have the freedom of a
Franklin, but does that mean they completely surrendered agency or allowed
themselves to be silenced by those who, in the manner of Vaughan, framed
their narrative accounts? Contra Sekora and Olney, a number of scholars in
the field have emphasized the collaborative nature of the slave narrative, the
ways in which black authors could use both the features of the genre and
their subordinate relation to their sponsors to develop their own voices and
perspectives. To take an extreme example of such collaboration in a text that
on first glance can seem anything but collaborative (or a slave narrative): In
the 1831 *The Confessions of Nat Turner*, in which the condemned slave rebel
Turner tells his life history to his white racist inquisitor Thomas Gray, there
remains the distinct possibility, as Eric J. Sundquist has suggested, that
Turner used Gray to publicize the Americanness of his rebellion (Turner
had originally planned the slave conspiracy for July 4, 1831), to display the
Christian spirituality that informed his plot, and to exacerbate white fears of
possible black terror to come. From within the double enclosure of his jail
cell and the confessional narrative as framed by Gray, Turner, as Sundquist
explains, resourcefully conveyed his story of black resistance and thus can be
thought of as one of the "authors" of the *Confessions*. In his classic study of
what he calls "The First Century of Afro-American Autobiography,"
William L. Andrews similarly shows how blacks worked with and against
their white sponsors to tell their own stories on their own terms; and in an
important study of nineteenth-century black women's writings, Xiomara
Santamarina highlights the "conflicted collaboration" between black author
and white sponsor, finding even in Sojourner Truth's 1850 *Narrative*, which
the "illiterate" Truth produced with the help of the white abolitionist
amanuensis Olive Gilbert, a black-authored emphasis on the value of her
slave labor that conflicted with Gilbert's somewhat naive celebration of
Northern market culture.[3]

Truth's skeptical account of black "freedom" in the racist North went against the grain of most antebellum slave narratives, which, despite their depictions of Northern racism, typically charted the movement of the black male narrator from what Douglass termed "the tomb of slavery, to the heaven of freedom." This movement, or progress, was hailed by sympathetic readers of the time as typically American, a raced version of Benjamin Franklin's archetypal account of his "American" rise from rags to riches. In a lecture of 1849, the abolitionist Unitarian minister Theodore Parker celebrated slave narratives as the most distinctively American literature yet produced in the new nation, the very texts, he asserted, which contained "all the original romance of Americans in them." For Parker, slave narratives offered black voices and perspectives that could not be found "in the white man's novel" and that harkened back to the revolutionary spirit of the nation's founding. Clearly, he discerned in these narratives much more than the political desires of their white abolitionist sponsors.[4]

Still, recent book-history approaches to African American literature have raised new questions about the genre of the slave narrative. Michaël Roy, for instance, asserts that "slave narratives did not constitute a monolithic genre"; and he goes on to argue that because each work "occupied a different space in antebellum print culture," specific texts must be analyzed in relation to such factors as their material form, circulation, and intended audience.[5] While I am sympathetic to such approaches, which are useful for all forms of writing and not just slave narratives, I continue to think that there is considerable value in studying narrative tactics, self-characterization, and intertextuality in works that, both in their own time and beyond, were regarded as constituting something like a genre. That said, I agree with Roy that the texts we call slave narratives are hardly monolithic. The remaining pages of this chapter will focus on examples of what I take to be the distinctive voices and perspectives of the slave narrative – the black voices, or messages, that emerge from their not entirely white "envelopes" and that can be productively examined in relation to a tradition of American autobiography initiated at the time of the American Revolution. Central to that tradition is Benjamin Franklin, whose autobiography served as a model for numerous slave narratives to come, even those narratives authored by formerly enslaved black women.[6]

Franklin's autobiography was written over a nearly twenty-year period (1771–90) and was not published during his lifetime. With its interest in temperance, self-examination, and virtue, the autobiography has its sources in the tradition of the Protestant spiritual autobiography, which charts the individual's struggles against the temptations of the body in the larger context of the slow and uncertain progress toward salvation and grace. As Kathleen Clay Bassard and Yolanda Pierce have shown, spiritual narratives had a significant influence on slave narratives well into the nineteenth century.[7] In Franklin, that influence can best be discerned in the autobiography's second part, where he sketches out his project to achieve moral perfection. Bearing the impress of the Puritan Cotton Mather's call for regular self-examination, Franklin's sometimes comical account of his efforts to improve himself in all aspects of his life appealed to a number of black autobiographers, especially Frederick Douglass, who instructed his black readers of the *North Star* to find ways of imitating Franklin's example.[8]

But even more influential on the development of the slave narrative was the autobiography's first part, which depicts Franklin's flight from the puritanical constraints of Boston to the apparent freedom of cosmopolitan Philadelphia. At times, Franklin presents those constraints in language that evokes slavery, as in his descriptions of being beaten by his older brother (in the way of a flogging) during his apprenticeship. In a footnote on those beatings, Franklin portrays his resistance to his brother in revolutionary terms: "I fancy his harsh & tyrannical Treatment of me, might be a means of impressing me with that Aversion to arbitrary Power that has stuck to me thro' my whole life."[9] Though Franklin hadn't quite committed to the American Revolutionary cause by 1771, the year he drafted the first part of the autobiography, James M. Cox nevertheless persuasively argues that there was an intimate connection between the rise of autobiography in what would become the United States and the revolutionary energies of the nation's founding, and that such connections are nowhere more apparent than in Franklin's autobiography. As Cox explains: "What literally happens in the form of Franklin's work is that the history of the revolution, in which Franklin played such a conspicuous part, is displaced by the narrative of Franklin's early life, so that Franklin's personal history *stands in place of the revolution*."[10] The linking of the autobiographical self with the revolutionary ideals of the new nation would become central to the numerous slave narratives that drew on key aspects of Franklin's autobiography: the emphasis on the self-made life; the value of capitalist exchange and possessive individualism in the creation of a "free" self; the strategic uses of rhetoric, literacy, and deception in a competitive and inequitable social landscape; and the importance of contributing to the larger community. Slave narrators vary in their responses to Franklin, placing different emphases on different aspects of this "American" model, and in some cases challenging and subverting the model. Such varied black messages and autobiographical selves can be discerned in slave narratives despite the putative silencings and manipulations of their white sponsors.

The first slave narrative that shows the influence of Franklin is Venture Smith's 1798 *A Narrative of the Life and Adventures of Venture*. In the narrative's editorial preface, the white Connecticut schoolteacher Elisha Niles characterizes Smith as a black Franklin, or "Franklin . . . in a state of nature," for the way he "exhibits a pattern of honesty, prudence, and industry." In the remarkable life history that follows, Smith, who was taken from Africa and remanded into slavery, describes how he eventually managed to purchase his freedom, along with the freedom of his wife and children. In the manner of Franklin, he continues his economic rise in US culture, purchasing several homes and a farm, and developing a fleet of sailing vessels that soon makes him one of the more prominent traders of the day. Though the narrative can at times be chilling with its cold, economic calculus (for example, Smith states about his son who dies at sea that in "the loss of his life, I lost equal to seventy-five pounds"), there is every sense that this economic striver has, with the help of the Franklinian model, developed a strategy for survival in white racist culture. But as much as Franklin may have influenced Smith's thinking about how to present the upward arc of his life history, Smith's autobiographical account also departs from Franklin and works against Niles's framing preface. For, unlike Niles, Smith also emphasizes the impact of his childhood experiences in Africa on his resistance to slavery. Whereas the paternalistic Niles refers to Smith as "an untutored African slave," who, despite his success, remains something like an animal "in a state of nature," Smith in his narrative's opening section offers a very different sense of his African background. In particular, he celebrates his African father for choosing to sacrifice his life rather than betray his people to their tribal enemies. In Smith's narrative, it is his father, as much as Franklin and other American Revolutionaries, who teaches him about the value of "liberties and rights."[11]

With his appeal to liberties and rights, Smith departs from a spiritual narrative like the free black Briton Hammon's 1760 *Narrative*, and attempts to instruct possible black readers about the importance of the secular values of self-reliance and industry if they hope to rise in market culture. Though Smith depicts both the African and republican sources of his self-reliance, subsequent black autobiographers would place an even greater emphasis on Franklinian self-possession and the related political ideals of what they regularly present as an unfinished American

Revolution – unfinished for the simple reason that equality and liberty remain unavailable across the color line. In the *Life of William Grimes, the Runaway Slave* (1824), for instance, Grimes emphasizes the connection of industrious labor to black uplift, portraying himself as Franklinian in his efforts to make money and improve his social standing, even if that means becoming a lottery agent in New Haven. At the same time, he makes clear that blacks face enormous obstacles in attempting to rise like Franklin because of the pervasiveness of whites' antiblack racism. The story that Grimes ultimately tells about both Northern and Southern culture is one of anger and frustration, building to a chilling American Revolutionary declaration of his plan to will his previously flogged body to the nation so that his skin "might be taken off and made into parchment, and then bind the constitution of glorious, happy, and *free* America."[12] In this striking image, Grimes's scarred skin becomes a text of revolutionary resistance that tells the story of violation but also of the possibilities for a regenerated America.

Franklinian uplift and critique is for course central to Frederick Douglass's autobiographical narratives. Although there is much in his 1845 *Narrative* suggestive of the possible influence of Smith, Grimes, and other "black bourgeois autobiographers,"[13] the *Narrative* can also be read in relation to the tradition of spiritual autobiography that Franklin tapped into for part two of his autobiography. In his prefatory letter to the *Narrative*, the white abolitionist William Lloyd Garrison remarks on how slavery "entombs the godlike mind of man, defaces the divine image, reduces those who by creation were crowned with glory and honor to a level with four-footed beasts." Douglass gives some credence to that view in his autobiographical account, but he also poses a challenge to Garrison, showing how the slaves' sorrow songs and his own personal story demonstrate blacks' spiritual resiliency. Throughout the *Narrative*, Douglass, in the tradition of Puritan autobiography, depicts himself as fighting off the temptation to succumb to the tug and pull of the body, even as he strives to show that the conditions of slavery take a toll on the body. Still, Douglass's efforts to resist various forms of degradation testify to a desire for spiritual progress that has its most poignant expression in his famous apostrophe to the sailing vessels on the Chesapeake "robed in purest white." When, at the end of the *Narrative*, Douglass describes taking up the "severe cross" of leadership, he signals to white and black readers alike that he can assume this role because he has achieved a Christ-like or Mosaic spirituality.[14]

But as important as the spiritual narrative is to the *Narrative*, Douglass seems most indebted to the motifs of uplift, self-making, and possessive individualism central to Franklin's autobiography.[15] Like Franklin, Douglass depicts himself at the outset of his autobiography as stultified by a culture that attempts to keep him in his "proper" place. The move from the constraints of the Eastern Shore of Maryland to the relative freedom of Baltimore has important parallels with Franklin's move from Boston to Philadelphia, for the more cosmopolitan city exposes Douglass to greater intellectual and economic opportunities. Like Franklin, he learns by imitation, teaching himself to read and write on his own, and like Franklin, he strategically uses deception and deceit whenever such modes can forward his pragmatic ends. Whereas Franklin rises at a steady pace, Douglass repeatedly confronts the obstacles, or what Franklin terms the "harsh & tyrannical Treatment" and "arbitrary Power," that will forever be in his way in a slave culture. In attempting to overcome those obstacles, Douglass conceives of himself and his like-minded compatriots as American revolutionaries who "did more than Patrick Henry, when he resolved upon liberty or death." In this and several other instances, there is a harmonious relationship between the white envelope and black message, for Garrison, too, describes Douglass as akin to "PATRICK HENRY, of revolutionary fame." What Garrison fails to note is that whites' antiblack racism continues to thwart Douglass even after he escapes to the North. In the Franklinian manner of Venture Smith and William Grimes, Douglass attempts to rise in Northern culture after he makes his way to New Bedford, but he soon faces the racist resistance of white workers who do not seem all that different from the racist workers at the docks of Baltimore's Fells Point. Choosing to join hands with the white abolitionists he meets in Nantucket, Douglass nevertheless presents himself at the conclusion of his *Narrative* as a black freedom fighter devoted to "the cause of my brethren."[16]

In his 1855 *My Bondage and My Freedom*, a major expansion and revision of the 1845 *Narrative*, Douglass explores at greater length the cultural and institutional pressures that make it next to impossible for a black man to become a Benjamin Franklin. Having broken with Garrison and the Massachusetts Anti-Slavery Society in the early 1850s, Douglass takes even greater pains in *Bondage* to link himself with his black "brethren." This is a calculated rhetorical shift on the part of Douglass, who had mostly presented himself in the *Narrative* as a heroic individualist, despite his acknowledgment of his fellow slaves. Douglass deliberately enlarges upon the Franklinian model in *Bondage* by registering a greater sense of his communal ties to other rebellious blacks. In the *Narrative*, Douglass celebrates his self-reliant resistance to the slave-breaker Covey; in *Bondage*, by contrast, he describes the assistance he receives from other slaves who enable that resistance. Consistent with the black communitarian vision of the 1855 autobiography, Douglass in this self-published work dispenses with the "white envelope" of Garrison's and Wendell Phillips's somewhat condescending prefaces, and goes with a new preface by the black abolitionist James McCune Smith. Significantly, Smith presents Douglass in a Franklinian mode as a "Representative American" who, through his initiative, hard work, and self-restraint, manages to raise himself "from the lowest condition in society to the highest." At the same time, Smith follows Douglass's lead in noting that the persona of *Bondage* has close connections to black culture, and is much more than a shining example of black self-elevation. Douglass is also an exemplary American Revolutionary with a "special mission" of helping both the free and enslaved blacks to achieve "the exercise of all those rights" from which they have "been so long disbarred."[17]

In Douglass's and many other slave narratives of the antebellum period, the Franklinian model is regularly put to the service of linking the individual uplift of the black persona to the revolutionary cause of freedom for all blacks. And yet, as indebted as the slave narrative is to Franklin's autobiography, the fact is that most slave narrators cannot do what Franklin does at the outset of his autobiography: provide an authorizing family genealogy. In the *Narrative*, Douglass alludes to his unknown white father; in *Bondage* he focuses more on his black mother. McCune Smith reads Douglass's account of his mother's "deep black, glossy complexion" and "native genius" as an effort to show that "for his energy, perseverance, eloquence, invective, sagacity, and wide sympathy, he is indebted to his negro blood."[18] But ultimately Douglass and McCune Smith can only speculate about Douglass's genealogical history. The absence of known genealogies can be taken as a defining feature and subject of most slave narratives of the period, which is why so many begin with the vague but boldly annunciatory phrase, "I was born." But that bold "I was born" also serves as a kind of self-silencing, for the alternative would be for the former slaves to begin their narratives with an acknowledgment that they owe their existence to the rape of their black mother. All this said, these black autobiographers generally find ways of telling this story. In his 1845 *Narrative*, Douglass addresses the rape of his mother obliquely by describing the violation of his Aunt Hester almost immediately after acknowledging the uncertainties of the genealogical line on his paternal side. In this way, Hester serves as a surrogate for his mother. Watching her naked body being whipped by the master, the young Douglass has intimations of the traumatic truth of sexuality on the plantation. In their subsequent autobiographical narratives, William Wells Brown and Henry Bibb address matters of gender and sexuality more directly and with an even greater sympathy for the plight of the female slave.

Bundled with a testimonial letter from the white abolitionist Edmund Quincy and a preface by J. C. Hathaway of the Boston Anti-Slavery Society urging readers to take up the abolitionist cause, William Wells Brown's *Narrative* of 1847 would appear to be indebted to Douglass's *Narrative* and thus to Franklin's autobiography, as well. As in Franklin and Douglass, he describes how he learns to read and write through imitation and trickery. As in Douglass, Brown implicitly and explicitly invokes American Revolutionary ideals when he fights against arbitrary authority. But at the end of his *Narrative*, Brown underscores the irony that in order to achieve his freedom he will have to take refuge with the enemy of the American Revolutionaries, as Douglass did right after publishing his *Narrative*, by "fleeing from a Democratic Republic, Christian government, to receive protection under the monarchy of Great Britain." Given the failure of the United States to live up to its revolutionary ideals, Brown, like Douglass, emphasizes that the slave must develop strategies for survival, specifically by learning how to deceive the masters. In his repeated use of deception, Brown resembles the Franklin who deceived his brother and Keimer, and yet because, as Brown says, "slavery makes its victims lying and mean," it is difficult for him to adhere to Franklin's famous (and problematic) maxim: "Use no hurtful Deceit." In order to survive, Brown works for a slave trader in "blacking" slaves who are being sold at auction (he colors their hair to make them look younger), and in one of the more memorable scenes of deception in his *Narrative*, he describes how he escaped from a flogging by giving the written orders for his own flogging to an innocent free black, who suffers the punishment in Brown's place. Though Brown says that he "deeply regretted the deception I practised upon this poor fellow," it is clear from the overall narrative that his art of deception, which can be credited with helping him to escape from slavery, is integral to his autobiographical art.[19] (The art of deception is also integral to such later works as Henry Box Brown's *Narrative* [1851] and William and Ellen Crafts's *Running a Thousand Miles for Freedom* [1861].) For in the manner of a Franklinian trickster, Brown, like Douglass, rhetorically shapes his stories for particular audiences and occasions, and in subsequent autobiographical narratives tells different versions of the same story. His narrative inventiveness increasingly allows him to distance himself from the sometimes callous persona he created for the version published by the Massachusetts Anti-Slavery Office in 1847.

In all of his autobiographical narratives, Brown tells the story of the corporeal violations that can't quite be told directly, in part because of a hesitancy about breaching Victorian norms of propriety (similar issues would come up in Harriet Jacobs's 1861 *Incidents*), but mostly because of what the ex-slave Henry Bibb calls in his 1849 slave narrative the "despair in finding language to express adequately the deep feeling of [the] soul." That story is the sexual violation of Brown's mother and sister, which is touched on in J. C. Hathaway's preface, though mainly as yet more evidence of "the irresponsible control of the pale-faced oppressor." (For a fuller discussion of issues of self-control in Brown, see Chapter 6, below.) But much more is going on in the *Narrative* than polemics; Brown gets at something internal and psychological in ways that are altogether different from what we see in Franklin. Like Douglass, Brown begins his story with the words "I was born," a phrase that, despite its seeming simplicity, points to the rape of his mother. Whereas Douglass imagines a version of that rape through the flogging scene with his Aunt Hester and then moves the focus to his own initiatives at uplift and escape, Brown in his *Narrative*, in ways that are barely acknowledged by the abolitionists who preface and publish the work, addresses the pain and guilt that he feels knowing that he owes not only his existence but also his escape and freedom to the enslavement and sexual violation of the women of his family. For this reason, Brown's various autobiographical narratives – the *Narrative*, his autobiographical preface to *Clotel* (1853), his *Memoir* (1859), and other stories he would tell about his life – regularly stage scenes in which his mother and sister encourage him to escape despite their ongoing sufferings. Whether these moments actually occurred in Brown's life history is beside the point: these scenes serve both to vindicate and excuse what Brown must have considered as his act of abandonment. His sister, who is eventually sold to Natchez and vanishes forever from his life, offers Brown a kind of benediction right before her sale: "If we cannot get our liberty, we do not wish to be the means of keeping you from a land of freedom."[20] Brown's rendering of a similar benediction from his mother before she is sent to the New Orleans slave market is less a cleansing absolution than an authorial confession to the lingering effects of his survivor's guilt. The self-reliant Franklinian ex-slave is not so self-reliant after all.

We see a similar emphasis on gender and sexuality in Henry Bibb's *Narrative* (1849), a work that, like Brown's, seems to follow the Franklinian-Douglass autobiographical model even as it veers from it. Like Douglass's *Narrative*, Bibb's comes bundled with testimonials from its authorizing white editor, in this case Lucius C. Matlack, who rather conventionally says that Bibb's text promises to "be instrumental in advancing the great work of emancipation in this country." But as is true for many of the slave narratives that Olney, Sekora, and others regard as driven by convention and shaped by abolitionists, Bibb's autobiographical narrative has a distinctive story to tell, which he relates with a creative artistry that, as in Brown, covers up and attempts to rationalize his abandonment of others. Like Douglass, he begins with the "I was born" that suggests the violation of his mother, and then describes the hardships of slavery, his desire for escape, his efforts to run a Sabbath school, and the impact of American Revolutionary ideology on his active pursuit of freedom. Alluding to the Declaration of Independence, and in this way positioning himself in relation to the revolutionary fathers, he proclaims his belief that "every man has a right to wages for his labor; a right to his own wife and children; a right to liberty and the pursuit of happiness; and a right to worship God according to the dictates of his own conscience."[21] Franklin couldn't have put such sentiments any better than that.

But the autobiographical focus of Bibb's *Narrative* soon shifts from his rise in the culture to his "marriage" to "a mulatto slave girl named Malinda," a woman whom he claims to have loved so profoundly that he was willing to link himself to her with a slave marriage, despite knowing that "such a step would greatly obstruct my way to a land of liberty." Like Brown, he emphasizes that the status of his wife and (later) daughter as property makes them vulnerable to the sexual predations of their male owners. When Bibb states that "no tongue, nor pen ever has or can express the horrors of American Slavery," it is clear that, in the manner of Brown, he is simply unable or unwilling to directly address the implications of that propertied relationship, beyond stating that he regrets "being a father and husband of slaves." Bibb's efforts throughout the *Narrative* to free his family from slavery enact his own revolutionary anger at the authority of the master. But the autobiographer who can seem so caring about his nonlegal wife, and who is quite open about the fact that his mother and her mother before her had been sexually violated by slaveholders, nonetheless turns against his wife in unsettling fashion when, at the conclusion of his life history, he refers to her "degradation" for "living in a state of adultery with her master." Bibb fails to ask important questions about volition and the power of the master, and he uses the news of his wife's putative "fall" to justify his marriage in 1848 to the Boston antislavery activist Mary Miles. Having escaped to Detroit, he says about his former wife from the relative comfort of his situation in a free state: "Poor unfortunate woman, I bring no charge of guilt against her, for I know not all the circumstances connected with the case. It is consistent with slavery, however, to suppose that she became reconciled to it."[22] One of the large arguments of the relatively few slave narratives written by women is that there is no reconciling to such degradation.

   Precisely because slave women bear the burden of white patriarchy on their bodies, their narratives tell different stories from those of formerly enslaved black men, though there are broad overlaps. Critics have argued that male-authored slave narratives emphasize Franklinian "possessive individualism," "rivalry ... between men," and the pursuit of individual "mastery," while those authored by black women emphasize "community, interdependence, heritage, and culture."[23] But there are risks to conceiving of these differences in such binary terms. Numerous autobiographies by black male narrators display an interest in community and interdependence (Bibb's *Narrative*, Douglass's *Bondage*, and Samuel Ringgold Ward's *Autobiography* [1855] are especially compelling examples), and self-sufficiency and revolutionary independence are crucial to such key texts as Truth's *Narrative* and Jacobs's *Incidents*, despite the fact that both Truth and Jacobs portray themselves as mothers in ways that black male narrators obviously cannot. As Joanne Braxton demonstrates in her pioneering study of a black women's autobiographical tradition, slave narratives like Jacobs's *Incidents* evolve, in part, "from the autobiographical tradition of heroic male slaves," in which the "disguise and concealment" are put to the service of the larger "quest for freedom."[24] To be sure, Truth's *Narrative* and Jacobs's *Incidents* are more focused on matters of sexual exploitation and social interdependencies than most male-authored slave narratives. But these works also display important debts to the Franklinian tradition of American Revolutionary autobiography. Truth, after all, is a freedom fighter, and one of the principal motifs of the overall narrative is her effort to obtain the freedom of her son after making a "declaration" of independence that she would do just that. Similarly, near the beginning of *Incidents*, Jacobs sets forth her own revolutionary dictum: "He that is *willing* to be a slave, let him be a slave." In this ideological context, Jacobs's decision to fight back against Dr. Flint, her willingness to match her "might" against that of the master, has more in common with Douglass's revolutionary decision to fight back against Covey than most critics have acknowledged.[25]

   That said, matters of sexuality and gender are at the center of Truth's and Jacobs's autobiographical narratives, both of which tell distinctive stories that depart from the frames established by their white editors. Because Truth's 1850 *Narrative* was dictated to Olive Gilbert and presented as a third-person account, this particular version of Truth's life history would at first glance appear to be an unlikely source for a frank perspective on sexuality and gender, especially given that the editor's preface concludes with a conventional appeal to white readers that "the following Narrative may increase the sympathy that is felt for the suffering colored population of this country, and inspire to renewed efforts for the liberation of all who are pining in bondage on the American soil." But the story Truth tells about her relationship with her children is hardly conventional. The evidence suggests that the five children Truth gave birth to while a slave in New York State were the children of her slave "husband" Thomas, and that, as indicated by Truth's successful lawsuit in 1827 for the return of a son, she became empowered as a mother in ways that the Southern black women in Brown's and Bibb's narratives never could. And yet Truth's *Narrative* describes sexual rivalries and violations that are similar to what Jacobs would later write about in *Incidents*. Truth initially wishes to marry a slave named Robert, but that union is denied by Robert's master. (There is a similar such scene in Jacobs.) The forced marriage to Thomas that follows shortly thereafter thus clearly serves the needs and desires of her master, who then develops an oddly proprietary watchfulness over Truth's children. The master's kind interest in the children is described by Truth (or Truth/Gilbert) as "proof of her master's kindness," but the extent of that kindness raises questions about his relationship to those children. As Truth elaborates in her *Narrative*: "If her master came into the house and found her infant crying, (as she could not always attend to its wants and the commands of her mistress at the same time,) he would turn to his wife with a look of reproof, and ask her why she did not see the child taken care of. . . . And he would linger to see if his orders were obeyed, and not countermanded."[26] Whatever the relationship of her master to the children, this account nonetheless captures the sexual rivalry between the white wife and the black slave woman that is nowhere commented on in the framing preface and conclusion. Instead, that rivalry is artfully built into the texture of Truth's overall story of how her freedom was constrained not only by her labors in the field but also by her sexual vulnerability in the master's home.

Jacobs's *Incidents*, which is framed by a preface by her white "Editor" Lydia Maria Child and an appendix with testimonial letters from black and white friends, addresses similar matters of female vulnerability in US slave culture. In her editorial preface, Child states that she may be accused of "indecorum" in promoting a narrative that is so frank about sexuality, but in *Incidents* itself, Jacobs turns the matter of decorum against her white readers, and in certain respects against Child, making it clear that the standards for "pure" female behavior have no relevance to the exigencies of the life of a slave girl. It is "with deliberate calculation," she says, that she chose to have children with a white man in her neighborhood in order to avoid sexual relations with her master; and though her grandmother and uncle originate the idea, she presents her later decision to hide out in a crawl space for nearly seven years as similarly made with "deliberate calculation" in order to thwart her master and gain freedom for her children. Throughout the narrative there are mentions of the various white and black people, mostly women, who come to Jacobs's aid, but without her Franklin-like independence and deceptiveness, her plotting would not have succeeded. When she states, for example, with respect to her master, that "I resolved to match my cunning against his cunning," Jacobs invokes the tradition going back to Franklin, and that manifests itself in numerous slave narratives, of learning how to manipulate appearances in order to rise in the culture (or, in this case, to survive and eventually escape from slavery). By taking refuge in a crawl space for seven years, Jacobs also draws on, or invokes, the Thoreauvian tradition of pursuing spiritual regeneration in a place made sacred by the autobiographical narrator. Whether intended or not, Jacobs's "Loophole of Retreat" has parallels with the Concord jailhouse of Thoreau's "Resistance to Civil Government" (1849). If for Thoreau "the true place for a just man is . . . a prison," for Jacobs the true place for a just woman in slavery is a self-imprisonment that liberates her body from the sexual labors and violations of patriarchy. Inspiring Jacobs's creative stratagems and eventual escape are her desires, consistent with the ideals of the revolutionary Franklin, for "pure, unadulterated freedom" for herself and her children. But her narrative ends, like most slave narratives, with an understanding that freedom will remain illusory in the North until slavery is no longer the law of the land. Jacobs thus concludes with a Stowe-like instance of direct address – "Reader, my story ends with freedom" – that has the ring of irony given that her freedom is the result of a slave sale transacted in New York City. Once again, the Franklinian revolutionary model has its limits for blacks in a slave culture, even in the supposedly free North.[27]

Jacobs's concluding direct address to her reader conveys her awareness of the rhetorical constraints on her autobiographical narrative. She is writing to Northern whites whom she knows will never completely fathom her experiences and may never be able to see her as anything but a fallen woman. Jacobs presents her experiences from within the "white envelope" that has been created by her sympathetic editor, Lydia Maria Child, and yet she remains in control of her story by virtue of her rhetorical resourcefulness and willingness to move beyond the constraints of her authorizing editor. There are similar constraints on virtually all of the slave narratives that I have discussed in this chapter, but also similar signs of agency and resourcefulness on the part of black authors, who did what they could to tell their stories in the narratives that bore their names. If some or all of these writers worked in an American Revolutionary tradition that had its most influential exemplar in Benjamin Franklin, they did not blindly or unselfconsciously follow in that tradition, and female authors in particular had their own distinctive stories to tell about the limits of Franklinian individualism, or what Maurice O. Wallace has termed the "possessive freedom-dream."[28] All of these writers called attention to the constraints on black freedom in the North, and worked with the revolutionary form inscribed in Franklinian/American autobiography. In post–Civil War autobiographical narratives, and in the neo-slave narratives of twentieth-century US fiction, African American writers such as W. E. B. Du Bois and Sherley Anne Williams would take up the continued challenges facing blacks in a white racist culture while honoring the agency and vision of the slave narrators – or black autobiographers – who inspired their work.[29]

CHAPTER 6

"Whiskey, Blacking, and All"
Temperance and Race in William Wells Brown's Clotel

For William Wells Brown and other nineteenth-century African American writers, temperance was both an aesthetic and a problem. As an aesthetic, temperance provided ways of representing interconnections among black elevation, racism, corporeality, and violence. As a problem, temperance spoke to possibilities of individual and social reform but often failed to address institutionalized forms of racism in the larger culture. Brown's 1853 novel works with the aesthetic and wrestles with the problem.

In the March 18, 1852, issue of *Frederick Douglass' Paper*, Douglass printed an editorial supporting New York State legislation modeled on the 1851 Maine Law, which banned the manufacture and sale of liquor. Around the same time, he began printing numerous articles championing Harriet Beecher Stowe's *Uncle Tom's Cabin* (1852). By 1853, Stowe's antislavery novel and temperance emerged as dominant, even linked, concerns of his newspaper, and these interrelated interests were addressed in a letter from William Wells Brown printed in the issue of August 26, 1853. Writing from London on August 2, 1853, Brown proclaims that "'Uncle Tom's Cabin' is still doing a great work; its popularity and its wide circulation is not only arousing the dormant feeling of that generous love of freedom and lofty enthusiasm which, a few years ago, burst from the limbs of the beaten and outraged slaves of the West Indies, but will do much to create a desire for the elevation of the laboring classes in Europe, and especially in Great Britain." Brown's rhetoric initially suggests that the "laboring classes," like the slaves of the West Indies, are the victims of brute exploitation and arbitrary authority, but as the letter continues he increasingly places the burden for the "elevation" of the working poor on the poor themselves, whom he portrays less as "wage slaves" than as "slaves" of the bottle:

> It is true that much can be said of the sad position in which a large portion of the people are placed, but very much of their degradation is brought upon

98

by themselves. – The amount of drunkenness is frightful. . . . It is enough to horrify any one to go amongst these people, who seem abandoned to the varied evils that neglect, ignorance, and vice have produced. . . . Many of these appear so worn in countenance, form, feature, and expression, that one is almost led to doubt whether they are of the same species with the well-organized and the noble of the race. – Through the vice of intemperance and its degrading influences, the lofty lineaments of their better nature gradually wear away, until nothing is left but the attributes of the idiot or the fiend.[1]

In this anxious meditation on the corporeal and moral degradation brought about by intemperance, Brown suggests that "drunkenness," a form of self-enslavement, transforms the white working classes into a different "species" from the human race.

Brown develops similar connections among temperance, slavery, and race in his 1853 *Clotel; or, The President's Daughter: A Narrative of Slave Life in the United States*, generally regarded as the first novel published by an African American. In a revealing scene on a stagecoach late in the novel, a Connecticut minister, who "went the whole length of the 'Maine Law,'" tells the passengers of how he used to keep "spirits about the house" before he became a "teetotaller."[2] He did so, in part, because his servant, "who was much addicted to strong drink" (191), insisted that he needed whiskey on hand to mix with the boot blacking. Suspicious of the servant's demands, the minister one morning himself pours the whiskey into the boot blacking. He triumphantly describes the servant's response to his experiment: "He took the blacking out, and I watched him, and he drank down the whiskey, blacking, and all" (191). More explicitly than in Brown's letter on English poverty, the rhetoric of this account suggests, with an uncomfortable literalism, that to drink intemperately is to transform oneself into a "black" slave to the bottle. The depiction of the servant is consistent with Paul Gilmore's argument that Brown regularly made use of minstrel imagery in order to present himself "as a self-sufficient manipulator of the literary marketplace and its dependence on mass cultural images of blackness."[3] But the fact that the servant's race is never mentioned only underscores the transracial applicability of the lesson encoded in this anecdote.

Geoffrey Sanborn has recently argued that Brown includes the stagecoach scene in *Clotel* as part of his aesthetic of performance, diversion, and showmanship. As he remarks, "None of the interchanges [on the stagecoach] involve the main characters . . . and none . . . affects the plot. At no point, moreover, is there a reference to race or slavery." But as my brief discussion of the exchange on the Maine Law suggests, temperance has much to do with race; and throughout the novel, temperance and race have much to do with slavery. Moreover, the stagecoach scene has a good deal to do with the plot because it exposes Clotel to the national culture while moving her from Cincinnati back to Virginia as she searches for her daughter, Mary. To be sure, the scene does add to the fun of reading what Sanborn terms the "herky-jerky, variety-show-style narrative" that is *Clotel*.[4] But the extended conversation about the Maine Law is far more than showmanship. It is but one of a number of moments in which temperance is linked to the novel's larger concerns about race, slavery, and the unfinished work of the American Revolution. For Brown, temperance served aesthetic and political purposes; and his longstanding interest in the reform and its discourses helped to energize his first novel and his overall career.

From the mid-1830s to the time of his death in 1884, Brown participated in a number of African American temperance organizations committed to the belief that the free blacks could elevate themselves in the United States by liberating themselves from liquor. At his most optimistic, Brown argued that if blacks could overcome "the enslaving appetite" for drink, as he termed intemperance in *The American Fugitive in Europe* (1855), they might one day overcome slavery itself.[5] And yet Brown, like Nathaniel Paul, knew full well that black elevation was extraordinarily difficult in a racist slave culture. Aware that a progressive model of temperance risked absolving white racist culture for its role in enslaving and subordinating blacks, Brown and other black temperance reformers sought to expand their concerns beyond the problem of controlling blacks' drinking habits in order to portray whites' antiblack racism and desires for mastery as themselves forms of intemperance. In *Clotel*, as I elaborate below, many of the most intemperate figures are whites, not blacks. Over the course of the novel, Brown shows how the lack of restraints on whites' "enslaving appetite" for drink, power, and sexual gratification works to perpetuate the enslavement of blacks in the South and the marginalization of free blacks in the North. The novel's fragmentary collage technique, with its dislocating shifts among various characters and scenes, allows Brown to display a wide range of intemperate actions among a wide range of characters, thereby challenging easy dichotomies of temperance and intemperance along racial lines. The result is a novel that, despite its problematic metaphor of "blacking," destabilizes race and (perhaps unwittingly) challenges idealistic conceptions of the transformative power of temperance. That said, progressive models of temperance reform have an important place in the novel, and it is with Brown's optimistic belief that temperance could contribute to the struggle against slavery and racism that I want to begin.

In the "Narrative of the Life and Escape of William Wells Brown," which prefaces the 1853 London first printing of *Clotel*, the third-person biographer (probably Brown) comments on Brown's temperance work in Buffalo following his escape from slavery in 1834:

> In proportion as his mind expanded under the more favourable circumstances in which Brown was placed, he became anxious, not merely for the redemption of his race from personal slavery, but for the moral and religious elevation of those who were free. Finding that habits of intoxication were too prevalent among his coloured brethren, he, in conjunction with others, commenced a temperance reformation in their body. Such was the success of their efforts that, in three years, in the city of Buffalo alone, a society of upwards of 500 members was raised out of a coloured population of less than 700. (69)

As the three-time president of this society, Brown sought to help the free blacks to assume "a position," as Josephine Brown remarks in her 1856 biography of her father, "where they could give a practical refutation to the common belief, that the negro cannot attain to the high stand of the Anglo-Saxon."[6] In this respect, his goals were of a piece with those of the black temperance movement of the period. Numerous black reformers argued that the free blacks should make a concerted effort to control their drinking so that they could elevate themselves in US society and thereby convince whites of the errors of proslavery ideology.[7] For example, the Report of the Committee on Temperance delivered at the 1833 "Third Annual Convention, for the Improvement of the Free People of Colour in These United States" warned that whites could claim that blacks were better off in slavery when they observed "degraded men, clustering around those fatal corners, where '*liquid fire*' is dispensed"; and the report went on to blame black intemperance, not white racism, for "*four fifths* of the pauperism known among us." Though William Whipper, the founder of the American Moral Reform Society, contested the notion that blacks were "more intemperate than whites," he nonetheless argued in his 1834 presidential address to the Colored Temperance Society of Philadelphia "that we must be more pure than they, before we can be duly respected." Martin Delany, who in 1834 helped to organize a black temperance society in Pittsburgh, drafted a resolution at the 1841 State Convention of the Colored Freemen of Pennsylvania calling on blacks to adopt "TOTAL ABSTINENCE" so that they might gain "the esteem of all wise and virtuous men." For, as Stephen Meyers put it in the February 10, 1842, issue of his temperance/abolitionist newspaper, *Northern Star and Freeman's Advocate*: "[W]henever it can be said (and not gainsayed) that the free blacks are a sober, industrious and intelligent people, capable of self government, the only argument in favor of slavery falls to the ground."[8]

In their writings, Brown and other black temperance reformers of the period can appear to be placing undue emphasis on the ways in which, as Douglass remarks in his 1845 "Intemperance and Slavery," a "large class of free people of color in America . . . has, through the influence of intemperance, done much to retard the progress of the anti-slavery movement." But by the 1840s these reformers had also taken up the more radical agenda of highlighting abuses of white power through the rhetoric of temperance. In "Intemperance and Slavery," for instance, Douglass, after seeming to blame intemperate free blacks for their degraded status in the United States, quickly shifts his attention to racist whites of the North and South, whom he presents as exhibiting analogous forms of intemperance far more insidious than the putative drunkenness of Northern blacks. He lambastes the white racist mob that attacked 1,200 black members of Philadelphia's Moyamensing Temperance Society during the August 1, 1842, celebration of West Indies emancipation. And by insisting that prior to his escape from slavery "I was not a slave to intemperance, but a slave to my fellow-men," he makes clear, through analogy and metaphor, that for the most part it was the slaveowners, not this particular former slave, who evinced intemperance.[9] Commenting on slavery's tendency to promote "intemperance," the white abolitionist Theodore Weld writes in his influential *American Slavery as It Is* (1839): "Arbitrary power is to the mind what alcohol is to the body; it intoxicates. Man loves power. It is perhaps the strongest human passion; and the more absolute the power, the stronger the desire for it." Brown similarly remarks in an 1847 lecture delivered to the Female Anti-Slavery Society of Salem: "Give one man power *ad infinitum* over another, and he will abuse that power; no matter if there be law; no matter if there be public sentiment in favor of the oppressed." "Drunk" on unlimited power, the individual enslaver, like the alcoholic, becomes a "slave" of appetite.[10]

As the Female Anti-Slavery Society setting of Brown's 1847 lecture suggests, the discourse of intemperate appetite was often gendered as an attack on patriarchal power. In her biography of her father, Josephine Brown points to the pronounced vulnerability of the female slaves: "If there is one evil connected with the abominable system of slavery which should be loathed more than another, it is taking from woman the right of self-defence, and making her subject to the control of any licentious villain who may be able to purchase her person."[11] Brown repeatedly represents such violations in his writings, in large part because of traumatic events that he mourned throughout his life: the sexual violations of his mother and sister. (Brown barely mentions his three brothers in his autobiographical narratives.) As he remarks in the prefatory "Narrative" to *Clotel*: "[N]othing could be more heart-rending than to see a dear and beloved mother or sister tortured by unfeeling men" (50). The violation of his mother was a particularly painful source of guilt for Brown because without that violation he would not have been born; he owes his very existence to the intemperate patriarchal violation that is the focus of his social critique. In his autobiographical "Narrative," Brown depicts the innkeeper Mr. Freeland, to whom Brown is briefly hired out, as representative of the "tyrannical and inhuman" slaveholder par excellence: "he was a horse-racer, cock-fighter, gambler, and, to crown the whole, an inveterate drunkard. What else but bad treatment could be expected from such a character?" (50). That large question becomes a haunting one when Brown's mother is sent to the New Orleans slave market, to be sold to one of the Freelands of the world, and his sister, who had been purchased "for the master's own use" (56), is sent to a slave pen for another's master's own use. Similar concerns about the "enslaving appetite" of the masters haunt the opening chapters of *Clotel*. ·

The narrator asserts at the beginning of *Clotel* that the relative lack of existence of "the real Negro, or clear black" (81) provides the "best evidence of the degraded and immoral condition of the relation of master and slave in the United States of America" (81–82). Brown writes in his 1853 *Three Years in Europe*, published the same year as *Clotel*, that the increasingly white complexion of the slaves "is attributable, solely to the unlimited power which the slave owner exercises over his victim."[12] It is attributable, in short, to the sexual domination that slavery vouchsafes the patriarch, a power which is depicted in *Clotel*'s opening chapters as a form of intemperance that corrupts master and slave alike. The forever offstage (because dead) Thomas Jefferson emerges as the *ur*-intemperate master for having fathered two daughters by Currer, the slave women who formerly "kept house" (85) for him.[13] As a sign of the corruption resulting from such hypocritical exploitation, Currer in effect prostitutes her daughters, Clotel and Althesa, by sending them to balls in the misguided hope that they might become, as their mother once was, "the finely-dressed mistress of some white man" (84–85). By depicting the daughters first at a "negro ball" (86) and then (with their mother) at a slave sale, Brown suggests that there is little difference between the two institutions, insofar as both put slave women at the mercy of white men. Brown presents the slave sale as an occasion in which grossly physical masters, "joking, swearing, smoking, spitting" (87), compete to purchase female bodies for sexual purposes. While Currer and Althesa are sold to a slave speculator and sent downriver to New Orleans, Clotel is purchased by Horatio Green, the son of a wealthy Richmond gentleman, who claims to have fallen in love with her. As the novel develops, however, it becomes increasingly clear that the seemingly "fortunate" Clotel is also at the mercy of a master's intemperate appetite.

As is well known, Brown, in telling Clotel's story, drew on Lydia Maria Child's "The Quadroons" (1842), breaking Child's narrative into several sections and changing names, but otherwise adhering so closely to the story as to lift numerous passages word for word.[14] Child's story clearly appealed to Brown for the way it conjoins antislavery and feminist discourses to suggest that, from the very start, intemperate desires govern a white master's decision to make a slave woman into his mistress. Green initially rents a country cottage for Clotel, where she gives birth to a daughter, Mary. But increasingly he spends extended periods of time with his male friends in the city, and though Brown (Child) never comments on the obvious – that he would have been drinking with these friends – he portrays Green as "drunk" with ambition when he chooses to marry Gertrude, the daughter of "a very popular and wealthy man" (101). In the widely read antebellum temperance fictions of T. S. Arthur, economic desires and political ambition are presented as intoxicants that "enslave" mind and body.[15] Brown similarly presents Green's ambition as analogous to those moments in temperance tracts when the young man takes the first drink that precipitates the inevitable decline: "[T]his new impulse to ambition, combined with the strong temptation of variety in love, met the ardent young man weakened in moral principle, and unfettered by laws of the land" (102). Green's initial "taste" of power stimulates desires for more; lacking in "the idea of restraint" (102), he succumbs to appetite. His metaphorically intemperate ambition is literalized in his descent into alcoholism: "While [Clotel] was passing lonely and dreary hours with none but her darling child, Horatio Green was trying to find relief in that insidious enemy of man, the intoxicating cup" (149).

Through his appropriation of Child's story, Brown develops a damning portrayal of slavery as a patriarchal institution that stimulates, rather than restrains, the intemperate desires of the white male masters. Because the masters inevitably become "enslaved" to these desires, even a man with some moral potential – like the Reverend John Peck, who purchases Currer – can find himself succumbing to the temptations of power. Originally from Connecticut, Peck, invited by his uncle to Natchez,

Mississippi, marries a woman with a slave plantation and soon becomes a proslavery advocate who uses the Bible to justify his mastery. That such mastery makes him into a beast of sorts is made clear by his daughter, Georgiana, who tells the story of how her father joined in the pursuit of fugitive slaves with "those nasty negro-dogs" (143), and eventually did the work of the dogs in killing one of the fugitive slaves. The depiction of the parson's descent into dog-like bestiality is consistent with Brown's depiction throughout the novel of the consequences of governing "by decrees and laws emanating from . . . uncontrolled will" (176).

Given Brown's gendered focus on patriarchal exploitation and domination, and his admiration for Stowe, it is not surprising that the white woman Georgiana should emerge as one of the more exemplary characters in the novel. Like her father, Georgiana has been educated in the North, but in her case that education has opened her eyes to the evils of slavery. When she moves back to the South, she takes note of the differences between the two sections. As Brown remarks, she "had the opportunity of contrasting the spirit of Christianity and liberty in New England with that of slavery in her native state, and had learned to feel deeply for the injured Negro" (109). In some respects she has recovered the lost spirituality of her fallen father.

Following the death of her father to cholera, Georgiana, in alliance with Carlton, a Northern freethinker whom she marries after converting him to Christianity, adopts a plan of "gradual emancipation" (162) for the slaves of her plantation. Consistent with arguments made by Douglass, W. C. Nell, and other black leaders of the period (including Brown), Georgiana rejects her husband's initial suggestion that she work with the American Colonization Society and ship her approximately one hundred slaves to Liberia, insisting that blacks have earned the right to regard the United States as "their native land" (160).[16] (She later remarks that it would be better to deport "the vicious among the whites" [183].) In an effort to set an example to her Southern neighbors, she resolves to demonstrate blacks' capacities for temperate industry by paying them for their labors and allowing them to use their earnings to purchase their freedom. Georgiana's belief that it is ultimately the slaves' responsibility to display their industry places an enormous burden on the slaves. However, the rhetorical and political dimensions of her plan are similar to what I noted in writings by black temperance reformers of the period, and it is clear that Georgiana is viewed positively by Brown as "The Liberator" (159). As described in the novel, Georgiana's plan produces the very changes in her slaves that black temperance reformers like Whipper argued would contribute to black elevation: "They became temperate, moral, religious, setting an example of innocent, unoffending lives to the world around them, which was seen and admired by all" (163).

The need for the slaves to demonstrate their capacities for temperate industry assumes even greater urgency when Georgiana, suffering from consumption, decides to liberate her slaves before she dies. Summoning them before her as a group, she delivers her emancipation proclamation:

> "From this hour, . . . you are free, and all eyes will be fixed upon you. I dare not predict how far your example may affect the welfare of your brethren yet in bondage. If you are temperate, industrious, peaceable, and pious, you will show to the world that slaves can be emancipated without danger. Remember what a singular relation you sustain to society. The necessities of the case require not only that you should behave as well as the whites, but better than the whites. . . . Get as much education as possible for yourselves and your children. An ignorant people can never occupy any other than a degraded station in society; they can never be truly free until they are intelligent." (182–83)

In order to help her former slaves elevate themselves in the United States, Georgiana has purchased land for them in Ohio, "where I hope you will all prosper" (183). On that purchased land, to pick up on the John Winthrop–like rhetoric of her speech, the liberated blacks would assume the status of something like a "city upon a hill," with "all eyes" watching their progress. Should the liberated slaves fail to prosper, so she implies, they would only reconfirm whites' racist notions of blacks' unsuitability for freedom.

Georgiana's emancipation program thus raises a number of questions. We might ask, for example, how far the former slaves' adoption of temperate industry will take them in light of the existence of Ohio's racist "Black Codes." Surely Brown would have been aware of the fate met by the slaves of the Virginian John Randolph, mentioned in the novel's first paragraph. Randolph similarly bequeathed land in Ohio for his liberated slaves, who were unable to claim it because of the opposition of white farmers.[17] We might also ask what would keep the industrious slaves from succumbing to the lure of the market and becoming "slaves" to their speculative ambition for material gain. Relatedly, we could ask whether it is so easy to dismiss Southerners' critiques of market capitalism as a form of "wage slavery."[18] It is notable, for example, that the moment Georgiana's slaves adopt their temperate, industrious habits, the surrounding slave-owners, rather than becoming convinced of the slaves' capacities for free-dom, want to purchase them to work on their plantations. In this respect,

Georgiana's experiment implicitly suggests that the more industrious are the black workers, the more they will be exploited.

Brown attempts to elide such questions, contradictions, and problems by inserting into the novel, just before Georgiana announces her emancipation plan, a Manichaean mythic account of the origins of regional differences in which the good Puritans are presented as begetting the temperate ideals of free labor in the North and the bad colonizers at Jamestown are presented as begetting the intemperate practice of slavery in the South. Despite the fact that the Puritans slaughtered Indians and bought and sold slaves, Brown memorializes the *Mayflower* as the "parent" of the "labour-honouring, law-sustaining institutions of the North" (181), while damning the "low rakish ship hastening" (180) to Jamestown as the "parent" of "idleness, lynch-law, ignorance, unpaid labour, poverty, and duelling, despotism, the ceaseless swing of the whip, and the peculiar institutions of the South" (181).[19] According to this myth, the differences between the sections' founders created the nation's "parallel lines" (188) of freedom and slavery. As an advocate of free labor, Georgiana wants to end such parallelism by reforming the South, but she can only succeed if the North is as committed to free labor for people of all races as the Pilgrims of this mythic account. Brown would like to think that such is the case – hence his commitment to black elevation and self-help – but when, later in *Clotel*, he casts a critical eye on the North, the regions don't seem all that different. Northern prejudice against blacks, Brown writes in an account of Jim Crow practices on a train, is "another form of slavery" (171). In a concession that relieves blacks from the onus of demonstrating their abilities to rise in a "free-labor" economy, Brown likewise notes, following his account of the death of Georgiana, that racists throughout the United States attempt "to retard the work of emancipation for which she laboured and so wished to see brought about" (185). That such efforts by white racists may be regarded as forms of intemperance is made clear in the episode immediately following Georgiana's liberation of her slaves: Clotel's ride in the stagecoach where she hears the Connecticut minister's story of how his servant "drank down the whiskey, blacking, and all."[20]

The light-skinned Clotel, who had been sold to a slave trader by the vengeful Gertrude, eventually escapes from slavery by disguising herself as a white gentleman accompanied by a black servant, the intelligent and industrious slave William.[21] While William continues on to Canada after the escape, Clotel, still dressed as an "Italian or Spanish gentleman" (186), takes a stagecoach to Richmond in pursuit of her daughter, Mary. In an anachronistic moment typical of the ironies generated by Brown's use of historical collage, those aboard the stage discuss the "contemporaneous" politics of the election of 1839–40 and the Maine Law of 1851 (the irony is that the Whigs' presidential nominee of 1839, "Old Tip" William Harrison, wins his "log cabin" campaign by freely distributing hard cider and whiskey to his supporters). With reference to his home state, the Connecticut minister who supports the Maine Law makes a point similar to what Brown asserts in his 1853 letter to *Frederick Douglass' Paper*: that social prosperity is "attributable to the disuse of intoxicating drinks" (188). The linkage between temperance and prosperity set forth by the minister reinforces Brown's mythic notion of sectional origins and differences; Connecticut, in this account, keeps alive the putative freedom-loving spirit of the Puritans. And yet Brown, through the response of the proliquor Southerner aboard the stage, suggests that the North's commitment to temperance is little more than a self-aggrandizing fiction, for the Southerner tells a hilarious tale of visiting his "teetotaling" relatives in Vermont and discovering a secret world of rampant drinking. When he spends time with the family group, the Southerner hears "nothing but talk about the 'Juvinal Temperance Army,' the 'Band of Hope,' the 'Rising Generation,' the 'Female Dorcas Temperance Society'" (188). But as soon as he is alone with one or two members of his family, he is offered drinks from hidden stashes of rum and brandy. As a result, the Southerner proclaims, "during the fortnight that I was in Vermont, with my teetotal relations, I was kept about as well corned as if I had been among my hot water friends in Tennessee" (190).

Though most of the stage's passengers applaud the story, Brown is hardly sympathetic to the Southerner's joy in Northern hypocrisy. If anything, the tale underscores the need for the restraints of Maine Law legislation. Thus Brown gives the final word to the Connecticut minister, who, in addition to sharing his account of his servant's "blacking," offers a follow-up disquisition on the connections between intemperance and slavery. He proclaims to the group (to extract just a portion of his long speech):

> "Look at society in the states where temperance views prevail, and you will there see real happiness. The people are taxed less, the poor houses are shut up for want of occupants, and extreme destitution is unknown. Every one who drinks at all is liable to become an habitual drunkard. . . . *I have known* many young men of the finest promise, led by the drinking habit into vice, ruin and early death. *I have known* many tradesmen whom it has made bankrupt . . . *I have known* . . . kind husbands and fathers whom it has turned into monsters. *I have known* honest men whom it has made villains – elegant and Christian *ladies* whom it has *converted into bloated sots*". (190)

The litany of intemperate "husbands and fathers" reinforces Brown's focus on the ways in which men, by succumbing to their desires for mastery, sexuality, and money, become slaves of appetite. The image of women becoming "*bloated sots*" adds to the urgency of his antitemperance message. Moreover, the broad-based nature of his indictment suggests, against the grain of Brown's origin story of sectional differences, that the sections are not so "parallel" or different after all. That said, in the context of the novel, the minister's warnings on social and moral decline speak mainly to Southern men, specifically to the life trajectory of the Southerner Horatio Green, whose intemperate actions generate much of *Clotel*'s plot.

In this respect, Green may be viewed as a stand-in for Thomas Jefferson, whose role in the production of the Declaration of Independence and Currer's children makes him the ultimate patriarchal originator of not only the plot of the novel but also, metaphorically speaking, the plot of the nation. Persisting as a perpetual challenge to this national "plot" is a counterplot: black rage and rebellion. In a famous passage, which Brown reprints in *Clotel*, Jefferson in his 1785 *Notes on the State of Virginia* offers a nightmare vision of the possible enactment of that plot, describing how "ten thousand recollections, by the blacks, of the injuries they have sustained; new provocations; the real distinctions which nature has made; and many other circumstances, will divide us into parties, and produce convulsions, which will probably never end but in the extermination of the one or the other of the race."[22] Brown's political perspective is quite different from Jefferson's, insofar as he rejects essentialist or biological notions of racial difference and believes that African Americans have earned their rights to citizenship. But he presents a similarly anxious vision, in an account late in *Clotel*, of the aftermath of Nat Turner's rebellion: "Without scruple and without pity, the whites massacred all blacks found beyond their owners' plantations: the Negroes, in return, set fire to houses, and put those to death who attempted to escape from the flames. Thus carnage was added to carnage, and the blood of the whites flowed to avenge the blood of the blacks. These were the ravages of slavery" (203). Such violence may be regarded as the well-deserved "ravages" of Jeffersonian (national) hypocrisy and expediency. And yet, as sympathetic as Brown may be to black rebels, his emphasis on the rage of Turner and his swamp-dwelling coconspirator, the fictional Picquilo, who "imbrued his hands in the blood of all the whites he could meet" (202), conveys an anxiety that revolutionary violence is also a form of intemperance in which "low and vindictive passions" (201) could in effect enslave those who succumb to them.[23]

Concerns that revolutionism, however legitimate and necessary, can lead to a loss of self-government inform Brown's writings from the 1840s to the 1870s. Commenting on the French Revolutions of the 1790s and 1840s in *The American Fugitive in Europe*, for example, Brown attacks Marat as "that blood-thirsty demon in human form" and praises Lamartine as a more temperate leader who, "by the power of his eloquence, succeeded in keeping the people quiet" and in rational control of their minds and bodies. Along the same lines, he celebrates the black revolutionaries Toussaint L'Ouverture and Madison Washington as models of self-restraint. Indicative of Toussaint's self-control and "humanity," as Brown points out in a lecture of 1854, was his decision to help "his master's family to escape from the impending danger." Brown similarly praises Madison Washington, the leader of the 1841 slave uprising on the *Creole*, for throwing himself between the rebellious slaves and white enslavers, "exclaiming 'Stop! no more blood,'" after the black rebels had gained control of the ship. As Brown remarks in *The Black Man, His Antecedents, His Genius, and His Achievements* (1863), Madison Washington's "act of humanity raised the uncouth son of Africa far above his Anglo-Saxon oppressors." As for Nat Turner, Brown depicts him in two texts of the 1860s as a temperate revolutionary whose "acts, and his heroism live in the hearts of his race." Indicative of his clear-headed response to his white oppressors, Turner, Brown informs his readers, was a teetotaler who "never tasted a drop of ardent spirits in his life." Appropriately, he was hung by a "poor old white man, long besotted by drink."[24]

To return to *Clotel*, it is noteworthy that however much Brown may be concerned about the "intemperate" rage of Turner and Picquilo, he presents their violence as a direct response to forms of white intemperance and thus as a mostly positive form of black agency. For example, just prior to the account of the Turner rebellion, Brown tells the story of how Althesa's daughters (Jefferson's granddaughters), Ellen and Jane, become objects of the sexual desires of male enslavers following the deaths of their mother and their white stepfather, Morton. Depicted at the slave market as "shrinking from the rude hands that examined the graceful proportions of their beautiful frames," Ellen poisons herself after being purchased by an old man, while Jane, purchased by "an unprincipled profligate" (197), witnesses her lover killed by her "master" and subsequently dies of grief. The conjunction in the novel of the cholera epidemic, which kills off many of the slaveholders, and Nat Turner's rebellion, which similarly "seizes persons who were in health, without any premonition" (195), suggests that Brown to some extent shares in Turner's and Picquilo's rage against white enslavers. For that reason, he chooses to emphasize the temperate side of his black revolutionaries as well. He does so, in part, by describing Picquilo (his stand-in for Turner) as a man who is domestically inclined, working with his wife to make the Dismal Swamp into a habitable refuge: "He had met a negro woman who was also a runaway; and, after the fashion of his native land, had gone through the process of oiling her as the marriage ceremony. They had built a cave on a rising mound in the swamp; this was their home" (202). Brown's depiction of the Dismal Swamp as a domestic space for temperate revolutionaries had an impact on Stowe, whose second antislavery novel, *Dred* (1856), similarly shows its eponymous black rebel transforming the swamps into a haven in a heartless world. As one of the novel's escaped black slaves declares after arriving at Dred's refuge: "Bress de Lord, dere an't no whiskey here!" Soon he is industriously "hoeing in the sweet-potato patch."[25]

Anticipating that his white readers would feel threatened by the rage of the swamp-dwelling, domestic, but ultimately revolutionary Picquilo, Brown in the concluding chapters of *Clotel* shrewdly attempts to transmute black rebellion into a more conventional account of black elevation through his characterization of the slave George Green. Despite the fact that he participated in Turner's rebellion, Green emerges as a model of temperate industry and fidelity, and is "as white as most white persons" (210). With the notable exception of his skin's complexion, George resembles the temperate and intelligent slave William, the "full-bodied Negro" (167) who helps Clotel escape from her slave master and then refuses to abide by Northern Jim Crow laws aboard a train. Suggestive of his link with William, George is introduced into the novel immediately following the account of Clotel's heroic escape from a District of Columbia slave prison and her suicidal dive into the Potomac River "within plain sight of the President's house and the capital of the Union" (205). Her suicide can be viewed as an act of temperate revolutionism that, through an extraordinary act of self-control, puts on display the hypocrisy of Jefferson's nation while preserving her body from the violations, sexual and otherwise, of "profane and ribald" (207) fugitive slave hunters. George, too, is presented as a temperate revolutionary. Though sentenced to hang for participating in Turner's rebellion, he chooses to risk his life during a fire to save "valuable deeds belonging to the city" (211), thus prompting the "humane" city authorities to postpone for a year his scheduled execution (thereby making clear the limits of progressive models of black elevation in a slave culture). George's control over his body, as evidenced by his seemingly contradictory acts of joining with Turner and then later risking his life to save whites' legal documents, emerges as one of his most praiseworthy traits.

George eventually escapes from slavery when his beloved Mary, Clotel's light-skinned daughter, exchanges clothes with him and takes his place in jail. In a novel that so insistently focuses on male intemperance, as manifested in sexual domination and exploitation, it is oddly appropriate that Mary's crossdressing strategy temporarily makes Brown's light-skinned hero into a woman. Though George reassumes his male identity after making his way to Canada, for the rest of the novel he evinces an androgynous disposition that only further develops his heroic status. A model of temperate Franklin-like industry, he works by day, studies by night, and when it becomes clear that he cannot help Mary, who is sold South, he journeys to Liverpool, takes a job in a Manchester mercantile house, and after ten years becomes "a partner in the firm that employed him, and was now on the road to wealth" (217). Though "African blood coursed through his veins" (224), George keeps his racial identity a secret. In the improbable happy ending of the novel, George, during a vacation in France, is reunited with Mary, now Mrs. Devenant. Incredibly, she had escaped from slavery with the help of the Frenchman Devenant, who fell in love with her because she resembled his dead sister. As in many popular domestic novels of the period, the brother-sister aspect of the marriage spiritualizes it into a symbolically nonsexual one, though the fact is that Devenant leaves behind a son when he dies a few years after the marriage.[26] By contrast, Brown suggests that George, over the course of his upward rise, keeps his sexual desires in check. Brown celebrates him at the end of the novel, then, not for his manly linkage with Nat Turner or his manly rise in free market culture but for his womanly devotion: "the adherence of George Green to the resolution never to marry, unless to his Mary, is, indeed, a rare instance of the fidelity of man in the matter of love" (225).

In terms of the novel's presentation of numerous sexual violations of (slave) women as indicative of men's "enslavement" to sexual appetite, George's sexual continence and fidelity, his adherence to the conventional values of a "true woman" (120), emerges as the novel's ultimate act of temperance, contributing significantly to what black reformers regularly argued temperance could bring about: his economic, social, and moral elevation. And yet, because George's particular rise occurs not in the United States but in Britain, Brown conveys his skepticism about the ability of temperance to ensure blacks' moral and social elevation in the United States. Even as the novel draws on black temperance reformers' discourse of black elevation, it challenges the movement's somewhat naïve assumptions. Lurking in the Dismal Swamps, the vengeful Picquilo, Nat Turner's coconspirator and "heir," suggests an alternative route to black elevation through the creation of black community and the adoption of revolutionary violence.[27]

Despite his insights into the limits of the reform, temperance would remain central to Brown's antebellum and postbellum writings, both as a metaphor for unrestrained patriarchal power and as a program for black elevation. In the late 1850s he regularly lectured with Frances Ellen Watkins Harper on the interrelated topics of "slavery, temperance, and the elevation of colored Americans." Though he briefly championed black emigration to Haiti in the early 1860s, Brown embraced the Union after Lincoln issued the Emancipation Proclamation, and in his revised versions of *Clotel*, which he retitled *Clotelle*, he transformed the figure of the "white" and womanly George into the full-blooded black Jerome. In the 1864 version, Jerome's intelligence and dignity work to convince Linwood (modeled on Horatio Green) to free all of his slaves; but in the 1867 version, Jerome, who attempts to vindicate his manhood and rights to citizenship by fighting in the Civil War, is cruelly sacrificed by a white Union officer who commands him to retrieve the dead body of a fellow white officer. Jerome comes under fire, and his "head was entirely torn off by a shell."[28]

Jerome's needless death points to Brown's disillusionment with racial politics in the United States in the years immediately following the Civil War. But as Alonzo D. Moore writes in the "Memoir of the Author" prefacing Brown's *The Rising Son; or, The Antecedents and Advancement of the Colored Race* (1874), Brown renewed his "efforts, in connection with his estimable wife, for the spread of temperance among the colored people of Boston." As part of his continuing commitment to black elevation, Brown in 1868 created the "National Association for the Spread of Temperance and Night-schools among the Freed People of the South," and he became one of the first blacks initiated into the Massachusetts Grand Division of the Sons of Temperance. He participated in the 1870 State Convention for the Promotion of a Prohibitory Political Party in Massachusetts, and for the rest of the decade campaigned for prohibition. His temperance work had an influence on Pauline Hopkins, who in 1880 won an essay contest sponsored by Brown for blacks at Boston high schools on the topic of "The Evils of Intemperance and Their Remedies."[29] Soon after Brown's death in 1884, his wife was elected president of the local branch of the Women's Christian Temperance Organization.

Given the failure of Reconstruction in the South by the late 1870s, however, we might question the value of black temperance in the face of white "intemperance." Brown addresses this issue in complex and disturbing ways in his last major work, the autobiographical *My Southern Home; or, the South and Its People* (1880). In 1867 Brown remarked that the Southern secessionists who fomented the Civil War were "[d]runk with power";[30] and in *My Southern Home* he depicts power-crazed Southerners as suffering from an extended hangover. In response to white Southerners' continued demands for mastery, Brown urges blacks to be more temperate than whites, warning black waiters, for instance, against following the "bad example" of the "great deal of drinking" they view "in white society of the 'Upper Ten.'" Like his white heroine Georgiana in *Clotel*, he continues to place an extraordinary responsibility on the blacks themselves to achieve their elevation by adopting temperate, industrious behavior. "The time for colored men and women to organize for self-improvement has arrived," he states near the end of the book, and he offers this recipe for black elevation: "To elevate ourselves and our children, we must cultivate self-denial. Repress our appetites for luxuries and be content with clothing ourselves in garments becoming our means and our incomes. The adaptation and the deep inculcation of the principles of total abstinence from all intoxicants. The latter is a pre-requisite for success in all the relations of life."[31] As in the phrase "whiskey, blacking, and all," Brown's use of the word "all" here extends temperance beyond the literal act of drinking to encompass various aspects of bodily self-control. And he suggests at the end of *My Southern Home* that such self-control could help to make blacks "white."

In a troubling revision of the gender politics of *Clotel*, where black women are often the victims of white male intemperance, Brown in *My Southern Home* suggests that black women often exhibit the most intemperate behavior, blaming them for becoming insatiable consumers rather than responsible (re)producers. Under the influence of the alcohol that white merchants freely distribute to blacks who patronize their stores, the women succumb to an appetite for consumption that "amounts almost to madness," refusing to "stop buying until their money is exhausted." Brown's image of intemperate consumption expands to a gendered image of intemperate drinking: "a drunken girl – a drunken wife – a drunken mother – is there for woman a greater depth? Home made hideous – children disgraced, neglected, and maltreated." In terms of Brown's metaphorics of color and intemperance in *Clotel*, such a mother would be contributing to the "blacking" of her children, and a similarly provocative use of color imagery appears in the concluding chapter of *My Southern Home*. For even as Brown urges his black male readers to take pride in their racial identity – "Black men, don't be ashamed to show your colors, and to own them" – his utopian hope in the book, similar to Douglass's in the 1880s after he married the white Helen Pitts, is for a postracial world of human equality. That can happen, at least in part, Brown suggests, through racial amalgamation. Calling upon blacks to consider emigrating to the North, where they will "come in contact with educated and enterprising whites, [which] will do them much good," he proclaims that "history demonstrates the truth that amalgamation is the great civilizer of the races of men."[32] In order to encourage such amalgamation, Brown suggests, black women need to create temperate homes in which they would raise children that "educated and enterprising whites" would want to marry. Brown's advocacy of "civilizing" marriages between blacks and whites in particular would allow us retrospectively to view the relationships between Jefferson and Currer (Sally Hemmings), Horatio and Clotel, and Morton and Althesa, however exploitative they may have been in the antebellum discursive context of *Clotel*, as predictors and rehearsals of the deracialized union between blacks and whites that Brown in this final work envisions as the ultimate fruit of temperance.

CHAPTER 7

Beautiful Warships
The Transnational Aesthetics of Melville's Israel Potter

The past fifteen years or so have seen a renewed interest in aesthetics and American literary studies.[1] *The return to aesthetics can be taken as a response to what some regard as a problem with the New Historicism: a tendency toward reductionist readings of literary works as inevitably complicit with dominant forms of power. A focus on aesthetics encourages a greater attention to what authors actually do with form and language. As Wai Chee Dimock has argued, a focus on aesthetics also encourages a more transnational or global perspective on literary history.*[2] *Much recent work on aesthetics and American literary history draws on the writings of Immanuel Kant. Rejecting narrow notions of nation-bound reading or writing during a time of revolution in Europe, Kant championed a cosmopolitan aesthetics, which he believed had the potential to bring about world peace. Inspired by Kant, Shakespeare, Milton, the Bible, and a wide range of other texts and writers, Melville developed his own perspective on transnational aesthetics and revolution. In Israel Potter (1855), his relatively neglected novel about the American Revolution and one of the great transatlantic novels of the nineteenth century, Melville embraced the marginal and the ugly (his version of the Kantian sublime) in order to challenge American exceptionalism and suggest connections between aesthetics and democratic practice.*

In her provocative treatise on aesthetics, *On Beauty and Being Just* (1999), Elaine Scarry comes to beauty's defense. Challenging those who regard beauty as merely a cultural, political, or historical construction, she attempts to revitalize Kantian notions of common sense (*sensus communis*) in order to argue for universal notions of objective beauty. She remarks on how the process of aesthetic contemplation in effect liberates individuals from the particularities of their time and place: "But simultaneously what is beautiful prompts the mind to move chronologically back in the search for precedents and parallels, to move forward into new acts of creation, to move conceptually over, to bring things into relation, and does all this with a kind of urgency as though one's life depended on it." At stake in such aesthetic engagement, Scarry says, is nothing less than social justice, the desire to produce a better world through the creation, reproduction, and contemplation of beauty. In Scarry's formulation, beauty, which she never really defines, is what we all know is beautiful. Working in the mode of consensus, she focuses on the artistry of Matisse, the loveliness of palm trees and gardens, and the joy "we" all experience at the sight of beautiful faces, with the implication that we all would take pleasure in the same beautiful faces, whether spotted in Cambridge, Massachusetts, or the sub-Sahara. Insisting in a Kantian mode that shared notions of beauty have played a crucial role in leading humankind toward greater possibilities of freedom, she opines that beauty may help to bring forth a world without war. "Beauty is pacific," she declares, and thus "[w]e can be forgiven, in a discussion of beauty, for not wishing to speak about war ships."[3]

This chapter speaks about warships, and it raises questions about the consensual notion of beauty that Scarry celebrates. As Mark Canuel has noted, Scarry's championing of normative, even conventional markers of beauty, such as Matisse's flowers, "risks making [aesthetic] experience a means toward furthering the inclinations of others." For Canuel, a challenge to Scarry's somewhat coercive aesthetics can be found in Kant's discussion of the sublime – that which is elusive, mysterious, and frightening. Whereas Scarry presents the sublime as a destructive masculine power, Canuel argues that the sublime has a crucial place in Kant's philosophy in acknowledging the existence of feelings that are "simultaneously subjective and yet compatible with the disagreement and nonresemblance of others – with the incompatibility among, and nonheritability of, aesthetic experience."[4] According to Canuel, the Kantian sublime testifies to the radical subjectivity of individual observers, who may have widely different responses to such awe-inspiring forces and objects in nature as mountains, storms, and castles. Still, Canuel notes that, however anxious Kant may have been about the sublime, he presents it, like beauty, as having the potential to reveal truths that are larger than the individual. As Kant remarks in *Critique of the Power of Judgment* (1790) on the simultaneously threatening and illuminating possibilities of the sublime: "But in that which we are accustomed to call sublime in nature there is so little that leads to particular objective principles and forms of nature corresponding to these that it is mostly rather in its chaos or in its wildest and most unruly disorder and devastation, if only it allows a glimpse of magnitude and might, that it excites the ideas of the sublime."[5] To paraphrase Emily Dickinson, it is in the "glimpse" where the meanings lie.

Such a conflicted, even chaotic conception of "nature" informs what I am calling the transnational aesthetics of Melville's neglected *Israel Potter: His Fifty Years of Exile* (1855), a transatlantic novel that works against antebellum culture's tendency to monumentalize and aestheticize the American Revolution, finding its greatest inspiration in chaos, disorder, and devastation. In *Israel Potter*, war is presented as an inchoate succession of violent and banal episodes in which participants have virtually no understanding of what is at stake or why they are doing what they are doing. Terroristic attacks on innocent civilians, brutal hand-to-hand combat, rampant explosions bringing about the instant deaths of scores of combatants, mass imprisonments and impressments, blurrings of national identities and histories, and a lust for power constitute the Revolutionary War as depicted in Melville's novel. Ultimately, Melville's tragicomic novel of the American Revolution works to unsettle fixed meanings of wars, individual lives, and nations, presenting the Revolution in antiexceptionalist terms as just another war that gives birth to just another self-regarding nation. In the manner of Wordsworth and other Romantics inspired by the French Revolution, Melville, in a sublime mode that aggressively challenges normative ideas of beauty, emphasizes the beauty to be found in what many would regard as the ugly, the discarded, and the lowly. The idea that beauty can be located on "the merest rag of old printed paper," "a thin, tattered, dried-fish-like thing," or a "mean, sleazy paper," to cite Melville's descriptions of the possibly bogus and possibly revelatory "Chronometricals and Horologicals" tract in *Pierre* (1852), is a theme that Melville foregrounds from the outset of *Israel Potter*, which itself has sources in what Melville terms a "tattered" and "sleazy gray paper" that is "now out of print."[6] Specifically, Melville draws on *The Life and Remarkable Adventures of Israel R. Potter* (1824), a ghostwritten auto-biographical narrative of the historical Israel Potter (1754?–1826?), a for-gotten common man who allegedly fought in the Battle of Bunker Hill and, in Melville's fictional retelling, was also a key participant in the epochal naval battle between John Paul Jones's *Bonhomme Richard* and the British *Serapis*. As I discuss below, Melville's representation of the sublime and the beautiful in that clash between warships stands as the novel's key site of aesthetic (and political) contemplation.

Before turning to warships, however, it would be useful to address connections between aesthetics and revolution. In obvious ways, the American Revolution, and to a certain extent the French Revolution, which is mentioned near the end of the novel, are central to *Israel Potter*. The revolutionary moment was also central to the aesthetic thought of

Kant. Although he initially regarded the French Revolution optimistically as a moment of liberation in which, as Elizabeth Dillon puts it, "the liberal subject.... becomes aware of his or her freedom," Kant remained concerned about threats posed to aesthetics from perpetual revolutions and abuses of state power.[7] In "Idea for a Universal History with a Cosmopolitan Purpose" (1784), he therefore called for a new cosmopolitanism that would elevate transnational principles of justice over war, along with a world federation that would broker the peace among nations necessary for the creation and contemplation of art. The dream of a revolutionary world made stable for aesthetic contemplation, and then kept stable by art, is also central to Friedrich von Schiller's *On the Aesthetic Education of Man* (1795). Inspired by Kant, Schiller argues that "Art" itself offers an "absolute immunity from human arbitrariness," thereby allowing for the "building of a ... joyous kingdom of play and semblance, in which man is relieved of the shackles of circumstance, and released from all that might be called constraint, alike in the physical and in the moral sphere."[8] Art, in other words, provides possibilities for the preservation (or reconstruction) of human agency and community, even in a world unsettled by war.

But a large question raised by Kant's and Schiller's revolution-inflected aesthetics is whether the world consists of anything other than arbitrariness, the "shackles of circumstance," and "blind forces." In their writings on the sublime, which emphasize the limits of human knowledge, they both address the difficulty of discerning timeless principles of art and nature in a world seemingly lacking in solid ground. Schiller writes in *On the Sublime* (1801), for example, that it might make sense to give up on the possibility of achieving any insights at all: "Should one approach history with great expectations of illumination and knowledge – how very disappointed one is!" Addressing his own philosophical concerns about unknowability in ways that anticipate Schiller's, Kant in "Idea for a Universal History" surprisingly suggests that fiction, perhaps more than transcendental insight or traditional philosophical discourse, could become a potentially useful tool for discerning or philosophizing about the existence of reason in history. He explains: "It is admittedly a strange and at first sight absurd proposition to write a *history* according to an idea of how world events must develop if they are to conform to certain rational ends; it would seem that only a *novel* could result from such premises. Yet if it may be assumed that nature does not work without a plan and purposeful end, even amidst the arbitrary play of human freedom, this idea might nevertheless prove useful."[9] If Melville emphasizes anything in *Israel Potter*, his novel conceived as history, it is precisely the "arbitrary play of human freedom" at the revolutionary moment, and the relation of such arbitrariness to renewed possibilities of aesthetic expression that break away from what Russ Castronovo terms "the singleness implied by national identity."[10]

Resisting what had become a coercive fetishizing of the American Revolution, Melville experiments in *Israel Potter* with an aesthetics of demonumentalization and defamiliarization dependent on tropes of imitation, performance, and confusion. Such an approach to the Revolutionary War may seem jaded, and it certainly went against the patriotic grain of Melville's time. But the novel is ultimately rejuvenating in the spirited and often comical way that it presses readers to reflect on the value of wars that are made in the name of nations but not necessarily in the service of the ordinary people who inhabit them. As suggested somewhat obliquely (but still very powerfully) in the novel's simultaneously sublime and beautiful scenes with warships, Melville sought to recover what he regarded as the lost democratic possibilities of the American Revolution at his own cultural moment.

Melville knew the writings of Kant and Schiller. He owned or borrowed Schiller's complete works, and he refers to Kant in several of his novels.[11] In *Moby-Dick* (1851) and *Pierre*, he interrogates key tenets of Romantic idealistic philosophy, raising a number of questions about the nature of art, history, and providential design, and in his portrayal of the downward slide of the celebrity author Pierre, he suggests how ideas of the beautiful could be corrupted by nationalistic critics taken with genteel expressions of "Perfect Taste."[12] There is no *sensus communis* in *Pierre*, just American literary nationalists lacking in aesthetic understanding but powerful enough to establish their empty notions of beauty as the cultural norm. Melville's commercial struggles of the early 1850s only intensified his concerns about the coercive nature of institutionally sanctioned notions of what constituted meritorious American writing. *Israel Potter* appeared at a time when he had gone "underground," anonymously publishing short fiction in popular journals in the wake of his frustration at the relatively low sales of *Moby-Dick* and the humiliation of the mocking reviews and poor sales of *Pierre*.[13] As with *Benito Cereno* (1855), which draws on the historical Amasa Delano's *Narrative of Voyages and Travels* (1817), Melville strategically plays down his authorial identity in *Israel Potter*, not only by first serializing the novel anonymously in the July 1854 through March 1855 issues of *Putnam's Monthly Magazine* but also by working with a number of source texts that could be regarded as constraining rather than liberating his creative energies.[14] Signaling *Israel Potter*'s close connection to previously published texts, Melville seems intent on writing a novel about the American Revolution that refuses to rise above the level of a "minor" work and most certainly refuses to display itself as beautiful.[15]

In his prefatory dedication, "To His Highness the Bunker-hill Monument," Melville remarks about *Israel Potter*: "From a tattered copy, rescued by the merest chance from the rag-pickers, the present account has been drawn, which, with the exception of some expansions and additions of historic and personal details, and one or two shiftings of scene, may, perhaps, be not unfitly regarded something in the light of a dilapidated old tombstone retouched." Comparing his "tattered" novel to a tombstone – his comically irreverent image of the Bunker Hill Monument as a tomb for American Revolutionary ideals – Melville in this and other passages in the dedication modestly signals his indebtedness to the 1824 *Life and Remarkable Adventures*, stating that even "with a change in the grammatical person," from first- to third-person, his rendering of Potter's life as a patriot "preserves, almost in a reprint, Israel Potter's autobiographical story" (vii). Although Melville made a number of changes to his source text, which itself is crammed with errors and inventions, his mock-modest dedication rather aggressively undercuts any claims that his novel might make on the reader as a work of art.[16] By linking *Israel Potter* to the Bunker Hill Monument, he prods the reader to reflect on the monument's aesthetic claims, as well. A work of commemorative art, the monument was intended to stabilize nationalistic meanings, with its towering granite obelisk telling a single mythic story that would imbue all who viewed it with a sense of national belonging. As Daniel Webster declared to approximately two hundred former revolutionary soldiers at the site of the future monument, it would also imbue those who viewed it with a sense of "national prosperity."[17] Dedicating *Israel Potter* to a monument that, in Webster's terms, fails to encompass Potter's history of impoverishment, Melville implicitly suggests that one of the goals of his novel is to transform the Bunker Hill Monument from an image of beauty to an image of the sublime – a figure speaking to the multiplicity and radical subjectivity of meaning, and, thus, to the existence of more than one American Revolutionary story.

Melville describes the trials and tribulations of his eponymous hero in a passage that suggests a good deal about the philosophical perspective of his presentation of Potter's story: "The career of this stubborn adventurer signally illustrates the idea, that since all human affairs are subject to organic disorder, since they are created in, and sustained by, a sort of half-disciplined chaos; hence, he who in great things seeks success, must never wait for smooth water, which never was, and never will be; but with what straggling method he can, dash with all his derangements at his object, leaving the rest to Fortune" (114). Disorder, chaos, and derangement: these are the threatening but seductive instabilities of the Kantian sublime. Meaning in *Israel Potter*, as in most of Melville's fiction, is multiple, fractured, and elusive. What we are left with in Melville's "straggling method" of retelling Potter's life is an insistence on "organic disorder," which may or may not be meaningful in relation to the American Revolutionary mythos and for much of the novel doesn't seem all that beautiful.

Consider, for example, the novel's opening scenes, which in large part draw on the 1824 Potter narrative. In *Life and Remarkable Adventures*, the historical Potter, or more accurately the historical Potter's ghostwriter, adopts a first-person narrative in order to heighten Potter's identity as a self-conscious patriot in the American Revolutionary War, someone who, by choice, "took a distinguished part in the Battle of Bunker Hill."[18] Melville, by contrast, adopts a third-person narration in order to present what Peter Bellis terms "a succession of fragmentary and discontinuous episodes whose cumulative effect on the self cannot be gauged or represented."[19] Thus, while Melville terms Potter a "devoted patriot" (5) whose every action reflects his "fearless self-reliance and independence which conducted our forefathers to national freedom" (9), he portrays him as an almost volitionless wanderer who is pushed in different directions by unanticipated events and has little understanding of what he is doing at any particular moment. In this way, the term "devoted patriot" is almost immediately stripped of its meaning. In a highly compressed history of several paragraphs that subtly situates the eponymous hero's early life in a global context, Potter, "with the same indifference as porters roll their barrows over the flagging of streets" (9), moves from an unsuccessful courtship of a childhood sweetheart, to trading in skins and furs in Canada, sailing to the West Indies, escaping from captivity with the help of a Dutch and then an American ship, journeying to Puerto Rico and Eustacia, and finding work on a whaler off the coast of Africa, only to be discharged at Nantucket right around the time of the Battle of Lexington.[20]

The American Revolution similarly is presented as a random succession of events that (at least on the surface) fail to yield anything worthy of celebration or any clear sense of providential or historical design. Melville's distinctive approach to representing the American Revolution becomes immediately apparent in the account of Potter's participation in the Battle of Bunker Hill. Dismayed to learn that his beloved had married while he was still at sea, Potter briefly returns to farming, hears about the Battle of Lexington, enlists in the regiment of General Israel Putnam, and quickly finds himself within a chaotic scene of violence, the macabre highlight being Potter's effort to wrest a sword from what he fails to realize is the dismembered arm of a British soldier. The violence itself, which Melville presents in a rushed present tense, conveys the immediacy of chaos and the absence of patriotic meaning.[21] In Melville's artfully defamiliarizing account, soldiers on the ground, who can't grasp the larger picture (if there is one), fight in order to survive and find themselves fighting on one side or the other through mere happenstance and the contingencies of the moment.

Melville comically underscores the haphazard and provisional in his subsequent account of Potter's career, depicting how events toss him back and forth, often between countries, in the manner of a "shuttlecock" (123) or "Shuttle" (131). Shortly after participating in the Battle of Bunker Hill, Potter is taken prisoner on an English ship, but upon reaching England manages to escape dressed as an English sailor. Potter's first change of clothes initiates a succession of wardrobe changes that emphasize how easily identity can be altered and performed. As in *Redburn* (1849), *White-Jacket* (1850), and *Benito Cereno*, among other works, clothes are central to Melville's presentation of the fungibility of personal and national identity.[22] Potter dresses as an English sailor, a ditcher, and then a laborer, managing to work for Princess Amelia for six months while "few suspected him of being any other than an Englishman" (27). In a skillfully understated comic scene, he is recognized by George the Third as an American patriot, whom King George admires for his spunk, which leads Potter to admire the king he is fighting against. As the narrator archly remarks, "Indeed, had it not been for the peculiar disinterested fidelity of our adventurer's patriotism, he would have soon sported the red coat" (32). Potter takes on a new disguise when he is recruited to work as a spy for the American sympathizer Squire Woodcock, who is plotting with the Paris-based Benjamin Franklin. And yet Potter never understands the nature of his work or its possible relation to the revolutionary cause, and his confusion continues to be expressed in relation to clothing. When he returns from Paris to Woodcock's mansion, he becomes locked in a secret cell, finds that Woodcock is dead, assumes his clothes, and then dispenses with those clothes for the rags of a scarecrow. At which point the man in rags remarks to himself: "Ah! what a true patriot gets for serving his country!"

(81). A patriot, perhaps, and yet he remains befuddled about the role he is playing in the Revolutionary War.

Melville addresses Potter's repeated changes of clothes and circumstances in a passage that could be read as an ironic response to Kant's hopes for a philosophical novel that would reveal the providential design in history: "Thus repeatedly and rapidly were the fortunes of our wanderer planted, torn up, transplanted, and dropped again, hither and thither, according as the Supreme Disposer of sailors and soldiers saw fit to appoint" (84). In the context of the novel, the "Supreme Disposer" might be the author himself (Melville as the rewriter of the 1824 Potter narrative, which is to say, Melville as both copyist and revisionary artist), or the arbitrary and blind forces of nature whose meaning is elusive or nonexistent, perhaps little more than what the narrator terms "luck – that's the word" (119). As the chronicler of Potter's luck or changing fortunes, Melville thus becomes a very different sort of chronicler of US history from the popular patriotic storytellers of his day. In the revealingly titled chapter "In Which Israel Is Sailor under Two Flags, and in Three Ships, and All in One Night" (85), Melville presents arbitrariness, or luck, in relation to the contingencies of national belonging itself, chronicling how Potter is impressed onto the British warship *Unprincipled* and then taken onto a British revenue vessel, only to end up on John Paul Jones's warship when the sound of Jones's voice inspires him to go savage: Potter liberates himself by grabbing a British officer "round the loins, bedding his fingers like grisly claws into his flesh and hugging him to his heart" (89). This is just one more deliberately "unbeautiful" moment in which Potter is presented as "dash[ing] with all his derangements at his object, leaving the rest to Fortune."

Potter's serendipity in encountering Jones at sea initiates some of the most violent scenes of the novel. Here, in chapters that are written in the past tense but, like the account of the battle at Bunker Hill, have the feel of a breathless present, Melville depicts what some historians have come to call the modern era's turn to total war. He places the responsibility for such a turn in large part on Benjamin Franklin, the man who shrewdly puts Jones to the service of the American cause by placing him in command of a warship with unchecked authority over sailors eager to fight the British. But as with the Battle of Bunker Hill, Jones's war scenes are presented quite differently from what would be found in patriotic histories. Intent on destruction for the sake of destruction, Jones initiates a martial campaign of assaulting British civilian populations on the northern and western coasts of England, with no apparent larger motivation than a compulsion to destroy. With the help of Potter, he sets fire to a docked ship at Whitehaven, and as the townspeople swarm to the docks to see what is going on, "Israel, without a weapon, dashed crazily towards the mob on the shore." But Melville's focus is less on Potter's deranged savagery than on the spectacle of the burning boat, which is watched by "thousands of the people" (103). The narrator describes the scene: "The flames now catching the rigging and spiraling around the masts, the whole ship burned at one end of the harbor, while the sun, an hour high, burned at the other. Alarm and amazement, not sleep, now ruled the world" (104). Jones and Potter together have created a sublime spectacle that has awakened the multitudes. A similar sense of spectacle, both sublime and beautiful, informs Melville's subsequent representation of the clash between warships.

The battle between Jones's ship, with the Ben Franklin-inspired name *Bonhomme Richard,* and the British *Serapis* is generally regarded as the first major sea battle between "American" and British forces. In nineteenth-century US culture, it was celebrated in nationalistic terms as a crucial turning point in the Revolutionary War. Jones, who was adopted as an honorary US citizen, became famous for supposedly declaring, at the moment when all appeared lost, "I have not yet begun to fight." As with his telling of many other apocryphal accounts circulating in the popular literature of the time, Melville imports that proclamation into the novel (128), along with the outright fiction that the historical Israel Potter not only was on board Jones's ship but also was the American patriot responsible for naming the ship in honor of Ben Franklin's Poor Richard – a name that Jones seconds because of his admiration for Poor Richard's famous proverb "God helps them that help themselves" (115).

As Melville describes the scene, on a summer night of 1778, under a full moon off the coast of Yorkshire, hundreds of civilians gather on the cliffs to watch the approaching warships. But the promise of a traditional stately battle between two clearly defined sides quickly transmogrifies into utter pandemonium and "incredible atrocity" (127), as approximately half of the men on both sides are killed (the dead number into the hundreds). Death breaks down national distinctions – "The belligerents were no longer, in the ordinary sense of things, an English ship, and an American ship" (126) – and death trumps all in the cold waters off the northern British coast. "Into that Lethean canal," the narrator writes, "fell many a poor soul that night, – fell, for ever forgotten." Cannons burst apart, "killing the sailors who worked them" (125). Cartridges ignite and explode, and over "twenty men were instantly killed" (127). The French ship *Alliance* joins the fray and inexplicably fires on Jones's ship, killing many others. By the end of this horrific scene, Jones manages to gain control of the British vessel, even as his own ship sinks to the bottom of the sea. Melville concludes his extraordinarily vivid reimagining of the brutality of the encounter between the *Bonhomme Richard* and the *Serapis* with a rhetorical question: "In view of this battle one may well ask – What separates the enlightened man from the savage? Is civilization a thing distinct, or is it an advanced stage of barbarism?" (130). Kant couldn't have posed the question any better in his reflections on enlightenment and war.[23]

I refer to Kant to bring the discussion back to transnational aesthetics, for throughout the account of the clash between the *Bonhomme Richard* and *Serapis*, Melville self-consciously aestheticizes the violence so as to undercut its connection to national histories. It would be useful to look more closely at his representation of the battle. Departing from his sources in Robert C. Sands's *Life and Correspondence of John Paul Jones* (1830) and James Fenimore Cooper's *The History of the Navy of the United States* (1839), Melville presents the sea fight as if it were taking place on a stage, with the author (or Nature, or Fate, or God) playing director. Melville takes note of the "scenic atmosphere" (122), in which "an invisible hand came and set down a great yellow lamp in the east. . . . The lamp was the round harvest moon; the one solitary foot-light of the scene" (123). Playfully invoking both the man-in-the-moon stage director of *A Midsummer Night's Dream* and the "Man in the Moon" of Hawthorne's "My Kinsman, Major Molineaux" (1832), Melville begs the question of what sort of providential or contingent forces (or what the narrator calls "fickle power" [119]) might be responsible for bringing about this particular battle.[24] The fighting, which takes place over a three-hour span in a classically sublime oceanic and nighttime setting, is observed by thousands of spectators off the shores of Fife. As Melville explains: "[T]he Man-in-the-Moon was not the only spectator. From the high cliffs of the shores, and especially from the great [Yorkshire] promontory of Flamborough Head, the scene was witnessed by crowds of the islanders" (124). Whatever might be the suffering of the participants, and whatever the conflict might amount to in relation to national histories and what seems to be the jumble of the American Revolutionary War, in Melville's telling, the battle unfolds as artistic spectacle, a glorious dance between "partners in a cotillion" (124) for the "thousands" (121) in attendance.[25]

In his depiction of the battle between warships, Melville does more than simply set the stage. From beginning to end, he describes the contest in relation to longer and larger literary and cultural histories, to the point where the scene itself, however ghastly, participates in the production and reproduction of art. Again and again, Melville resorts to conceits, heroic similes, and literary and cultural analogies in an overwrought effort to enhance the aesthetic appeal of the scene. At times the writing can seem deliberately bad, but it is a badness, or "figurative excess," as Edgar Dryden nicely terms it, that ultimately gives meaning to the scene, even if that meaning can be understood as the undercutting of meaning.[26] And so Melville begins his account by stating that "a battle between two men-of-war, with their huge white wings, [is] more akin to the Miltonic contests of archangels than to *the comparatively squalid* tussles of earth" (122; Melville's emphasis). But rather than focus coherently on the Miltonic, Melville piles up analogies and imagery to the point where the reader's attention is focused less on the scene as observed by the novel's spectators on the cliff than on the self-conscious artistry of the analogies themselves. To note just a sampling from Melville's descriptive arsenal: the ships are "indistinct as the ghost of Morven"; the decks of the ships "dully resounded like drum-heads in a funeral march"; the *Serapis* circles "like a wheeling cock about a hen" (122); the moon casts "a dubious half demoniac glare across the water, like the phantasmagoric stream sent athwart a London flagging in a night-rain from an apothecary's blue and green window"; shots whiz back and forth "like shuttlecocks across a great hall" (123); the water between the two ships is "like that narrow canal in Venice" by the Bridge of Sighs; the warships themselves are like "Siamese Twins, oblivious of their fraternal bond"; Jones's men run from the gun deck "like miners from the fire-damp"; the masthead on the *Bonhomme Richard* resembles "the great tower of Pisa" (125); sailors plummet into the ocean "like falling pigeons shot on the wing"; men from Potter's ship "dropped hand-grenades upon her [the *Serapis*'s] decks, like apples"; the two ships are like the houses of the Guelphs and Ghibelines; the men frenziedly shedding their clothes resemble "fauns and satyrs" (126); sailors tend their guns "as Lowell girls the rows of looms in a cotton factory" (127); and, when the French ship *Alliance* mistakenly fires on the *Bonhomme Richard*, the ship burns "like the great fire of London, breaking out on the hells of the great Plague" (128). Just as Jones plays to the crowds on the cliffs, Melville plays to his literate reader. Melville concludes his account with an image reminiscent of the sinking of the *Pequod* in *Moby-Dick*: "About ten o'clock, the Richard, gorged with slaughter, wallowed heavily, gave a long roll, and blasted by tornadoes of sulpher, slowly sunk, like Gomorrah, out of sight" (130).

Of course much is bleak here, and aspects of the descriptions of the battle look forward to the mechanistic descriptions of the clashing warships in "A Utilitarian View of the Monitor's Flight," which appeared in

Melville's *Battle-Pieces* (1866). In that poem, as Hennig Cohen remarks, the "style is anti-poetic" and the "lines grind and clank like heavy machinery" in ways that help to reinforce Melville's insight in the concluding stanza: "War yet shall be, but warriors / Are now but operatives."[27] By way of contrast, the diction that Melville deploys to depict the sea battle in *Israel Potter* seems anything but mechanistic. Instead, an odd exuberance informs the portrayals of such lively human presences as Jones and Potter. Exuberant as well is Melville's display of his active creative imagination. Melville's aestheticizing of the violence, in a novel that so doggedly works against conventional notions of beauty, presses the reader in exhilarating ways to rethink the meaning of this celebrated historical moment. As part of what I am calling Melville's transnational aesthetics, the wide-ranging allusions complicate and undercut hermetic national narratives, provide larger historical and literary perspectives, and suggest that beauty can be found in, or constructed from, the most unlikely of places. Ironically, Melville's representation of the deadly combat between warships, whose national affiliations seem not to matter, does precisely what Scarry argues the contemplation of beauty should do, for Melville's allusive method "prompts the mind to move chronologically back in the search for precedents and parallels, to move forward into new acts of creation, to move conceptually over, to bring things into relation." Where Melville differs from Scarry is in his embrace of the sublime.

Daniel Herwitz describes the Kantian sublime as "our way of coming before the power of a universe whose spirit rushes beyond us: it is the experience of the utopian," providing a glimpse into "the supersensible substrate of our own humanity."[28] Melville implicitly conveys such utopian yearnings and intimations through his representation of the horrific but also potentially transformative violence unleashed by men on warships. In his reimagining of the clash between the *Serapis* and the *Bonhomme Richard*, Melville presents violence as having a certain democratic vitality consistent with the vitality exhibited now and again by the confused but indefatigable Israel Potter. As discussed above, the violence of the American and French revolutions had a significant impact on Kant's and Schiller's thinking about aesthetics and conflict, renewing their interest in the freedom-enhancing power of aesthetics. Kant specifically warned of the dangers of the revolutionary and postrevolutionary moment: "A revolution may well put an end to autocratic despotism and to rapacious or power-seeking oppression, but it will never produce a true reform in ways of thinking. Instead, new prejudices, like the ones they replaced, will serve as a leash to control the great unthinking mass."[29] In many respects, Melville in

Israel Potter would seem to agree with this assessment, for the novel's preface and conclusion suggest that the democratic impulses of the Revolution have been betrayed by cultural arbiters and elites. But in the spirit of Kant's and Schiller's more affirmative writings on the liberatory potential of the French Revolution, Melville also seeks to present revolutionary violence as having the potential to challenge old prejudices and lead to something new. With his figurative excess, he invokes transhistorical traditions of art in ways that would appeal to what Schiller calls "every finely attuned soul," even as the excesses of the descriptive rhetoric suggest the importance to Melville of attempting to rewrite or reimagine the patriotic stories that inform his source texts and have been embraced by his filiopietistic culture.[30]

In rendering the clash between the warships as spectacle, Melville makes this crucial scene into revolutionary art for the masses (both the fictional spectators and Melville's imagined readers). Russ Castronovo argues that crowds in literature traditionally speak to democratic energies and aspirations, and that "democracy, rendered as an aesthetic matter, returns compulsively to revolution even when sociopolitical change is exactly what beauty and art are supposed to make unimaginable."[31] Crowds prompt a refocusing of aesthetics away from elite perspectives and facile national histories; the battle between the warships is viewed by thousands from the cliffs of Whitehaven, and, consistent with the sublime's emphasis on tensions between radical subjectivity and the *sensus communis* of the glimpse, few if any of those spectators would have been able to decipher the scene, especially given that the "winning" warship is the one that sinks. The warships are as "indistinct, as the ghost of Morven," Melville writes, alluding to the Scottish poet James Macpherson's mystical *The Works of Ossian* (1765). What emerges unambiguously is the beauty of the spectacle itself. It is a beauty that in certain respects links crowds and sailors, reorienting the energies of the Revolutionary War in relation to a broader collectivity that has nothing to do with nations and everything to do with the visceral identifications prompted by violence.[32] In this scene of battle, Melville evokes such a collectivity not only through depictions of the crowd but also by noting the suffering of both the American and British fighters, another sort of crowd, who are injured and killed in a battle that is presented as a "co-partnership" (126) lacking in distinctly nationalistic meanings. The implication of this amazing scene, with its emphasis on crowds over nations, is that something further may follow from the battle between warships that would do justice to the battle's incipient democratic energies – but not in *Israel Potter*.

As Melville makes clear in the novel's dedicatory preface, *Israel Potter* is a historical novel that is constrained by Potter's life story and an unfolding history in which the common person has been forgotten. Following the battle scene, Melville, in a series of short, grim chapters, describes Potter's nearly fifty-year exile in England among the laboring classes.[33] Consistent with the figurative excess of the battle scene, Melville places a renewed emphasis in these closing chapters on the typological parallels between the American Israel Potter and the Israelites of the Old Testament, presenting England as similar to Egypt under Pharaoh. The narrator points to the ironies of Potter's situation at the moment when he is toiling in an English brickyard thousands of miles from the Promised Land: "He whom love of country made a hater of her foes – the foreigners among whom he now was thrown – he, who, as soldier and sailor, had joined to kill, burn, and destroy both them and theirs – here he was at last, serving that very people as a slave" (157).[34] But even as Melville analogizes Israel Potter to the enslaved chosen people of old, ironies remain, for this description highlights Potter's own savagery. Moreover, the narrator attributes to the beclouded Potter a guiding purpose and self-consciousness for which there is little evidence in the novel.

In the novel's concluding four chapters, which quickly move from the late 1770s to July 1826, Potter, after working as a brickmaker outside of London, marries a shop girl from Kent, with whom he has eleven children (ten die). As in the 1824 *Life and Remarkable Adventures*, Potter eventually earns his living repairing chairs, while holding onto his hope to return to his native country. In the final chapter, when Potter journeys back to the United States in 1826 with his one surviving son, the republican nation seems anything but the Promised Land Potter had dreamed of while laboring as an exile. Depicted as a sort of Rip Van Winkle figure, Potter, on the fiftieth anniversary of the Declaration of Independence, encounters a bustling, self-important postrevolutionary world and is nearly killed by a carriage driver racing madly through the streets near Boston's Faneuil Hall. (The historical Potter had returned in 1823; Melville changes the date in order to tease out the ironies attending the half-centenary celebration.) A frighteningly monolithic "patriotic triumphal" (167) crowd hails the heroes of Bunker Hill, but no one recognizes Potter, who is seeking a government pension for his service during the Revolutionary War. The prevailing mood of the final chapter is dismal and despairing as Potter recalls the failed dreams of his youth and quietly dies. Here is Melville's artfully understated final paragraph:

> He was repulsed in efforts, after a pension, by certain caprices of law. His
> scars proved his only medals. He dictated a little book, the record of his
> fortunes. But long ago it faded out of print – himself out of being – his name
> out of memory. He died the same day that the oldest oak on his native hills
> was blown down. (169)

Conflating the fading of the patriotic Potter with the fading of the long-
out-of-print Potter narrative of 1824, Melville concludes on a note consistent with the artistic self-abnegation and prickly ironies of his dedicatory
preface to the Bunker Hill Monument, where he states that he "durst not
substitute for the allotment of Providence any artistic recompense of
poetical justice." Both at the ending and in the preface, Melville suggests
that he has no choice but to surrender "my hero" (viii) to history, unable
(or unwilling) to redeem him through a crowd-pleasing nationalistic ending. But perhaps the best gloss on the ending of *Israel Potter* is provided not
retrospectively by Melville, as avowed self-abnegating artist, but prolepti-
cally by Schiller, as philosopher of history and art: "Thus little by little the
concrete life of the Individual is destroyed in order that the abstract idea of
the Whole may drag out its sorry existence, and the State remains for ever a
stranger to its citizens since at no point does it ever make contact with their
feeling."[35] For Schiller, the remedy to such stultifying forces is an art that
frees itself from the dictates of the nation and any other single, or "Whole,"
idea. Melville seeks a similar sort of freedom through a seeming renunciation of beauty in his embrace of Potter's "mouldy old rags" (152) – both the
clothes Potter adopts during his more than forty years in London and the
"dictated. . . . little book" which (again harking back to the language of
the preface) Melville claims to have rescued "by the merest chance from the
rag-pickers" (vii).

That opening remark on "the merest chance" is consistent with the
Kant-inflected transnational aesthetics that I am arguing has a significant
place in Melville's representation of the American Revolutionary moment.
Ultimately Melville is unable to discern clear patterns and meanings in
what he terms "that half-disciplined chaos," and thus *Israel Potter* implicitly warns of the risks of blindly following the lead of those, like Webster,
who remain ever confident in their ability to discern such patterns in the
history of a single nation. Consistent with the Kantian sublime, Melville
points to the limits, even failure, of his main character's cognitive abilities,
along with the "*unattainability*," as Kant puts it, "*of nature as a presentation
of ideas*" (Kant's emphasis).[36]

And yet, however bleak the ending, there is something rejuvenating
about the novel's comic energies and its hintings at the possibilities of

democratic collectivity and individual agency. Schiller enjoins his readers: "Live with your century, but do not be its creature."[37] Though at times exhibiting skills in performance and reinvention suggestive of his ability to exert some agency, Potter typically comes across as the creature of his age. It is the great performers of the novel – John Paul Jones, the imprisoned Ethan Allen taunting British spectators at Falmouth, and Benjamin Franklin – who more compellingly display an ability to channel the forces unleashed by the revolutionary moment. Franklin, whom Melville appears to be mocking for a hypocritical, time-bound pragmatism, may well be the novel's most canny portrayal of such a dynamically creative figure. "Having carefully weighed the world," the narrator declares, "Franklin could act any part in it," including taking on the roles of Englishman, Frenchman, and American. Given that aesthetics in the novel is often about performance, Franklin as "chemist, orator, tinker, statesman, humorist, philosopher, maxim-monger, herb-doctor, wit" (48) would seem to qualify as an artist himself.[38] Like the man-in-the-moon director of the battle between the two warships, Franklin is presented not only as the consummate performer but also as someone who deviously works behind the scenes to make things happen. It is Franklin who brings Jones and Potter together; it is Franklin who is involved in plots that are never made clear; and it is Franklin who commissions Jones and puts him in charge of a ship, to which Potter eventually attaches the name associated with Poor Richard. The narrator doesn't offer a final judgment on Franklin; it is Potter himself who is given the honor. Glancing through Franklin's almanacs while locked up in Franklin's Parisian domicile, Potter reflects on his enigmatic canniness: "Somehow, the old gentleman has an amazing sly look – a sort of mild slyness – about him, seems to me. His wisdom seems a sort of sly, too. But all in honor, though. I rather think he's one of those old gentlemen who say a vast deal of sense, but hint a world more. Depend upon it, he's sly, sly, sly" (54).

In its understated way, Melville's revolutionary *Israel Potter* is sly, sly, sly, pointing to the value of art and democratic revolutionism in a work that appears to be an artless chronicling of happenstance in history. In a comically antic novel that mixes fictional with historical characters, skews historical chronologies, and depicts such celebrated historical figures as Franklin, Jones, and Allen as tricksters, plotters, and killers, Melville restages the American Revolution in all of its sublime multiplicity and confusion, helping us to realize how little we know about the trajectories of history even as we discern that those trajectories might have gone in different directions from the self-aggrandizing nationalism depicted in the novel's final chapter. In *Israel Potter*, Melville provides no great new insights into the patterns and meanings of the chaos that is history because such insights will always be elusive. Instead, we are encouraged to imagine new stories from the "mouldy rags" we have been bequeathed, taking as one promising starting point the visceral identifications and broader collective democratic possibilities limned in the sublime beauty of warships.

CHAPTER 8

Antebellum Rome
Transatlantic Mirrors in Hawthorne's The Marble Faun

In the thirty years since the publication of Robert Weisbuch's Atlantic Double-Cross *(1986), transatlantic studies has moved in a number of directions. For Weisbuch, transatlanticism was about cross-influences between British and American literature, though with an American literary nationalist twist: American writers (he claimed) anxiously sought to break away from the tyranny of British literary traditions and develop their own unique national literature. Paul Giles in* Transatlantic Insurrections *(2001) toned down Weisbuch's literary nationalist perspective by arguing that the two literary traditions nourished one another and never became entirely separate or unique; and Leonard Tennenhouse further revised Weisbuch, asserting in* The Importance of Feeling English *(2007) that what American writers most desired was to become part of the great English literary tradition. This chapter, by focusing on Hawthorne's response to Rome, works against the US-England binary that has been central to transatlantic approaches in nineteenth-century American literary studies, even as it locates Hawthorne's thinking about Rome in relation to Anglo-American suspicions of Catholicism. In many respects, when Hawthorne and other antebellum travelers journeyed to Rome, they saw something quite different from what they encountered in England: a Roman Catholic social and political order that was the reverse mirror image of Protestant-democratic America. The surprise was that they also saw much in Rome that mirrored current conflicts and tensions in their own country. Hawthorne addresses the complexities of such mirroring in his fourth and final novel,* The Marble Faun *(1860).*[1]

In a letter of April 6, 1860, to his publisher and friend William Ticknor, Hawthorne commented on the enthusiastic early reviews greeting *The Marble Faun*: "I have been much gratified by the kind feeling and generous praise contained in the notices you send me. After so long absence and silence, I like to be praised too much. It sounds like a welcome back among my friends. But, in fact, if I have written anything well, it should be this Romance; for I have never thought or felt more deeply, or taken more pains." Traditionally, critics responsive to Hawthorne's high claims for *The*

Marble Faun have read the romance as a deeply felt meditation on art, history, and religion that has at its center an allegory of the Fortunate Fall. Swayed by Hawthorne's prefatory assertion that "Italy, as the site of his Romance, was chiefly valuable to him as affording a sort of poetic or fairy precinct, where actualities would not be so terribly insisted upon, as they are, and must needs be, in America," these readers tend to view 1850s Rome itself allegorically – as the "eternal city" of fallen man – and to avert their eyes, as it appears Hawthorne encourages them, from the more immediate political and social engagement, and prescient historicism, informing the romance.[2] It is no wonder that numerous modern commentators have found *The Marble Faun* to be a relative bore. Such is the occasional fate of "timeless" allegory.

The Marble Faun's great precursor text, Milton's allegory of the fall, was in part a mediated response to, and exploration of, the historical tensions underlying the English Revolution.[3] That fact should press us to be more attentive to the sociocultural and historicist dimensions of a Milton-inspired novel that Hawthorne wrote during a time when the Roman Catholic authorities and their allies had overcome one revolutionary challenge to their governing power and were attempting to contain future subversive threats. By insisting on *The Marble Faun*'s ahistorical "fairy" setting and then building to the notion that Donatello's murder of Miriam's Model encapsulates "the story of the Fall of Man" (434), Hawthorne has to be assigned some responsibility for the many ahistorical readings of the novel that have followed. Not only have the preface and allegorical thematizing deflected attention from the novel's account of the tense political situation in 1850s Rome, they have also deflected attention from the ways in which that account speaks to Hawthorne's concerns about the United States. I will be arguing that *The Marble Faun*, which ambitiously addresses myriad themes in the larger context of Western history, also addresses the more immediate situation of the pre–Civil War United States, not by alluding to the specifics of the American 1850s but rather through a historicism that explores more generalized cultural tensions in a foreign setting that, during the antebellum period, would have invariably prompted Americans to think about, and even see a version of, their own country.[4] It would not be inappropriate to call that foreign setting "antebellum Rome."

Central to the Puritans' millennialism, the specter of Rome as absolute Other – despotic, aristocratic, Catholic – continued to fascinate and appall the majority of antebellum Americans. During the 1830s, a decade that saw a significant rise in Catholic immigration, there was a concomitant heightening of concerns, voiced most dramatically in Samuel F. B. Morse's *A Foreign Conspiracy* (1834) and Lyman Beecher's *Plea for the West* (1835), about the threat posed by papal Rome to the young nation's political liberty and Protestant-republican character.[5] The writings of these prominent nativists, coupled with the concurrent popularity of convent novels by "Rebecca Reed" (1835) and "Maria Monk" (1836), contributed to a marked increase in the production and dissemination of anti-Catholic discourse – the seductions of which the emergent author Hawthorne could not always resist. For example, he observes in an 1836 sketch, "Churches and Cathedrals," that while the Church of St. Peter is "the wonder of the world, and undoubtedly the most sublime monument that mankind ever consecrated to the Deity, since the creation," it must not be overlooked that St. Peter's cost the Roman citizenry one hundred and sixty million dollars and continues to drain Rome's limited resources. For Hawthorne, the reader-oriented editor of and primary contributor to the *American Magazine of Useful and Entertaining Knowledge*, St. Peter's, a church he had yet to see firsthand, represents the corruption and degeneration characterizing Roman Catholicism as a sociopolitical power. Thus he asserts that St. Peter's "may as justly be numbered among edifices of state, as the royal palaces, the fortresses, and the national prisons."[6]

Two decades later, however, in *The Marble Faun*, Hawthorne suggests a very different attitude toward Roman Catholic luxury and decadence. With its numerous descriptions of European paintings and sculptures, the romance expresses an attraction to an aestheticized Catholicism. The attraction to Catholic art extends in the novel to other aspects of Roman Catholicism, particularly the practice of confession. In *The Scarlet Letter*, Dimmesdale's need for confessional relief eventually drives him, as the narrator remarks, "to practices, more in accordance with the old, corrupted faith of Rome": he begins whipping himself with a scourge. Perhaps Hawthorne wanted to suggest, as James Russell Lowell reported in an 1860 letter to Jane Norton, that Catholic confession would have provided Dimmesdale with a needed escape from the guilt-ridden culture of the Puritans. Hawthorne remarked in an 1858 notebook entry on the confessionals of St. Peter's: "If I had ... a murder on my conscience or any other great sin, I think I should have been inclined to kneel down there, and pour it into the safe secrecy of the confessional. What an institution that is!"[7] When, in a climactic scene of *The Marble Faun*, Hawthorne has the New England copyist Hilda, a "daughter of the Puritans" (54), actually enter one of St. Peter's confessionals in search of spiritual solace, it would appear that we have come a long way from the nativist "Churches and Cathedrals" and that a deliberately self-conscious rhetoric, directed at Hawthorne's American readers, means to call attention to that distance. Rather than moving Hilda quietly into the confessional, Hawthorne, in what Henry James terms the novel's "purest touch of inspiration,"[8] builds dramatically to her decision. We are told, for example, that Hilda, who "had not always been adequately impressed by the grandeur of this mighty Cathedral" (348), regarding it as "a gay piece of cabinet-work on a Titanic scale; a jewel-casket, marvellously magnified" (349), now suddenly perceives it "as a magnificent, comprehensive, majestic symbol of religious faith" (350). Tormented by having witnessed the Italian nobleman Donatello's murder of Miriam's mysterious Model, she surrenders to her inchoate desires – "She did not think; she only felt" (357) – seeks out a receptive priest, and then "passionately, with sobs, tears, and the turbulent overflow of emotion too long repressed, she poured out the dark story which had infused its poison into her innocent life" (357). In doing so, she experiences, unlike Dimmesdale, a soothing and restorative sense of relief: "When the hysteric gasp, the strife between words and sobs, had subsided, what a torture had passed away from her soul!" (357–58).

In antebellum convent fiction and nativist tracts, the confessional was invariably depicted as a site of sexual transgression. As the anonymous author of *Pope, or President?* (1859) maintained in a chapter titled "The Romish Confessional": "This seduction of women through the confessional is peculiar to no country: it is common to all – and must be from the unchanging nature of the Romish system."[9] Revising the standard treatment of confession in America's nativist tracts and convent novels – virginal American Eve at the mercy of satanic European priests – Hawthorne guides the reader to the surprising insight that the confessional, at least in this one instance, has served its office. Yet it does so not without the taint of confessional violation. Just prior to Hilda's confession, Hawthorne warns of the possibility of Catholic expediency (344); and in the account of the confession itself he portrays the priest as a Chillingworth-like psychological manipulator who leads Hilda "on by apposite questions that seemed to be suggested by a great and tender interest, and acted like magnetism in attracting the girl's confidence to this unseen friend" (357). Charles Eliot Norton warned in *Notes of Travel and Study in Italy* (1859) that the confessional allowed the papacy to maintain its despotic control: "Such a government can be carried on only by secret and corrupt means. The confessional becomes an instrument of the State, the secret police an instrument of the Church."[10] In *The Marble Faun*, as it turns out, soon after the confession Hilda is apparently betrayed by her selected priest and taken hostage by the Church to coerce Miriam and

Donatello into surrendering to papal authorities. These authorities – priests and armed soldiers – are ubiquitous in the novel; and it must be stressed that despite Hawthorne's seeming attraction to Roman Catholic rituals and institutions in certain scenes, the repeated descriptions of the French and papal militia suggest that he, too, remains concerned about Catholicism's tendencies toward despotism.

Hawthorne's conflicted perspective on Roman Catholicism, as enacted in the confessional and other key scenes of *The Marble Faun*, corresponds to a similarly conflicted perspective in American culture during the 1850s. This was the decade that saw the emergence of the nativist Know-Nothings and the publication of numerous anti-Catholic texts, such as Charles Frothingham's *The Convent's Doom* (1854) and Edward Beecher's *The Papal Conspiracy Exposed* (1855). But the 1850s also saw cultural commentators ranging from Hawthorne's friend George Stillman Hillard to James Jackson Jarves discovering in Rome a glorious artistry that prompted self-conscious discussions and, in some cases, revaluations of its supposedly despotic character. As the sometimes fiery anti-Catholic Jarves remarked on the Sistine Chapel in his 1856 *Italian Sights and Papal Principles*: "No one can enter this beautiful chapel, and behold the multitudes kneeling in silent adoration before the sacrament, without feeling stirred within him the spirit of devotion." In part, the renewed interest in Catholic Rome reflected social elites' concerns, exacerbated by conflict throughout the decade, that the institutions of antebellum culture were no longer regarded by "the multitudes" with a "spirit of devotion." Like their Victorian counterparts, whose Gothic revivalism expressed desires for a return to a harmonious organic order untroubled by class divisions and urban-industrial alienation, elites in particular began to yearn for a well-ordered world characterized by authority and deference. For a number of commentators and travelers of the period, the Roman Catholic Church's emphasis on hierarchy and patriarchy didn't seem all that lamentable during a decade that saw an increasing emphasis on such control in prisons, factories, and plantations – patriarchal institutions championed by their supporters as familial.[11]

Moreover, while Rome was regularly imaged in Whig and Republican "free-labor" rhetoric as the embodiment of a corrupt "slave power," one senses that underlying the Ruskin-influenced Gothic aestheticism of Jarves, Norton, and other American travelers in Rome during the 1850s and early 1860s was an attraction, less to the Church's institutional power, than to an idealized unity apprehended beneath the surface of Rome's unappealing sociopolitical condition. Swayed by Ruskin's evocative celebration of Gothic unity – an aesthetic, as he put it in *Modern Painters*, which binds "things separately imperfect into a perfect whole" – numerous American cultural commentators found in the Gothic an objective correlative, as it were, to their larger political and social desires for a "perfect whole." Writing in the spirit of Ruskin, Jarves, in his 1861 *Art Studies: The Old Masters of Italy*, joined past to present as he called upon Americans to put aside their anti-Catholic prejudices and reevaluate the early Italian painters: "The nobility and beauty of that art which is herein delineated were the fruits of the democratic energies and faith of mediaeval Italy; akin in spirit to those, which, in our own blood, are preparing our country for an equally glorious career in art; while Italy herself, as a united whole, is uprising to a new birth, to keep us company in the drama of progress."[12] The appeal of the Gothic's supposedly democratic and progressive power to create "a united whole" can be taken as yet another expression of what the historian George Forgie has shown to be the period's pervasive sentimental nostalgia for unifying origins – a nostalgia that spoke to the many Americans who feared their own nation was hurtling toward a disastrous fragmentation.[13]

In *The Marble Faun* Hawthorne evokes such nostalgia through his repeated reflections on Rome's buried past, or what he calls the city's "ideal life" (5). In Rome, he says, the traveler begins to feel "that the present moment is pressed down or crowded out" (6). Rome's "dreamy character" (6) liberates individuals from the particulars – the day-to-day exigencies – of their contemporaneous histories, providing a larger, more transtemporal framework for historical and religious contemplation. Only in Rome, then, as Hilda explains, could "[a] Christian girl – even a daughter of the Puritans – . . . pay honour to the idea of Divine Womanhood, without giving up the faith of her forefathers" (54). Motivated not by any worldly faith in Roman Catholicism but by a purer Christian faith, she feels unabashed about tending the Virgin's shrine from her "Dove-cote" (56). Similarly, a pure love of beauty impels her to copy the works of Old Master painters in "generous self-surrender" (60).[14] She responds to the shrine, to "the mighty Old Masters" (57), and to Rome itself ("Rome – mere Rome – will crowd everything else out of my heart" [111]) as her fellow American traveler Kenyon responds to the fading frescoes of Gothic cathedrals, "as symbols of the living spirit that made Catholicism a true religion, and that glorified it as long as it retained a genuine life" (303). Delighting in the "living radiance" (304) suffusing and in effect uniting Rome, Kenyon proclaims: "Christian Faith is a grand Cathedral" (306).

But Gothic revivalism, with its emphasis on "self-surrender" to a larger whole, is but one strain in the novel, as Hawthorne also strives to show that Rome's ideal unity owes much, during the 1850s, to the imposition of political and military power. William Ellery Channing (the nephew of the famous Unitarian minister of the same name) had written in his 1847 *Conversations in Rome*: "The proposition which the Pope lays down, like every European monarch, is – I have the power in my hands; I can only keep it by an armed force; there is the armed force – obey it! obey it!" Hawthorne likewise caustically commented in his notebook on the ubiquity in mid-1850s Rome of "French soldiers, monks, and priests of every degree, a shabby population smoking bad cigars."[15] In *The Marble Faun*, written just ten years after Louis Napoleon's troops helped to put down the Risorgimento and restore the Pope to power, Hawthorne continually reminds the reader of the coercive presence throughout Rome of the French military. Near Hilda's shrine to the Virgin, for example, is "a station for French soldiers, with a sentinel pacing in front" (51). Intermingling in Rome's streets and avenues are "priests, soldiers, nobles, artists, and women" (74). In the Pincian Garden "the red-trowsered French soldiers are always to be seen" (100), and the same soldiers patrol the Colosseum. Such is the harsh reality of Rome's occupied status that Kenyon cannot help musing on the bitter irony of Marcus Curtius's heroic self-sacrifice of throwing himself into a pit at the Roman Forum. At the time, Curtius may have preserved the Roman Republic, but he failed to stave off "the future calamities of Rome – shades of Goths and Gauls, and even of the French soldiers of to-day" (161).

Troubled by the Roman authorities' recourse to brute martial power, Hawthorne expresses a strong current of sympathy in the novel for the Anglo-Italian and probably Jewish Miriam Schaefer, who, unlike the self-surrendering copyist Hilda, defies the "Old Masters." Linked to such strongly independent women as Jael, Judith, Cleopatra, and the parricide Beatrice Cenci, the mysterious Miriam embodies a revolutionism at odds with the various reactionary forces depicted in the novel. To be sure, Hawthorne deliberately keeps the reader in the dark about the specifics of her prior involvement in "some plot or political intrigue" (465), but the analogy developed between Miriam and Beatrice Cenci hints at the nature of her past plotting. It occurred, we learn, soon after she repudiated a marriage, arranged by her father, to an older Marchese. Like Shelley's Beatrice Cenci, the victim of two tyrannous "fathers," her own and the corrupt pope who supports him, Miriam was pushed to rebel against the authority of Rome's fathers. In *The Cenci* (1819) Beatrice eventually commissions an assassin to kill her incestuous father. Although it seems safe to assume that Miriam's father is no Cenci, the Beatrice/Miriam analogy, underscored by Miriam's responsiveness to Guido's representation of Beatrice's suffering, suggests that Miriam, too, may have "commissioned" the assassination of a patriarch connected with the Roman Catholic political authority.[16]

The assassination possibility is highly significant, since it was the November 1848 assassination of the pope's handpicked prime minister, Count Pellegrino Rossi, that precipitated Rome's republican revolution – a revolution celebrated by many Americans as a signal expression, and even mirror image, of the Protestant-republican revolutionary ideals of 1776. Margaret Fuller, who regarded the assassination as "one of terrible justice," exclaimed on the Romans' uprising in an 1848 letter to the *New York Tribune*: "In Europe, amid the teachings of adversity, a nobler spirit is struggling, – a spirit which cheers and animates mine. I hear earnest words of pure faith and love. I see deeds of brotherhood. This is what makes my America." Similarly, Theodore Dwight wildly asserted in *The Roman Republic of 1849* (1851): "The grand secret which Americans have yet to learn, is this, that the Italians have suddenly, and without the suspicion of the world, become devoted Protestants."[17] Viewed through the lens of Fuller and Dwight, Miriam's implication in political plotting suggests that, despite her alleged ties to the Cenci family and the larger papal power structure, it is not improbable that Hawthorne conceived of her as an anti-Catholic revolutionary, perhaps even assassin, of 1848.

There are a number of clues which point to this more specific dimension of Miriam's past activities. For example, she reencounters her former Model in the catacombs of Saint Calixtus, by legend a hiding place for religio-political rebels, most famously the "pagan" Memmius. According to the narrator, Memmius was rumored to have been "a thief of the city, a robber of the Campagna, a political offender, or an assassin with blood upon his hand" (35). The assassination possibility, one of several choices, is given added weight, not only by its placement at the end of the sentence but also by the comment that Miriam's Model is the type "whom artists convert into Saints or assassins, according as their pictorial purposes demand" (19). Eventually her purposes demand that Donatello become an assassin, as both Donatello and Hilda see her request and, to a certain extent, commission the murder of the Model through her mesmerizing eyes. Immediately following the murder, Miriam conceives of Donatello and herself as conspirators who have betrayed republican principles (176), but when it is later learned that the Model had become a monk shortly after ending his initial association with Miriam, the murder can be viewed as a republican revolutionary assassination of a tyrannizing Catholic who sought to keep her in thrall.

In various ways, then, Hawthorne quietly suggests that Miriam earlier had participated with the Model, as she participates with Donatello, in a political assassination. The two murders are symbolically reenacted in the great carnival scene following Hilda's disappearance, with the political symbolism again pointing to Miriam's role as anti–Roman Catholic subversive and assassin. It is worth underscoring that Hilda disappears soon after she fulfills her promise to deliver a secret packet put together by Miriam to that vestige of corruption, the Palazzo Cenci. On her way there she passes through the Jewish ghetto, wherein, according to the narrator, the Jews "lead a close, unclean, and multitudinous life, resembling that of maggots when they over-populate a decaying cheese" (388). The passage is usually read as an unfortunate anti-Semitic lapse on Hawthorne's part; but viewed in its historical context the description is critical less of the Jews than of Catholic Rome, a "decaying cheese," which forcibly made the Jews into "maggots." Just prior to the 1848 revolution, the Roman authorities had allowed the Jews to live outside of the ghetto. Following the reinstatement of Pius IX, however, as historian Paul Baker notes, "Church authorities quietly withdrew the recently granted privileges, and the harsh treatment of the Jew was resumed."[18] Clearly, from the perspective of the papacy, the Jews were tied to the revolutionary activities giving rise to the Republic of 1849. That Miriam is identified as partly Jewish further links her to these activities, as does her apparent participation in extinguishing the Virgin's lamp shortly after Hilda vanishes. It was only in 1854, after all, that the pope declared the doctrine of Immaculate Conception, thereby identifying the Catholic Church more explicitly with Mary's purity. Ann Taves explains: "The concern with Mary's inviolability and purity reflected, most specifically, the papacy's concern with the political inviolability of the church in the Italian context."[19] In this respect, to extinguish the Virgin's lamp in post-1854 Rome is to express a subversive desire to "extinguish" the Roman Catholic Church's political authority.

The extinguishing certainly liberates Kenyon's heretofore self-suppressed anti-Catholicism, as he now looks at Rome, not only from the perspective of one despairing in the loss of his beloved but also as a Protestant-republican, as an American, repulsed by Roman Catholic tyranny and corruption:

> For here was a priesthood, pampered, sensual, with red and bloated cheeks,
> and carnal eyes. . . . And here was an indolent nobility, with no high aims or
> opportunities, but cultivating a vicious way of life as if it were an art, and the
> only one which they cared to learn. Here was a population, high and low,
> that had no genuine belief in virtue. . . . Here was a soldiery, who felt Rome
> to be their conquered city, and doubtless considered themselves the legal
> inheritors of the foul license which Gaul, Goth, and Vandal have here
> exercised, in days gone by. (411–12)

Though the narrator chastises Kenyon for his rigidities – "The sculptor
forgot his marble" (413) – the unfolding captivity plot and nativist rhetoric
encourage the reader to adopt an anti–Roman Catholic perspective that is
subversive and revolutionary, and in keeping with Miriam's.

The carnival itself is in keeping with Miriam's subversive energies, as its
very gaiety is associated, through the image of the catacombs, with
Miriam's prior conspiracy with her Model: "For a few afternoons of early
Spring, this mouldy gaiety strays into the sunshine; all the remainder of the
year, it seems to be shut up in the catacombs, or some other sepulchral
store-house of the past" (436). And as Hawthorne describes the scene, he
presents the carnival of the late 1850s as a ritual of revolution that restages
the Protestant-republican revolution of 1848. Rossi was assassinated during
a mob action; and at carnival, as "festive people fought one another with an
ammunition of sugar-plums and flowers" (439), there are two "assassina-
tions." The first to go is a Roman senator's coachman, struck "full in the
face" with a "well-directed . . . double-handfull of powdered lime, flung,"
suitably (and humorously) enough, by an exemplar of Protestant-republican values, "an impious New Englander" (443).

More ominous, however, as lime "hung like smoke over a battle-field"
(439), is the subsequent attack on Kenyon himself. Having been urged to
participate in the festival by Miriam and Donatello, Kenyon, so the rhetoric
suggests, has been set up to be the principal victim of the revolutionary
energies released from the catacombs and animating the carnival; in a sense,
during the carnival, Kenyon, "a mark for missiles from all quarters" (444),
role-plays as Rossi. At first he is surrounded by "[f]antastic figures, with
bulbous heads" (445); but then there appears an amorous gigantic woman
who, feeling slighted, "draw[s] a huge pistol . . . took aim at the obdurate
sculptor's breast, and pulled the trigger" (446). As in Miriam's paintings, a
vengeful woman performs the violent act, described here as a political
assassination. A costumed notary arrives and "offered to make the last will
and testament of the assassinated man" (446). Meanwhile, Donatello and
Miriam, dressed as a Peasant and Contadina, "appeared to be straying

through the grotesque and animated scene, taking as little part in it as himself" (447). Ironically, while Kenyon is unable to take part in the merriment, he most certainly takes part in the scene.[20] Similarly, as the masterminds behind the "assassination," Miriam and Donatello play the part that any good assassins would play – appearing to be uninvolved. That fiction of uninvolvement breaks down, however, when Donatello is arrested and Hilda appears on the balcony. Though the epilogue offers a completely unrevolutionary explanation of events, the "assassination" does precipitate Hilda's liberation from the Cenci palace (and, we later learn, from a convent), the price of which is paid by Donatello.

The carnival scene may be read, then, as a ritual reenactment of the revolutionary energies that brought into being the short-lived Roman Republic of 1849 and that continue to reside in the hearts and minds of the Roman people – as an enactment, in short, of energies that many of Hawthorne's antebellum Protestant-republican readers would have applauded. But in portraying Kenyon's fear and disorientation at carnival, in transforming Kenyon from nativist to "Rossi," Hawthorne expresses something very different from what Nina Baym terms "the author's disgust that yet another surrogate has been unable to survive social pressure."[21] As in the presentation of the hunted (and haunted) Coverdale at the carnivalesque masquerade described in *The Blithedale Romance* (1852), Hawthorne also expresses his unease that Miriam's energy (or Zenobia's) may erupt in a violent revolutionism that would subject the Kenyons (or Coverdales, or Hawthornes) of the world to a grotesque "merry martyrdom" (445). Sympathetic to Miriam's rebelliousness and imagination, while at the same time nervous – as he seems, actually, throughout his fiction – about the destabilizing, topsy-turvy effects of revolution, he presents Rome's annual carnival as a model safe outlet wherein the very revolutionism he so imaginatively (and patriotically) entertains is played out and defused.[22] "Everybody seemed lawless," the narrator writes of the gaiety; yet "nobody was rude" (441). Like the confessional, the carnival allows for a release of throttled energies within a circumscribed setting that keeps them in check. And though the narrator initially notes that a precautionary safeguard against these energies breaking loose is maintained by French and papal dragoons (441), he ultimately maintains that a recourse to force will not be necessary, for "to do the Roman people justice, they were restrained by a better safeguard than the sabre or the bayonet; it was their own gentle courtesy, which imparted a sort of sacredness to the hereditary festival" (441).

Hawthorne's idealization of the "gentle courtesy" at carnival, of the participants' willingness to "let loose their mirthful propensities, while muzzling those fiercer ones that tend to mischief" (441), is the idealization of an antebellum author who feared that a similar eruption of carnivalesque energies in America would not be so merry. While the Roman citizenry remains capable of attaining "a sympathy of nonsense; a true and genial brotherhood and sisterhood, based on the honest purpose – and a wise one, too – of being foolish, all together" (439), Americans, Hawthorne ruefully remarked in *The Scarlet Letter*, "have yet to learn again the forgotten art of gayety." The extended scenes on Donatello's fall from his idyllic Tuscan past, on the corruption of his "Sunshine," evocatively explore a pastoral playfulness that Americans, particularly New Englanders in Hawthorne's view, lost so long ago that virtually no traces remain on the collective mentality. (Such is the implication, say, of "The May-Pole of Merry Mount" [1836].) Contemplating the consequences of introducing a "Roman carnival" into antebellum America, a world, as he put it in an 1854 letter to Horatio Bridge, of "continual fuss, and tumult and excitement, and bad blood," Hawthorne confided to his notebook a year before writing *The Marble Faun*: "the whole street would go mad in earnest, and come to blows and bloodshed, were the population to let themselves loose to the extent which we see here."[23]

Preparatory to carnival, Hawthorne believed, joyless and conflict-ridden Americans, an amalgam of peoples lacking in a shared hereditary past, need to develop a sense of community that would impart to those above and below the spirit of "gentle courtesy." Given his perception of the current unavailability of such socially integrative ideals, however, Hawthorne during the mid-to-late 1850s, at least in his political writings, usually sided with the restraining forces of authority. For example, and rather chillingly, just prior to writing *The Marble Faun* he called for the reinstatement of legalized flogging on board American ships (a metonymy for the state), for his experience as consul and, arguably, his continued adherence to the antiabolitionist Democrats, led him to conclude that its banning had contributed to an upsurge in incidents of frustrated captains murdering their rowdy "foreign" seamen.[24] We may speculate, then, that it is precisely Hawthorne's discomfort with the restless masses that leads him, in effect, to close the door on Donatello's prison cell and present his fall as fortunate. Kenyon remarks on Donatello's moral and intellectual growth: "Out of his bitter agony, a soul and intellect (I could almost say) have been inspired into him" (282). Miriam declares that Donatello's Adamic fall brings "a higher, brighter, and profounder happiness" (434). By using Kenyon and Miriam to promote a moral and theological allegory of the soul's growth following the fall, Hawthorne can seem unconcerned about, and even blind to, the suffering and privation attending the individual's, or, more generally, the erstwhile republican Roman citizenry's fall into despotism. His is a partial sympathy tinged with social anxiety, which results in his acquiescence, uneasy and conflicting as it may be, in the containing (and restraining) potential of confessional, carnival, and prison.[25] The postscript concludes with Kenyon chuckling over the mystery of Donatello's ears – a gesture that transforms "republican" concerns about Donatello's unfortunate fate into mythological play.

Himself a historical participant in the period he is representing, Hawthorne – tourist, voyeur, and distinguished representative of the Democracy – cannot escape from a certain complicity in his characters' aestheticizing and allegorizing of their experiences. But it is a complicity that, to a large extent, is the subject of his romance, which explores from a historically contingent and implicated perspective the desire for an ideal unifying authority – moral, aesthetic, or political – in a world currently rife with conflict between the forces of revolution and reaction. That desire, among other things, speaks to Hawthorne's acute historicist perception of the desire informing the discursive trope of "antebellum Rome." In this respect, it is worth noting that in his 1852 campaign biography, *The Life of Franklin Pierce*, Hawthorne justified his friend's support for Jackson's veto of the Maysville Road bill by invoking the trope: "The peril to the individuality of the States, from a system tending so directly to consolidate the powers of government towards a common centre, was obvious. The result might have been, with the lapse of time and the increased activity of the disease, to place the capital of our federative Union in a position resembling that of imperial Rome, where each once independent state was a subject province, and all the highways of the world were said to meet in her forum." In his letters of 1860, with civil war impending, Hawthorne reaffirmed his position against consolidation. Writing to William Ticknor in February of that year, he proclaimed: "I go for a dissolution of the Union; and on that ground, I hope the Abolitionists will push matters to extremity." Similarly, ten months later, in a letter to Henry Bright, he maintained that "the Union is unnatural, a scheme of man, not an ordinance of God." However, when comparing America to Rome in an 1858 notebook entry, he lamented America's lack of unifying ideals and therefore its *difference* from Rome: "I wonder that we Americans love our country at all; it having no limits and no oneness; and when you try to make it a matter of the heart, everything falls away except one's native State; – neither can you seize hold of that, unless you tear it out of the Union, bleeding and quivering."[26] In this private meditation, unionism, rather than being "unnatural," possesses an organic but, regrettably, not a binding transcendental authority.

In *The Marble Faun*, revolutionary and conservative alike share in the desire to attain a degree of transcendental authority and to ground that authority in nature. Metaphorically, we might say, in their quest for foundational beliefs, in their evident discomfort with the sovereignty of their unshackled Protestant imaginations, Kenyon, Hilda, and even Protestant-republican Miriam resemble Roman Catholics. But because authority in Catholic Rome so often seems corrupt and despotic, the characters, and arguably Hawthorne himself (through his narrator), regularly resort to ahistorical psychological allegories that free them from any sense of complicity in the worldly ruling order. According to Kenyon, for example, mankind "craves a true ruler, under whatever title, as a child its father" (166). From this perspective, Hilda's retreat to the Virgin's shrine as "a child, lifting its tear-stained face to seek comfort from a Mother" (332), and Miriam and Donatello's responsiveness to the "patriarchal majesty" (314) of Pope Julius's statue at the square of Perugia, reflect "universal" longings to subsume self to a beneficent parental figure, a ruler, as the narrator reverentially describes Aurelius, "with an air of beneficence and unlimited authority . . . in [whom] the obedient subject would find his highest interests consulted" (166).

Viewed contextually, however, Hawthorne's use of a precise social setting and his appropriations and revisions of antebellum discourses of Roman Catholicism indicate that contemporaneous social tensions and confusions have exacerbated longings for a "true ruler," and not only in Rome, and perhaps not only among social elites. Thus the narrator describes Pope Julius, as captured in his statue, in terms very similar to the heroic Puritan protector of Hawthorne's early sketch "The Gray Champion" (1835): "An imaginative spectator could not but be impressed with the idea, that this benignly awful representative of Divine and human authority might rise from his brazen chair, should any great public exigency demand his interposition, and encourage or restrain the people by his gesture, or even by prophetic utterances worthy of so grand a presence" (314). In Rome, I would suggest, Hawthorne, like other American travelers of the period, discovers an absence – the spiritual void resulting from the passing of America's heroic revolutionary fathers and their founding ideals – and in *The Marble Faun* he explores the dynamic that would soon impel self-reliant Northern Protestant Americans to subsume themselves to the simultaneously "popish" and "prophetic" "representative of Divine and human authority": the fatherly, redemptive, unifying, but finally nonnegotiable force of Abraham Lincoln.[27]

Coda on Race

Early in 1862, Hawthorne traveled with his friend William Ticknor to Washington, DC, in order to get a closer look at the ravages of the war. He shared his thoughts in "Chiefly about War-Matters," published in the July 1862 *Atlantic Monthly*. With perhaps the pope in mind, he describes Lincoln, whom he met with the help of his friend Horatio Bridge, as "one of the potentates of the earth." But he also expresses his admiration for the down-to-earth president, and makes fun of him as well. (That part of the essay was cut from the *Atlantic* printing.) A large section of the essay is devoted to the militarization of the nation, as Hawthorne presciently laments: "Will the time ever come again, in America, when we may live half a score of years without once seeing the likeness of a solider, except if it be in the festal march of a company on its summer tour? Not in this generation, I fear, nor in the next, nor till the Millennium; and even that blessed epoch, as the prophecies seem to intimate, will advance to the sound of the trumpet."[28] Hawthorne's irreverence toward the president, his cringing at perpetual militarization, and his unwillingness to celebrate a war that had already killed thousands of Americans made him a persona non grata among many antislavery New Englanders.

"Chiefly about War-Matters" got under the skin of its readers in 1862, and, despite its antimilitarization and pacifism, it continues to get under the skin of recent commentators, who take it as just one more instance of Hawthorne's failure to address what many of us now regard as the great moral issue of his time. I argue in Chapter 1, above, and elsewhere that there is considerable evidence that Hawthorne was antislavery and regarded slavery as one of the world's "evils." Not only did he sign a Free Soil petition in 1852, he regularly depicted patriarchal power as a form of slavery, and thus brought together antislavery and feminist discourses in his characterization of such figures as Chillingworth, Judge Pyncheon, Westervelt, and Miriam's Model.[29] All this said, a passage in "Chiefly about War-Matters" has raised concerns about Hawthorne and race that have ramifications for how we might read *The Marble Faun*.

Early in the essay, Hawthorne describes seeing "contrabands," or fugitive slaves, in northern Virginia. He writes:

> So rudely were they attired, – as if their garb had grown upon them spontaneously, – so picturesquely natural in manners, and wearing such a crust of primeval simplicity, (which is quite polished away from the Northern black man,) that they seemed a kind of creature by themselves,

not altogether human, but perhaps quite as good, and akin to the fauns and rustic deities of olden times. I wonder whether I shall excite anybody's wrath by saying this.[30]

Hawthorne's noting of his (false) concern about the possible wrathful response of his readers suggests that he knew he was taking some risks in the mythological comparison. Still, there is no evidence Hawthorne's contemporary readers were bothered by the comparison of African Americans fleeing slavery to "fauns and rustic deities of older times." Instead it has been critics of our own time who have taken up the comparison in order to make somber pronouncements on the racist implications of Hawthorne's novel about a Roman "faun." Early in *The Marble Faun* we're told that the probably Jewish Miriam is rumored to have "one burning drop of African blood in her veins" (23) as the result of possibly being the daughter of a South American planter. Though that rumor isn't taken all that seriously, it has been enough to lead some critics to assert that Hawthorne's novel of "antebellum Rome," with its "black" faun and heroine, is essentially a white-supremacist novel indicative of Hawthorne's desire to rid the US nation of African Americans. Blythe Ann Tellefsen, for instance, argues that *The Marble Faun* points to "the vulnerability of white, Protestant-American identity to the influence of other ethnic, religious, and racial identities," and in this way makes the case for "racial isolation" by suggesting "that African Americans – Miriam and Donatello – cannot be reconciled to society and included in the nation's future." Arthur Riss similarly contends that the depiction of the fugitive slaves in "Chiefly about War-Matters" makes them into nonpersons, and then, like Tellefsen, he reads what he takes as the racism of the mythological comparison back onto *The Marble Faun*, arguing that in both the novel and the essay Hawthorne aestheticizes race as part of a larger effort to "explain (not evade) why the [black] race cannot become 'persons' even if they are emancipated."[31]

   There are considerable strains in the leaps from aesthetics to politics in Tellefsen's and Riss's pronouncements. It is worth observing that in the same passage on the mythological look of the fugitive slaves he encounters in Virginia, Hawthorne refers to "the Northern black man," with no suggestion at all of his mythological or nonperson identity. Might Hawthorne, who loved mythology, simply be taking on a playful role in the essay, pleased that he might annoy some of his somber readers? The more serious question to raise here is that of method. True, *The Marble Faun* to some extent depicts Miriam as a mixed-race character, but is Hawthorne talking about blood or culture when he describes her as possibly Jewish?[32] More importantly, what are we to make of an interpretive method that so confidently reduces *The Marble Faun* to an unambiguously white-supremacist novel similar to the later work of Thomas Dixon? And to put this very simply: Where in all of Hawthorne's writings does he actually say that blacks are nonpersons who do not merit citizenship? The answer, of course, is nowhere. Race is certainly an important constituent of the novel, but in ways that are not easy to pin down, especially given the mysteries surrounding Miriam's mixed-race background.

Hawthorne's portrayal of Miriam as possibly even black brings me back to "Chiefly about War-Matters." For there is a key moment in the essay that has gone uncommented on by those who insist on white-supremacist readings of both the essay and *The Marble Faun*, and that is Hawthorne's reflection on the origins of the nation, which he observes is not so white after all:

> There is an historical circumstance, known to a few, that connects the children of the Puritans with these Africans of Virginia, in a very singular way. They are our brethren, as being lineal descendants from the Mayflower, the fated womb of which, in her first voyage, sent forth a brood of Pilgrims upon Plymouth Rock, and, in a subsequent one, spawned slaves upon the Southern soil, – a monstrous birth, but with which we have an instinctive sense of kindred, and so are stirred by an irresistible impulse to attempt their rescue, even at the cost of blood and ruin.[33]

"They are our brethren," writes the putative white supremacist about the nation's miscegenated past, feeling "an instinctive sense of kindred" that leads him to consider attempting the rescue of the fugitive slaves. Hawthorne resists, in part because they already have found supporters. But in remarking on the "irresistible impulse" to come to the aid of the fugitive slaves, Hawthorne for just a moment, to read back from the essay to *The Marble Faun* one last time, resembles Donatello when he feels a similar impulse to come to the aid of Miriam, the woman in thrall to a patriarchal master. That moment leads to Donatello's Fortunate Fall. In the interstices of *The Marble Faun* and "Chiefly about War-Matters," Hawthorne may well be suggesting the relevance of the trope of Felix Culpa to a war of emancipation that he's more sympathetic to than he's willing to let on.

CHAPTER 9

Edward Everett Hale's and Sutton E. Griggs's Men without a Country

Toni Morrison's "Unspeakable Things Unspoken" (1989) did the influen-
tial work of helping to desegregate the color line in American literary
studies. This chapter follows in that spirit by discussing the relatively obscure
black writer Griggs in relation to the popular white writer Hale. The
chapter also considers both writers' views of the nation in a larger oceanic
context.

Edward Everett Hale's "The Man without a Country" (1863) was probably the most widely read short story in the United States from 1863 to 1945; Sutton E. Griggs's first two novels, *Imperium in Imperio* (1899) and *Overshadowed* (1901), the second of which was self-published, were barely noticed at the time of their publication. This chapter examines intertextual connections between Hale's popular short story and Griggs's first two novels, focusing on the authors' narrative figurations of nation (or country) in relation to debates on race, patriotism, and imperialism. In his first two novels, Griggs, I suggest, drew on, revised, and recuperated Hale's phenomenally popular short story, discerning in it something that was generally lost on readers of the nineteenth and early-twentieth centuries: its expression of anger at the US nation, and its thematic emphasis on the interrelationship between dispossession and patriotism.

Hale (1822–1909), a white Unitarian minister from Massachusetts, published "The Man without a Country" anonymously in the December 1863 *Atlantic*, and over the next several decades the story was republished numerous times under Hale's name (and always with a preface by Hale).[1] By the 1890s the widely reprinted and anthologized "The Man without a Country" had also become a standard school text. In the versions published between 1863 and 1898, Hale linked the story to goals that Griggs (1872–1933), a black Baptist minister from Texas, would have applauded: support for the Union cause in the Civil War, which included emancipation, and thus an implied support for Reconstruction. In the post–Civil War context, the antislavery and antiracist motifs of the story, including a scene in which Africans are liberated from a slave ship, would have been especially resonant for Griggs. I will be focusing on Griggs's appropriations and revisions of Hale's story. In particular, I examine Griggs's narrative strategies in *Imperium*, which resemble the narrative strategies of "The Man without a Country." His use of flag imagery and other patriotic icons in *Imperium* draws on similar imagery and icons in "The Man without a Country," and his conception of Texas as a site of black conspiracy overlaps with Hale's depiction of Texas's place in the Burr conspiracy. In *Overshadowed*, Griggs continues his textual conversation with "The Man without a Country" by boldly revising Hale's portrayal of the patriot at sea.

The author of a number of popular short stories, Hale published his most famous story in the midst of the Civil War, nine years before Griggs's birth. "The Man without a Country" tells the story of one Philip Nolan, an army officer who in 1805 joins with Aaron Burr in his alleged western conspiracy, which is implicitly analogized to Southern secession, and is captured and tried at a court-martial. When the court asks Nolan to affirm his loyalty to the nation, he shockingly declares: "D—n the United States! I wish I may never hear of the United States again!"[2] Granting his wish, the court subsequently sentences Nolan to a life at sea, and from the moment of his sentencing in 1807 to his death in 1863, Nolan resides on various US naval vessels in which Nolan's fellow sailors work strenuously to make sure he learns nothing about the United States. They censor newspaper articles, deny him access to ever-changing maps, and guard their conversations in his presence. As Nolan becomes infirm and aged, however, some information about the United States is leaked to him, though the sailors agree that no one will tell him about the Civil War. Aware that he's dying, Nolan reveals to an officer named Danforth that over the years he has built a shipboard shrine to the United States, which Danforth later describes in a letter to the story's narrator:

> The stars and stripes were triced up above and around a picture of [George] Washington, and he had painted a majestic eagle, with lightnings blazing from his beak and his foot just clasping the whole globe, which his wings overshadowed. The dear old boy [Nolan] saw my glance, and said, with a sad smile, "Here, you see, I have a country!" And then he pointed to the foot of his bed, where I had not seen before a great map of the United States, as he had drawn it from memory, and which he had there to look upon as he lay. Quaint, queer old names were on it, in large letters: "Indiana Territory," "Mississippi Territory," and "Louisiana Territory," as I suppose our fathers learned such things: but the old fellow had patched in Texas, too; he had

carried his western boundary all the way to the Pacific, but on that shore he had defined nothing.[3]

With the help of his shipboard shrine, Nolan displays US continental expansion up to the time of the Civil War, making the acquisition of Texas and westward movement to the Pacific key to his passion for US nationalism. In a sense, Nolan, like his shrine's majestic eagle, has himself taken Texas and the western territories as an imaginative act of patriotism, thereby redeeming his youthful traitorous act of attempting to secure the territories for Burr. After describing the shrine, Danforth reports on the death of Nolan, who leaves among his papers the epitaph that he wants engraved on a stone somewhere in New Orleans:

> In Memory of
> PHILIP NOLAN,
> *Lieutenant in the Army of the United States.*
> He loved his country as no other man has loved her; but no
> man deserved less at her hands.[4]

Ironically, then, "The Man without a Country" presents the life history of a man who could have entered the annals of American history as one of its most notorious traitors and instead ends up as an iconic figure of US nationalism. It is the paradoxical nature of this patriot-traitor that may well have caught Griggs's attention. In a provocative critical reassessment of the story, Carrie Hyde shows how nineteenth-century readers gained instruction in patriotic thinking not only from revolutionary heroes such as Patrick Henry and George Washington but also from "negative figures of citizenship" who are denied full political autonomy: "traitors, expatriates, and slaves," such as Major John André, Frederick Douglass, and even Burr himself. As she remarks about Hale's tapping into this tradition: "By prioritizing negative examples of citizenship, 'The Man without a Country' makes the pathos of dispossession a precondition for the patriotism of the protagonist and reader alike. As a result, Hale's seemingly simple allegory of loyalty interrogates the categories of political belonging – expanding readerly sympathy to the nation's outcasts as well."[5] Nolan is entrapped for over fifty years on a naval vessel, and his identification at a key point in the story with equally homeless African slaves speaks to the pathos of his own homelessness and sense of dispossession. Hale himself makes the connection between Nolan and black Americans in his 1886 preface to "The Man without a Country," stating that when he heard from a friend in Virginia about "the death of PHILIP NOLAN, a negro from Louisiana, who died in the cause of his country in service in a colored regiment, I felt that he had done something to atone for the imagined guilt of the imagined namesake of his unfortunate god-father."[6] Oddly enough, then, Hale proposes that a black Philip Nolan could atone for a white Philip Nolan who, in Hale's overall account, had nothing much to atone for.

Though "The Man without a Country" had a pervasive presence in late nineteenth-century American culture, we lack absolutely definitive evidence that Griggs read it, in part because we lack most of Griggs's letters and journals. And yet both Griggs's *Imperium* and *Overshadowed* portray black men and women who want to love their country and receive less at her hands, and there is considerable textual evidence that Griggs learned from Hale's famous story about what Hyde terms "outcast patriotism."[7] At various moments in Griggs's first two novels, the leading characters state, in effect, "D—n the United States," and make decisive moves to act on their anger. In *Overshadowed*, the main character chooses exile at sea, and in *Imperium* the two main characters, instead of building a shrine to Texas, develop plans (like Burr and Nolan at the opening of "The Man without a Country") to take Texas in order to create a new country. As I discuss below, Griggs's most direct "quotation" from "The Man without a Country" can be found at the end of *Overshadowed*, but the Texas plot in *Imperium* resonates with the account of Texas at the opening and close of "The Man without a Country." In Hale's story, the plot to take Texas is foiled by the US government; in *Imperium*, it is foiled by the narrator of the novel, Berl Trout. But Berl does more than foil the plot: as a participant-narrator he complicates our understanding of the plot. The participant-narrator of "The Man without a Country" similarly complicates interpretation of Nolan's story. Though there are significant differences between the narrators of "The Man without a Country" and *Imperium in Imperio* as characters (one is a white naval officer and the other a black ex-conspirator), there are enough similarities in the works' destabilizing narrative strategies to suggest that Griggs learned something about narrative from Hale, as well.

Both "The Man without a Country" and *Imperium* set up complicated relationships between the author and narrator that can frustrate, or inspire, interpretation. In the 1863 anonymous printing of "The Man without a Country," which a number of first-time readers probably took as nonfiction, the public life of Philip Nolan is told by Frederic Ingham of the US Navy, who first meets Nolan around 1820 and last sees him around the time of the war with Mexico. When Ingham notices Nolan's obituary in 1863, he decides to tell "this poor creature's story." With the help of legal and naval documents, letters, and oral history, the narrator pieces together an account that runs from 1805 to 1863. Remarking on Burr and Nolan's activities in 1805, Ingham confesses: "What Burr meant to do I know no more than you, dear reader," and he goes on to describe a number of other incidents that ultimately elude him. "I imagine his life," he says about Nolan's history, "from what I have seen and heard of it." Ingham initially encounters Nolan on a ship enforcing "our Slave-Trade treaty" and is moved by Nolan's efforts to return liberated slaves to their homeland in Africa. Eventually he loses touch with Nolan, and the final report of Nolan's death comes to the narrator from the naval officer Danforth, who sends a letter that allows Ingham to complete the story. But in ways that Hale may not have intended, the assembled story, with its conjectures and lacunae, suggests that US nationalism can be understood as a form of fantasy, and that patriotism has its greatest resonance when it is coupled with dispossession.[8]

Subsequent reprintings of "The Man without a Country" include an author's preface from Hale that insists on the fictionality of Philip Nolan (but not of the equally made-up Ingham), perhaps because there was a historical figure circa 1800 named Philip Nolan. He also discusses the story's Civil War context, conceding that there are different ways of reading a story that he no longer fully controls. In 1863 Hale aimed to encourage a patriotic love for the Union as the US nation, disturbed as he was by the 1863 absentee run for the Ohio governorship by Clement Vallandigham, a Southern sympathizer or Copperhead. And yet by the time the story was published in the *Atlantic*, Vallandigham had been convicted of treason by a military court and subsequently banished to the South by Abraham Lincoln. To some extent, then, the story had lost its original purpose. But perhaps that was all for the good. Declaring that the story "passed out of my hands,"[9] Hale implies it can do larger and more important cultural work in the service of US nationalism.

Much in "The Man without a Country," however, displays the darker and more disturbing sides of national power, and thus encourages reader identification with the traitor-patriot Nolan. At the close of his 1868 preface, Hale notes that a reader from Connecticut told him "the story must be apologized for, because it was doing great injury to the national cause by asserting such continued cruelty of the Federal Government through a half-century," a comment that perceptively links Nolan's "fit of frenzy" in damning the United States to the court's comparable juridical fit of frenzy in indefinitely banishing Nolan. Moreover, the narrator Ingham calls the decision to keep information about the United States from Nolan "a little cruel." Ingham describes his own post-1830s efforts to free Nolan, the man who heroically served the United States during the War of 1812, as "like getting a ghost out of prison. They pretended there was no such man, and never was such a man. . . . It will not be the first thing in the service of which the Department appears to know nothing!" Perhaps because he is aware of the possibilities for a darker reading of an arbitrary and heartless national power, Hale begins his 1868 preface with an assertion of the story's patriotic dimension, stating that he wrote it during the summer of 1863 "as a contribution, however humble, towards the formation of a just and true national sentiment, or sentiment of love to the nation."[10]

Griggs's *Imperium* begins with similar claims about the patriotic motives behind the storytelling, but those claims are made not by Griggs but by his narrator, Berl Trout. "I . . . pronounce myself a patriot," the narrator states in the prefatory "Berl Trout's Dying Declaration." However, the opening words of his preface are as follows: "I am a traitor." Like Hale, in other words, Griggs works with a complex thematic tension between the traitor and the patriot. What's vague at the outset is exactly what the condemned Berl means by terming himself both a patriot and a traitor. Is he talking about being a traitor to the US nation, or another social entity, or, as he says, "the whole human family"? Adding to the uncertainty is Griggs's own prefatory "To the Public," which introduces the narrator's preface. In his post-1863 printings, Hale established himself in his prefaces as the author of "The Man without a Country." Griggs, by contrast, presents himself as an editor rather than an author, which is to say that the Griggs of the preface seems to be more a fictional character than an actual historical author, even as he insists that he is telling a true story. He states that Berl "was a warm personal friend" of the African American characters whose parallel and sometimes intersecting lives we follow throughout the novel: the dark-skinned Belton Piedmont, who struggles to work his way up the social ladder from his humble rural origins, and the light-skinned Bernard Belgrave, whose wealth and privilege protect him from the sorts of hardships Belton regularly faces. As different as they are, by the end of the novel both are involved with a black nationalist conspiratorial organization dedicated to destroying the US nation. Berl, the novel's historian and narrator, not only "learned from their own lips the stories of their eventful lives" but also, in the tradition of Hale's Ingham, developed his narrative from "documents" which are now in the possession of Griggs, who asserts that he fulfilled Berl's "dying request by editing his Ms."[11] Griggs's opening gambit of presenting two prefaces raises questions about how to read the narrative that follows. As in "The Man without a Country," there is a participant-narrator, who, strangely enough, is not described or even clearly identified until the novel's concluding chapter, and a nagging sense that this narrator keeps us forever at a distance from the novel's main characters.[12]

Unlike "The Man without a Country," however, *Imperium*, which is supposedly constructed from documents and personal testimony, can appear to be a conventional third-person narrative. Still, there is a strong interpretive narrative voice that is best linked to the traitor-patriot Berl, who seeks to highlight the significance of the patriotic treason to come. Accordingly, we are told that Belton's mother's decision to send him to the school run by the learned racist Tiberius Gracchus Leonard in Winchester, Virginia, "vitally affected the destiny of the nation and saved the sun of the Nineteenth Century, proud and glorious, from passing through, near its setting, the blackest and thickest and ugliest clouds of all its journey." When Belton's benefactor, the white newspaper editor V. M. King, advises Belton to appeal to the good side of whites, the narrator portentously tells us: "This is one of the keys to his [Belton's] future life. Remember it." As someone who thinks well of whites, Belton attends the appropriately named Stowe University, and when he is caught spying on a black teacher at a faculty meeting, he pretends to be a chicken thief and makes his escape before he can be identified. The narrator remarks: "Thus again a patriot was mistaken for a chicken thief; and in the South to-day a race that dreams of freedom, equality, and empire, far more than is imagined, is put down as a race of chicken thieves." Iconic images of flags, as in Hale's story, are crucial to the representation of the black patriot, who is described by his white benefactor King as "living ... beneath the American flag, known as the flag of freedom." Consistent with the presentation of Belton's desires for freedom and equality in an American mode, the white president of Stowe University urges him to "play a part in the adjusting of positions between the negro and the Anglo Saxon races of the South," and in so doing become one of America's "true patriots."[13]

But as we follow Belton's history as a patriot, we see him increasingly disillusioned by the virulent racism of Southern whites. He joins with the unemployed blacks of Virginia who "grew to hate a flag that would float in an undisturbed manner over such a condition of affairs." (Griggs regularly uses the nautical "float" in relation to the flag.) In a striking scene conveying the emasculation he experiences while unemployed, Belton disguises himself as a woman in order to spy on white culture, and is very nearly raped. When his wife gives birth to a light-skinned baby, he connects his near-rape to the possible rape or adultery of his wife. His (mis)reading of his wife leads to further alienation from the country, which is again underscored (by Berl as portentous narrator) through the image of the flag: "But ah! what were his feelings in those days toward the flag which he had loved so dearly, which had floated proudly and undisturbed, while color prejudice, upheld by it, sent, as he thought, cruel want with drawn sword to stab his family honor to death." Moving to Cadeville, Louisiana, to assume the presidency of a black university, Belton faces such intense racial hatred that he can only ask "what kind of a country he had entered." In the most melodramatic (and unforgettable) scene of the novel, Belton is lynched after helping a young white woman locate a song in her hymnal, and a Dr. Zackland takes the body to his medical office, where the still-living Belton stabs Zackland in the throat and leaves him dead on the dissecting table. Although Belton is arrested for murder, he gains his freedom through a Supreme Court ruling brought about by the intervention of his long-lost lawyer friend, Bernard. The narrator sums up where Belton is at this point in the novel: "Thus ends the tragic experience that burned all the remaining dross out of Belton's nature and prepared him for the even more terrible ordeal to follow in after years."[4] This is the moment when Belton could easily say, "God d—n the United States!" And indeed his subsequent actions suggest that he'd uttered or thought a version of such sentiments.

I have focused on the struggles of Belton because he is the character who most clearly embodies the Nolan role of traitor-patriot. It is Belton, and not the privileged Bernard (typically read as the novel's most radical figure), who initially embraces the Texas-based secretive black Imperium in Imperio (nation within the nation) and is initially presented as its leader. But *Imperium* presents two black men without a country, Belton and Bernard, and in crucial ways shows how these eventual antagonists are not so very different after all. Griggs had depicted the dark-skinned Belton working in relation to black communities, while the light-skinned Bernard attends Harvard (with the help of his white senator father), wins a congressional election, when the "masses of colored people rallied around his flag,"[15] and falls in love with the dark-skinned Viola Martin, who eventually kills herself rather than marry a light-skinned man whom she fears will "whiten" the black race and contribute to its extinction. Her suicide note charges Bernard to work against miscegenation, and Bernard vows to follow her edict. In short, when the Imperium in Imperio hinted at in Berl's preface is finally introduced, about two-thirds into the novel, both main characters are at a loss. And it is here, in Griggs's account of black patriots and traitors in Texas, that key themes and motifs of Hale's story come to the forefront of the novel.

"The Man without a Country" begins in the immediate wake of the Louisiana Purchase with Burr's apparent plot to take a huge swath of western territory, including land that would eventually become part of the state of Texas. In this respect, Hale's story provides an important prehistory to the Civil War. By thwarting Burr's alleged conspiracy, the United States maintained its hold on southwestern lands, a crucial precondition for the eventual war with Mexico, the admission of Texas as a slave state, and the national crisis over slavery that the Compromise of 1850 failed to resolve. Griggs evokes that history by naming the Louisiana doctor "Zackland" – an allusion to Zachary Taylor, who played a key role in the Mexican war. Even more cutting is the name of the Imperium's capital building, Thomas Jefferson College, which ironically honors the man who set forth the nation's egalitarian ideals only to become the slaveholder who made the purchase that led to the slave state of Texas. Given Hale's strong antislavery position, Texas has an odd place in his story. The dying Nolan is "wild with delight" at the hints he's received that Texas has become part of the Union, and accordingly he gives Texas a central spot in his shrine to the United States. But the specter of Texas ultimately disrupts the story, for the simple reason that, ever since the 1830s, Southerners who dreamed of extending US slavery into the southern Americas had desired the acquisition of Texas as a slave state. As described in "The Man without a Country," naval officials watching over Nolan at the time of Texas annexation wonder "whether they should get hold of Nolan's handsome set of maps, and cut Texas out of it, – from the map of the world and the map of Mexico."[16] As the map imagery makes clear, Texas has been "cut" from Mexico. But Hale doesn't follow up on what seems to be a critique of the way imperialism serves the interests of the slave power, perhaps because he expected the Civil War to bring about the end of slavery and, as a result, change the nature of US global expansionism. Nevertheless, by bringing Texas into the story, indeed into Nolan's shrine, Hale would seem to be doing contradictory and even incoherent cultural work, closing his eyes to the connections between the acquisition of southwestern lands for slaveholders, which he strongly opposed, and the expansionism that he appears to be celebrating through the image of Nolan's eagle "clasping the whole globe."

Because he wrote his novel at a different historical moment, and from a very different perspective, Griggs had a clearer view of Texas's connection to histories of slavery and racism.[17] If the black Imperium were successfully to take back Texas, Griggs seems to be suggesting, the group would to some extent rewrite, or unwrite, the US nationalist history of slavery and empire limned in Hale's story. But there are ambiguities in Griggs's presentation. Is the Imperium conceived as a reformist challenge to the US nation or as a hostile, separatist alternative? In his initial account of the Imperium, Belton tells Bernard of its founding during the post–Revolutionary period by an unnamed, influential black scientist. As celebrated by Belton, this organization, whose "Capitol at Waco was decorated in American flags," is inspired by American Revolutionary ideology and is in large part devoted to revitalizing that ideology in response to the dire developments of the post-Reconstruction moment: the Supreme Court's overturning of the Civil Rights Act of 1875, and the ongoing attacks on and lynchings of blacks. The black members of the Imperium, Belton believes, are patriots who are worth dying for. For that reason, when he recruits the lighter-skinned social insider Bernard to assume the presidency of the Imperium, he subjects him to a bizarre loyalty test, pretending to have turned against the Imperium and urging Bernard to expose the conspiratorial organization or die (to the point where he stages a mock execution). But Bernard resists Belton's threats, and defiantly asserts to his friend, who of course secretly agrees with him, "I think ... those whom you call conspirators are a set of sublime patriots."[18]

At the moment when Bernard assumes the presidency, then, the two friends from very different backgrounds appear to share a vision of the patriotic goals of the organization, even if there is something vague about whether their fundamental loyalty is to the Imperium or the US nation. In his presidential speech, Bernard rises to the occasion, reporting on injustices against blacks with respect to labor, civil rights, education, and other areas, while remarking on problems that had already been exposed through the account of Belton's experiences in the South.[19] The speech takes an even more aggressive turn, however, when Bernard urges blacks to resist volunteering to fight in the Spanish-American War, demanding to know why African Americans should serve a country that "treats us in a manner to make us execrate it." When the Imperium's Congress responds to Bernard's speech with the chant of "War! war! war!," Belton, who had recruited Bernard and experienced whites' anti-black racism on numerous occasions, abruptly has second thoughts about the subversive organization he had hitherto embraced.[20]

Belton may have role-played as a critic of the Imperium when he tested Bernard's mettle for leadership, but in response to Bernard' long speech, he gives one of his own, criticizing his friend and the Imperium while affirming his loyalty to the US nation. He now insists that his experience of dispossession has only added to his love of country, and he makes his case by invoking a key patriotic image that is also central to Nolan's shrine:

> "The Anglo-Saxon has seen the eyes of the Negro following the American eagle in its glorious flight. The eagle has alighted on some mountain top and the poor Negro has been seen climbing up the rugged mountain-side, eager to caress the eagle. When he has attempted to do this the eagle has clawed at his eyes and dug his beak into his heart and has flown away in disdain; and yet, so majestic was its flight that the Negro, with tears in his eyes, and blood dripping from his heart has smiled and shouted 'God save the eagle.'"[21]

Belton concludes his speech by calling on blacks to continue to emigrate to Texas in order to influence the popular vote as a constituent part of the United States – a plan that has some similarities with Hale's 1845 US-nationalistic *How to Conquer Texas, before Texas Conquers Us*, which called on antislavery people to emigrate to Texas in order to create voting majorities that would bring about "the conquest of Texas, by the peaceful weapons of truth, of freedom, of religion, and of right."[22]

Surprisingly, the heretofore warmongering Imperium's Congress unanimously approves Belton's speech, but a new crisis develops when the two leaders secretly meet at night and Bernard, in the manner of Aaron Burr, proposes a more radical plan that would accomplish what Burr failed to accomplish (if this was indeed his intention): the taking of the Southwest. Clearly treasonous, Bernard proposes "A PLAN OF ACTION FOR THE IMPERIUM IN IMPERIO" in which blacks would infiltrate and ultimately subvert the US Navy, build up a stockpile of weapons in Texas, secretly negotiate with foreign countries, and "hoist the flag of the Imperium" at Texas's capital city of Austin, while giving Louisiana to the foreign power that chooses to aid the black rebels (thereby in effect undoing the history of the Louisiana Purchase). Belton responds to Bernard's image of the flag of the Imperium with the flag of the United States: "Our Imperium was organized to secure our rights within the United States. . . . Our efforts have been to wash the flag free of all blots, not to rend it; to burnish every star in the cluster, but to pluck none out."[23] Stars are indeed "plucked out" of the flag in Hale's story because of the mandate that Nolan should know nothing about any developments concerning the United States, such as the addition of new states. Here, Belton is concerned that Bernard's plan would result in states truly being plucked out.

In his 1868 preface, Hale insists that one of his goals in "The Man without a Country" is to develop "love to the nation"; and in his story that love is cast in relation to the flag and other national symbols. Belton's expression of his opposition to Bernard's radical vision brings together a number of Hale's themes about the love of country and its symbolic incarnations. Belton declares to Bernard:

> "I love the Union and I love the South. Soaked as the Old Glory is with my people's tears and stained as it is with their warm blood, I could die as my forefathers did, fighting for its honor and asking no greater boon than Old Glory for my shroud and native soil for my grave. This may appear strange, but love of country is one of the deepest passions in the human bosom. . . . I shall never give up my fight for freedom, but I shall never prove false to the flag."

Like the dying Nolan, Belton looks forward to his end, providing Bernard with instructions for his burial that Bernard will indeed honor. Even when facing execution for his decision to resign from the Imperium, he refuses to back down, putting "duty to country above everything else." Just before being shot on Bernard's order, he offers his last words, which, like Nolan's closing words in his death letter, are meant to provide his epitaph: "Tell posterity . . . that I loved the race to which I belonged and the flag that floated over me; and, being unable to see these objects of my love engage in mortal combat, I went to my God, and now look down upon both from my home in the skies to bless them with my spirit." He is subsequently shot and killed, with the narrator stating in the concluding sentence of the chapter: "On the knoll where he fell he was buried, shrouded in an American flag." Hale's naval officer Danforth remarks on the death of Nolan: "And now it seems the dear old fellow is dead. He has found a home at last, and a country."[24] The same could be said for Belton.

Had *Imperium* ended with this penultimate chapter, we would have a man without a country who, in death, nonetheless has more of a country (and home) than his countrymen. It is the pathos of Belton's patriotic martyrdom that has persuaded many critics that Belton speaks for the historical Griggs. For example, Coleman writes, "In the denouement of the novel, Belton's conservative, perhaps even ultraconservative, remarks and resolutions are cast as the morally correct choice against Bernard's more militant program." But cast by whom? As Coleman goes on to remark, "This is all, of course, presented through an unreliable narrator, whose conservative aphorisms end up sounding like Griggs's personal opinion."[25] But do we know Griggs's personal opinion outside of the dynamic formalistic workings of the novel itself? We need to consider the novel's problematic ending, which, by bringing us back to its deliberately enigmatic beginning, points to Griggs's revisionary reworking of a key aspect of Hale's story.

As in "The Man without a Country," the account of the hero at his final moments is mediated by a character-narrator. The mysterious Berl Trout of the novel's opening now reveals himself as one of the five executioners of Belton. Repentant about his actions, he takes the Belton position that the Imperium should keep in reserve, but not renounce, the option to use violence. He then chooses to do what Belton himself had told Bernard was worthy of death: expose the Imperium. Concerned about the weapons that Bernard and the Imperium have stockpiled, Berl states at the end of his narrative, as he announced at the start: "I decided to prove traitor." But he's a traitor not to the US nation but to the Imperium, even as he upholds the group's reformist aims, offering the hope "that all mankind will join hands and help my poor downtrodden people to secure those rights for which they organized the Imperium, which my betrayal has now destroyed."[26]

Berl appeals to humanity in "the spirit of conservatism" for the rights of blacks, but on the basis of the systemic racism that we've read about in the novel, we should resist linking his naïve optimism directly to Griggs's own views. Might the specter of Bernard's rage also be seen as a mandate for social change? For example, consider the extraordinary public memorial that the Imperium erects in a seat of its Congress for former member Felix Cook, who was attacked and murdered by white racists: "a golden casket containing his heart, which had been raked from the burning embers on the morning following the night of the murderous assault."[27] Those burning embers suggest a still-burning anger. In this respect, I would suggest that Griggs conceives of Berl's conservatism and Bernard's rage in dualistic rather than binary terms. Again, it is worth remembering that it is Belton who recruited Bernard and taught him that betrayal of the Imperium was an act of treason worthy of death. In the end, Belton doesn't categorically reject Bernard's radical plan; instead, he asks for a four-year waiting period. Viewing the two men without a country as one, we can regard Bernard's final remarks on Belton, which are also the novel's final remarks on the US flag, as an effort to revise "The Man without a Country" by suggesting the limits of Hale's patriotic vision for black Americans: "Float on proud flag, while yet you may. Rejoice, oh! ye Anglo-Saxons, yet a little while. . . . [E]xhume Belton's body if you like and tear your flag from around him to keep him from polluting it!"[28] A similar rage against white supremacist US nationalists can be discerned in Griggs's subsequent novel and his other extant writings of the time, even as the image of the Imperium Congress's honoring of the burnt heart in a casket attests to the tortured nature of the sentimental nationalism that will remain a significant part of Griggs's work.

"The Man without a Country" moves from the patriot's renunciation of the United States to an embrace of a US nation including Texas, and in certain respects (however ironically or socio-critically) *Imperium in Imperio* follows that trajectory. In his next novel, the 1901 *Overshadowed*, Griggs ends where Hale's story begins: with his protagonist renouncing the nation and assuming a life at sea. In effect, Griggs's protagonist makes himself into a Nolan-like icon whose oceanic exile parodically revises, even as it pays homage to, Hale's story. Working with and against "The Man without a Country," Griggs limns the importance of (self-)exile to black patriotism. The title of Griggs's second novel, published two years after *Imperium*, may have also drawn from Hale. Consider again the famous description of the eagle in Nolan's shrine: "The stars and stripes were triced up above and around a picture of Washington, and he had painted a majestic eagle, with lightning blazing from his beak and his foot just clasping the whole globe, which his wings overshadowed." *Overshadowed* was published at a time when Hale was celebrating turn-of-the-century US military actions abroad, while Griggs was increasingly concerned about the global destructiveness of the eagle's beak, foot, and wings. It was also written during a time when Hale's "The Man without a Country" had come to be read, with Hale's help, as an unambiguously patriotic championing of the war against Spain. In a new preface written expressly to celebrate the invasion of Cuba, Hale offered a reading of the story that robbed it of its ambiguities and complexities, stating in jingoistic terms:

> [T]he calm historical fact is that we are at war with Spain. In that war it is time again for young men and young women, and old men and old women, for all sorts of people, to understand that the Country is itself an entity. It is a Being. The Lord God of nations has called it into existence, and has placed it here with certain duties in defence of the civilization of the world. It was the intention of this parable ["The Man without a Country"], which describes the life of one man who tried to separate himself from his country, to show how terrible was his mistake.[29]

A short story that could be read as antislavery and as a profound meditation on outcast patriotism was now, with Hale's help, put to the service of imperialism. Hale thus contributed to the process of making his story of nation building into what many have come to regard "as a transparent patriotic parable."[30] Griggs sought to recover the story's tensions and complexities.

In his 1902 novel, *Unfettered*, Griggs's main character, Dorlan Warthell, initially opposes the war with Spain and subsequent invasion of the Philippines as military actions intended to further the agenda of white racist imperialists, only to be persuaded by the woman he loves that the Northerners managing the invasion are doing the laudable "work of leading the Filipinos into all the blessings of higher civilization."[31] But in an earlier November 1900 letter to the *Indianapolis World*, Griggs offered a more jaundiced perspective on US imperialism, blaming McKinley's Republican Party for enslaving "the colored peoples of the Philippines and for worsening the plight of black citizens in the United States." Disillusioned by the continuing erosion of rights for blacks in the Jim Crow South, Griggs invokes US ideals going back to the Revolutionary period in urging blacks to support the Democratic Party under the leadership of William Jennings Bryan, arguing that the Democrats, long-reviled by African Americans, currently advocated "that same political freedom for which Patrick Henry pleaded."[32] And yet by the time of the 1901 *Overshadowed*, Griggs would appear to have little faith that the US nation was capable of living up to such revolutionary ideals.

As with all of Griggs's novels, the plotting of *Overshadowed* is complicated and at times confusing. In order to tease out the Hale dimension, I focus here on the plot-line involving Astral Herndon, the African American who by the end of the novel is a man without a country.

Set in Richmond, Virginia, the novel opens with Astral courting Erma Wysong, the daughter of a white father and black mother. After Astral moves North to pursue his schooling, the white James Lawson, son of a former governor, attempts to seduce Erma, asking one Dolly Smith to serve as his go-between. As it turns out, Dolly, the sister of Erma's dead mother, was years earlier put in a similar position by Lawson's father when he sexually pursued Erma's mother. Shortly after the birth of Erma, Lawson's half-sister, the Smith family falls apart: the mother dies of grief and the father banishes his two daughters from his household. Now seeking revenge on the prominent white family, Dolly goes public with what she knows about the Lawsons' history of sexually exploiting black women, only to be tarred and feathered by a white mob that does not want its city's blood secrets aired in public. Shortly thereafter, she commits suicide. Right around the same time, Erma's younger half-brother, John, experiences his own troubles. Fired from the Bilgal Iron Works because the labor union will not accept blacks as members, he kills the union chief who had earlier declared, "If a foe stands in our way and nothing will dislodge him but death, then he must die." Initially John is not suspected as the killer, but when his conscience bothers him, he confesses to his sister. Inspired by the hopeful tenor of Booker T. Washington's speech on the "Race Problem,"[33] which Washington had recently delivered in Richmond, Erma urges her brother to confess, which he does, with the predictable result: he's sentenced to death. Perhaps also inspired by the speech, several members of Virginia's House of Delegates begin meeting with educated young black women in order to better understand black people, again with the predictable result: one Horace Christian, a politician who had earlier participated in a black lynching, sexually violates Erma's friend Margaret. In a characteristically Griggsian textual moment of dark irony and violence, an honorable white man, the speaker of the house Lanier, gets the intoxicated Christian to dress up in blackface and manages to have him hanged instead of John. So the white lyncher is lynched, allowing John to escape to Florida, where he deliberately commits a crime in order to ease his conscience by serving a prison term. As I say, complicated!

At this point Astral returns to the novel, still in love with Erma. Despite the opposition of aristocratic light-skinned blacks, who are bothered by Astral's dark complexion, the two are married and have a child, Astral Herndon Jr. Seven years later, John appears in their home as an escaped convict, worn down by the Florida prison system, and dies before Erma's eyes. Erma immediately dies in response, and policemen arrive on the scene and assault Astral. He's delirious at first, but he manages to attend Erma's funeral and declares that he cannot allow her to be buried in the racist United States. The good Lanier urges Astral to change his mind, insisting that "with all its faults, this country is by far the greatest on earth." Still, he says he'll support whatever Astral decides to do, and Astral, given the antiblack violence that has been featured throughout the novel as the defining characteristic of the nation, has pretty much reached Nolan's state of mind when he declares "God d——n the United States!" Unlike Nolan, however, who's sentenced to life at sea by a vindictive court, Astral self-sentences himself to an undetermined time at sea. Traveling to New York harbor with his son and the bodies of Erma and her brother, he embarks on a ship whose destination his friends and associates assume is Africa. But that's not his choice; he chooses to live at sea. When "in mid-ocean," "[t]he caskets containing the remains of the two departed were gently lowered into the depths of the ocean and committed to the keeping of the waves." Then, with his son by his side, Astral offers this closing speech:

> "My son, . . . your mother had been buried in these domains, because here there abides no social group in which conditions operate toward the

overshadowing of such elements as are not deemed assimilable. And now, I, Astral Herndon, hereby and forever renounce all citizenship in all lands whatsoever, and constitute myself A CITIZEN OF THE OCEAN, and ordain that this title shall be entailed upon my progeny unto all generations, until such time as the shadows which now envelope the darker races in all lands shall have passed away, away, and away!"[34]

This is a remarkable rewriting of "The Man without a Country," as the protagonist embraces a new form of citizenship that appears to signal disconnection from the US nation. But the large thrust of the novel is to depict the ocean as an extranational space of natural rights that can serve as a model for national reform. For critics invested in Griggs's notion of "The Science of Collective Efficiency," which he elaborated in his 1923 *Guide to Race Greatness*, the seeming individualism of Astral's self-exile has been taken as a mark of his failure.[35] But read in relation to Hale's story, and in relation to Griggs's anger about the condition of African Americans circa 1900, Astral's final speech and decision to remain at sea can be understood as a testament of his patriotism *and* as a form of collective leadership that evinces his conviction about the need for social change.[36] In effect, Astral has made himself into an icon, "A CITIZEN OF THE OCEAN," who, like Hale's iconic "The Man without a Country," has the potential to inspire collectivities. The narrator of Hale's story, Ingham, insists on seeing Nolan as an icon, telling his readers that he offers Nolan's history "by way of showing young Americans of to-day what it is to be A MAN WITHOUT A COUNTRY." It should be noted, then, that by the end of Hale's story, when Nolan has emerged as an inspiring superpatriot, he embraces not the United States but the sea. In a passage that apparently resonated for Griggs, the dying Nolan requests of the naval officers who have him in custody: "Bury me in the sea; it has been my home, and I love it."[37] In the ocean burial that concludes *Overshadowed*, Griggs in effect takes back "The Man without a Country" from those – including Hale – who were using it to legitimate US imperialism, showing that, as Hale implies in his 1868 preface, exile from one's country in the service of a deeper patriotism might not be such a "terrible . . . mistake."

In an act of authorial revision and recuperation, Griggs finds wisdom in a work that Hale at the same historical moment sanctimoniously links to US wars abroad. Hale's story came to serve as war fodder for patriotic Americans during World War I and World War II, becoming even more popular than it had been in the nineteenth century, while Griggs's neglected novels retained their power – in the way of the patriotic outcast – by remaining overshadowed and without a country.

CHAPTER 10

Frederick Douglass in Fiction
From Harriet Beecher Stowe to James McBride

The chapters in this volume take various critical approaches to race and transnationalism in nineteenth-century American literature. But the opening chapter on Toni Morrison suggests that writers themselves are some of the best "theorists" we have on these often interrelated topics. That insight informs a number of other chapters, including this one, which focuses on post-1960s novelists who develop critical perspectives on race and transnationalism with the help of Frederick Douglass.

Frederick Douglass (1818–95) was a serial autobiographer who regularly told stories about his life that would often change depending on the rhetorical occasion. As discussed in Chapter 5, in his 1845 *Narrative of the Life of Frederick Douglass*, Douglass presents his rebellion against the slave-breaker Covey as a form of passive resistance consistent with his Garrisonian moral suasionism. In his 1855 *My Bondage and My Freedom*, however, Douglass presents the same rebellion as involving a more active aggression consistent with his turn to radical abolitionism. His accounts of figures like John Brown, Abraham Lincoln, and his former master Thomas Auld also vary depending on when and where he chooses to discuss these people. Despite such discrepancies, or perhaps precisely because of them, Douglass's autobiographical writings are best viewed as a kind of collage that helps us to better understand his emergence as an abolitionist, his relationship over a long period of time with his white and black family, his attitude toward political action, his thoughts on race, and his friendships with famous white leaders such as Lincoln and Brown. The critic Paul John Eakin observes that autobiographers resemble fiction writers in the way they create personae, develop narratives, and manipulate detail in their pursuit of truths larger than "objective" reconstructions of their life histories.[1] Douglass the autobiographer as a kind of fiction writer is my point of departure for a discussion of Douglass as a writer whose fictions of autobiography inspired later writers to represent him in their fiction. I'm particularly interested in the role Douglass plays in post-1960s novels that address race, transnationalism, and the legacy of John Brown. But first I want to turn to notable examples of nineteenth-century and early twentieth-century novelists who engaged Douglass in their fiction.

Harriet Beecher Stowe greatly admired Douglass's 1845 *Narrative*, and when she began work on *Uncle Tom's Cabin* (1852) she wrote him for additional help in describing a slave plantation. The evidence suggests that Douglass in some ways *is* in *Uncle Tom's Cabin* in the descriptions of the novel's slave plantations. But he's there, as well, in the character of George Harris, the mixed-race black who sounds like Douglass the orator and author of the *Narrative* whenever he points to the contradictions of an American Revolution that failed to produce equality for all. Soon after the publication of *Uncle Tom's Cabin*, Douglass delivered his most famous speech, "What to the Slave Is the Fourth of July?" (1852), which can sound as if it was influenced by George Harris, the very character inspired by Stowe's reading of Douglass. Early in 1853, Douglass published a novella, *The Heroic Slave*, which challenges the racialism of Stowe's novel by depicting a dark-skinned man who, unlike Stowe's dark-skinned Uncle Tom, uses violence to oppose slavery. In response, Stowe puts a different Douglass in her next antislavery novel, the 1856 *Dred*. Learning from *The Heroic Slave*, she creates a dark-skinned rebel, Dred, modeled more on Nat Turner than Douglass, who violently resists slavery from his refuge in the Great Dismal Swamp. Because Stowe ultimately doesn't approve of violence, she includes a scene in which a Christian slave named Milly tells Dred that violence goes against God's wishes. At an antislavery meeting in 1852, Douglass and Sojourner Truth had a widely publicized exchange on just this topic, with Douglass calling for violent resistance against the slave power, while Sojourner Truth invoked the Bible to argue against such violence. By importing that exchange into her novel, Stowe makes her black rebel, at least in this scene, into a version of the Douglass who needs to pay more attention to the religious discourse of Truth (and Stowe). Still, because the radical-abolitionist Douglass had such an impact on her political imagination, Stowe conceives of the dark-skinned Dred as truly revolutionary.[2]

Stowe refers to Douglass just once by name in her first two novels, mentioning Douglass and Samuel Ward as examples of black editors who "have risen to highly respectable stations in society." That reference, which comes in the final chapter of *Uncle Tom's Cabin*, challenges the novel's Liberian colonizationist ending by suggesting that African Americans have a role to play in the United States. Such a

suggestion anticipates the more complex ending of *Dred*, which concludes with the principle black characters choosing between emigration
and migration, with some moving to a black agricultural colony in
Canada and others making their way to New York City. A subscriber
to *Frederick Douglass' Paper*, Stowe had read about blacks' dissatisfac-
tion with the colonizationist ending of *Uncle Tom's Cabin*, and she
publicly renounced colonizationism in 1853. But with her remarks on
the US-based editor Douglass at the end of *Uncle Tom's Cabin*, she
reveals that she had already renounced the movement in 1852.[3]

References to Douglass can be found in other nineteenth-century
novels, but, as in Stowe, they're mostly brief. Still, given Douglass's status
in the culture, such instances helped authors to think through their
perspectives on race and transnationalism. In Maria Amparo Ruiz de
Burton's 1872 *Who Would Have Thought It?*, a fascinating novel about a
girl who initially looks black to the eye but turns out to be, like Ruiz de
Burton herself, from an aristocratic Mexican family of "pure Spanish
blood," the author explores what recent critics call comparative racialization. Working against the white-black binary, Ruiz de Burton presents
Mexican whiteness in relation to what Jesse Alemán terms "the vulgar
Anglo-Saxonism of the novel's Northerners," as well as against "Native,
Irish, and African Americans, who all remain on the racialized margins of
white Mexican privilege." At a time when Ruiz de Burton felt that white
Mexican Americans of the upper classes were viewed as second-class
citizens who could be lumped together with African Americans, she inserts
near the end of her novel a pamphlet by a "vulgar" Anglo-Saxon, one Beau
Cackle, that attacks President Grant for having "dared to slight a colored
gentleman, no less distinguished a citizen of African descent than Mr. Fred.
Douglass. Yes, this monster of tyranny, this horrible usurper ... this
Ulysses Grant, not only did not invite Mr. Fred. Douglass to a diplomatic
dinner, but he did not order to be destroyed a steamer in which Mr.
Douglass was refused a seat at the dinner-table." For committing this
"heinous" crime, Grant, according to Cackle, who cares not a whit about
African Americans, should be impeached.[4] Ruiz de Burton's ironic point is
that a seeming concern for African Americans, whom she regards as
inferior to Mexican elites, can help to shore up the power of Northern
whites and further marginalize Mexican Americans. Her novel can seem
reactionary and even mean-spirited in the way that it celebrates Mexican-
American whiteness at the expense of blacks and other white ethnics. Still,
with the help of Cackle's false sympathy for Douglass, Ruiz de Burton
makes a critical intervention into the nation's racial politics during the

Reconstruction period by developing comparative and hemispheric perspectives on post–Civil War racial formations.

Douglass has a similarly small but important place in Sutton Griggs's *The Hindered Hand* (1905). The black nationalist Griggs brings Douglass into his novel in order to warn blacks about the dangers of straying from their racial identity, especially at a time when white supremacists like Thomas Dixon are engaged in what Griggs, in the novel's appendix, calls the "cultivation of race hatreds." Was the mixed-race Douglass similarly exhibiting race hatred when he married the white woman Helen Pitts in 1884? That is the suggestion of the main female character of *The Hindered Hand*, a mixed-race woman named Tiara, who initially turns against Ensal Elwood, the black man who courts her, when he dubs her "Tiara Douglass." Rejecting that sobriquet out of hand, she states, "I cannot endure the name Douglass." She then challenges Ensal: "I perceive that you are an admirer of Frederick Douglass. Do you approve of his marriage to a white woman?" That question pushes him to rethink his assumptions about Douglass, and by the end of the novel Ensal embraces his blackness, marries Tiara, and journeys with her to Africa. In the appendix, Griggs speaks in his own voice about Douglass: "The marriage of Frederick Douglass to a white woman created a great gulf between himself and his people, and it is said that so great was the alienation that Mr. Douglass was never afterwards the orator that he had been."[5] Rejecting what he regards as the assimilationism of Douglass, Griggs insists on the importance of black racial pride to the struggle against the Dixons of the post-Reconstruction nation.

Contra Griggs, other instances of Douglass in novels of the first half of the twentieth century are mostly passing references that suggest writers' admiration for Douglass as one of the nation's great African American leaders. In Pauline Hopkins's *Contending Forces* (1900), for instance, the narrator refers to "the brilliant genius of a Frederick Douglass," and in James Weldon Johnson's *The Autobiography of an Ex-Colored Man* (1912), the first-person narrator calls Douglass one of his "heroes" and describes how "pictures of Frederick Douglass" grace the black music club he regularly visits. A picture of Douglass has a more prominent place in Ralph Ellison's *Invisible Man* (1952). When the unnamed first-person narrator joins the Brotherhood (i.e., the Communist Party), the leader, Brother Tarp, gives him a portrait of the "great man" and asks him what he knows about Douglass. The narrator responds, "Not much. My grandfather used to tell me about him though." The critic David Messmer writes about this moment: "Ironically, despite all of his education and familiarity with other prominent African American authors, Ellison's narrator is only aware of Douglass through oral and visual histories." But the narrator's relative ignorance makes good sense given that at the time of the setting of the novel virtually nothing by Douglass was in print. That would change during the 1950s when the Marxist scholar Philip Foner, who would have understood the communist Tarp's enthusiasm for Douglass, brought out his pathbreaking five-volume edition of Douglass's writings. That edition, however, failed to include one important group of Douglass's writings: his autobiographies.[6] Those autobiographies were reprinted during the 1960s, which is why Douglass began to appear in more substantial ways in fiction after the 1960s.

Updike, Race, and the 1960s

During his lifetime, Douglass was known as a great orator and not as the author of autobiographies. His best-known autobiography, the 1845 *Narrative*, sold around ten thousand copies and went out of print in the early 1850s. His second autobiography, the 1855 *My Bondage and My Freedom*, sold less than that and went out of print within a few years. His third autography, *Life and Times of Frederick Douglass*, published in 1881 and revised in 1892, was a publishing disaster and may have sold fewer than a thousand copies. That, too, went out of print. In 1941 the small publisher Pathway Press brought out an edition of the six-hundred-page *Life and Times*. But the publishing event that helped to create Douglass the autobiographer that we know today was the inclusion of his 1845 *Narrative* in the newly inaugurated John Harvard Library Series of great American books in 1960. Not surprisingly, when the *Narrative* appeared in this prestigious series after being out of print for over a hundred years, it found immediate traction at the time of the Civil Rights Movement. Doubleday published its own trade edition in 1961; a year after that, Collier Books brought out an edition of Douglass's 1881/1892 *Life and Times*; and in 1967 the *New York Times*'s Arno Press reissued the 1855 *My Bondage and My Freedom*, which had also been out of print for over a hundred years. Douglass was suddenly everywhere in the popular print culture of the 1960s, including being featured on the cover of the November 22, 1968, *Life Magazine*. Around this time, the United States Postal Service issued a Douglass stamp, and bridges, roads, and schools were given his name. Perhaps more importantly, during the 1960s many civil rights leaders turned to Douglass's autobiographies to proclaim that he was one of the great freedom fighters in American history, with Martin

Luther King Jr. presenting his own activism as in the tradition of Douglass. There were some dissenters. Malcolm X, for instance, declared that Douglass wasn't radical or violent enough and was too much the white accommodationist.[7] But my point is that Douglass during the 1960s as a figure in his autobiographies was once again a figure in US culture. It is not all that surprising, then, that in the first major instance of Douglass in fiction after the recovery and (really) rediscovery of his autobiographies, we get not Douglass himself as a fictional character in a historical novel set in the nineteenth century, but a Douglass autobiography as it has an impact on American lives during the 1960s. Indeed, one of the major "characters" in John Updike's 1971 *Rabbit Redux* is a Douglass autobiography.

Set in the late 1960s at the height of the Civil Rights Movement, *Rabbit Redux* is the second novel in Updike's "Rabbit" tetralogy, which he began in 1959 with *Rabbit, Run* and concluded in 1990 with *Rabbit at Rest*.[8] I am not alone in observing that the four novels about Harry "Rabbit" Angstrom of small-town Pennsylvania are engaged with race. In the first novel of the series, *Rabbit, Run*, the white Rabbit Angstrom, a former high school basketball star, joins a group of white teenagers playing basketball; the series ends in *Rabbit at Rest* with Rabbit dying of a heart attack while playing basketball with black men in a black neighborhood in Sarasota. Along the way, Rabbit regularly expresses his anxieties about blacks, Asians, and other minorities, while at the same time appearing to be something of a hipster in rejecting small town or suburban conformity.[9] In the 1971 *Rabbit Redux*, Rabbit, who is separated from his wife, signals that rejection by first inviting into his home a young white woman, Jill, who has run away from her wealthy family in suburban Connecticut. Rabbit subsequently takes in Jill's new acquaintance, a black radical named Skeeter, recently back from Vietnam, who carries around with him a copy of Douglass's 1881/1892 *Life and Times*. Unlike Malcolm X, Skeeter regards Douglass as a radical.

In *Rabbit Redux*, Douglass's autobiographies are registered as living, influential presences in 1960s culture.[10] And Douglass's words are hardly presented as familiar or domesticated in the way of canonical writing; they're incendiary, as we see in a dramatic moment at Rabbit's house when Skeeter decides to hold "a kind of seminar, about Afro-American history." During this group meeting, consisting of Skeeter, Jill, Rabbit, and Nelson (Rabbit's teenage son), the only black writer actually quoted is Douglass, whose words, at Skeeter's coercive urging, Rabbit reads out loud from Skeeter's marked-up copy of *Life and Times*. A version of the first passage that Skeeter has Rabbit read to the group can be found in all three of

Douglass's autobiographies. It's the scene when Douglass as a boy secretly watches his Aunt Esther being punished by the slave owner Aaron Anthony, who is furious with his attractive black woman slave for consorting with the slave Ned Roberts. Anthony disrobes Esther and whips her. This is part of what Rabbit reads to the group: "*Esther's wrists were firmly tied, and the twisted rope was fastened to a strong iron staple in a heavy wooden beam above, near the fireplace. Here she stood on a bench, her arms tightly drawn above her head. Her back and shoulders were perfectly bare. Behind her stood old master, cowhide in hand, pursuing his barbarous work with all manner of harsh, coarse, and tantalizing epithets.*"[11] The master's whip has a phallic dimension, and Updike, well before critics began to write on the topic, clearly understands that there is something pornographic about this recurring scene in Douglass's three major autobiographies.[12] As Rabbit reads this passage to Skeeter, Jill, and his son, the drugged-up Skeeter takes out his anger about the past violation of the black woman by violating the white woman, ripping Jill's clothes and viciously insulting her. It's a sad and angry moment in which Updike conveys the black character's Douglass-inflected rage while also perhaps playing to white phobia about black rage.

The scene continues with Skeeter demanding that Rabbit read from one of the most famous passages in all of Douglass's autobiographies: the moment when the teenage Douglass fights back against the slave-breaker Covey. Again, Skeeter aggressively directs him to a marked-up page in his copy of *Life and Times*, and this is part of what Rabbit reads to the group: "*The fighting madness had come upon me, and I found my strong fingers firmly attached to the throat of the tyrant* [the slave-breaker Covey]. . . . *I felt supple as a cat, and was ready for him at every turn. Every blow of his was parried, though I dealt no blows in return . . . I flung him on the ground several times when he meant to have hurled me there. I held him so firmly by the throat that his blood followed my nails. He held me, and I held him.*" As Rabbit reads from this famous scene, Skeeter begins to take off his clothes, and when Rabbit gets to the moment when Douglass declares that he has achieved "*a resurrection from the dark and pestiferous tomb of slavery, to the heaven of comparative freedom,*" Skeeter ejaculates onto Rabbit's sofa. All along, Rabbit has been obsessed with Skeeter's sexuality, so in the context of their developing relationship there's something appropriate about the exhibitionism and violation attending the reading. It's also appropriate that both passages that Skeeter prompts Rabbit to read are about interracial violence, though what's particularly interesting about Douglass's description of his rebellion against Covey is the emphasis on male physical intimacy across the color line. "*He held me, and I held him*," Douglass writes about himself and Covey wrestling on the ground. Such intimacy both intrigues and terrifies Rabbit, who watches Skeeter masturbate, and then drops "the book as if hot" and runs upstairs. "He has escaped. Narrowly," he thinks. But from what? As Updike presents the scene, and as the novel develops, Rabbit has escaped from his attraction to Skeeter, the man that this white outsider or hipster both identifies with and fears. Near the end of the novel, Rabbit faces down neighbors who demand that Skeeter leave at once, and as a result Rabbit loses his house: the neighbors set it afire and Jill dies in the blaze. Skeeter flees with the help of Rabbit, who drives him out of town. In their final scene together, Rabbit extends his hand in farewell, and Skeeter spits into the center of his palm. Initially shocked by this second ejaculatory moment, Rabbit "chooses to take the gesture as a blessing."[13]

In many respects, Updike's novel is of a piece with Norman Mailer's 1957 "The White Negro," William Styron's 1967 *The Confessions of Nat Turner*, and Saul Bellow's 1970 *Mr. Sammler's Planet* – works by white men obsessed with the supposed hypersexuality of black men.[14] But I find Updike's novel more satisfying and illuminating than those other writings, in part because he gives Douglass a voice in the 1960s, having him in effect speak to characters across a century about race in America, and in part because Updike (whatever his own racial anxieties) is keenly interested in white male racial anxieties as a topic for exploration in his fiction. Updike also conveys something more complex about black anger. Whatever we, or Updike, think of Skeeter, he is a character who takes pride in his blackness and who is not easily appropriated in the way of Mailer's "White Negro." In *Rabbit Redux*, Updike, with the help of Douglass's final autobiography, brings to life and critically engages the racial confusions, tensions, anxieties, and promises of the 1960s at the moment when Douglass's autobiographies were coming back into print and contributing to conversations about just these issues. Updike is perceptive about the potency of Douglass's insights into race in the United States, and oddly enough Douglass in this novel as a textual presence is perceptive about the black anger and white anxiety characterizing the 1960s.

There are other notable instances of Douglass in the 1970s American fiction. In Ishmael Reed's 1976 *Flight to Canada*, Douglass is mentioned early on as part of a mélange of historical and invented characters, and Raven, the novel's main character, learns to read by the sort of trickery reminiscent of Douglass in his autobiographies. Octavia Butler's 1979 *Kindred*, about black time travelers moving back and forth between 1970s Los Angeles and antebellum Maryland, mentions Douglass on several occasions, but more importantly the novel's pre–Civil War setting on Maryland's Eastern Shore was probably shaped by Butler's reading of Douglass's autobiographies. (Douglass was born and raised on the Eastern Shore.) But I want now to jump forward chronologically to recent novels that more fully engage Douglass. First I discuss four novels that address the transnational Douglass, and then I turn to three novels that reimagine the Douglass who had a long interracial friendship with the militant John Brown. Those novels in particular point to the unfinished work not just of the American Revolution and the Civil War but of Douglass himself.

Transnationalism: Ghosh, Adichie, McCann, Bradbury

Douglass spent his childhood and teenage years as a slave on Maryland's Eastern Shore and in Baltimore. It was only after the publication of the 1845 *Narrative* that he began to emerge as a transatlantic reformer and global citizen. The Indian-Bengali writer Amitav Ghosh and the Nigerian writer Chimamanda Ngozi Adichie present even the young Douglass as significantly connected to the larger world by focusing on what could be called the circulatory routes of the enslaved Douglass and his *Narrative*.

In *Sea of Poppies* (2008), the first novel of his *Ibis* trilogy, Ghosh works in part as a theorist, implicitly taking on Paul Gilroy's *The Black Atlantic* (1993), which had called for a reimagining of the history of slavery through the "chronotopes" of slave ships moving "across the spaces between Europe, America, Africa, and the Caribbean." In the manner of the comparative racialization of *Who Would Have Thought It?*, Ghosh enlarges Gilroy's transatlantic perspective on slavery to include the Asian coolies who were being transported to the British colony Mauritius via the Indian Ocean and the Pacific in the wake of Britain's Slavery Abolition Act of 1833. Douglass figures in all of this through the character of Zachary Reid, the second mate of the *Ibis*, a former slave ship that has been retrofitted in a Baltimore shipyard in order to meet the new demand for coolies. Like Douglass, Reid is a black from Baltimore, and like Douglass he has been working at William and George Gardner's shipyard in Fell's Point. Presented at the opening of the novel as having recently arrived in Calcutta in 1838, the year Douglass escaped from slavery, Reid, who despite being the light-skinned son of a freedwoman in Baltimore, can be thought of as a stand-in for Douglass, particularly in the way he is deployed, as Jacob Crane remarks, "as a surrogate throughout the novel for black Atlantic memory."[15]

But Douglass is also central to Reid's own memory as he recalls, shortly after his arrival in Calcutta, his last day at the Gardners' shipyard. That memory is the one direct reference to Douglass:

> He [Zachary Reid] saw again a face with a burst eyeball, the scalp torn open when a handspike had landed, the dark skin slick with blood. He remembered as if it were happening again, the encirclement of Freddy Douglass, set upon by four white carpenters; he remembered the howls, 'Kill him, kill the damned nigger, knock his brains out'; he remembered how he and the other men of colour, all free, unlike Freddy, had held back, their hands stayed by fear. And he remembered, too, Freddy's voice afterwards, not reproaching them for their failure to come to his defence, but urging them to leave, scatter: 'It's about jobs; the whites won't work with you, freeman or slave: keeping you out is their way of saving their bread.' That was when Zachary had decided to quit the shipyard and seek a berth on a ship's crew.

Reid's memory draws on a moment in Douglass's *Narrative* that dramatizes the tensions between black slaves and white ethnics in 1830s Baltimore, but Ghosh makes two significant changes. He calls Douglass "Freddy Douglass," when at the time he was Frederick Bailey. (Douglass changed his name after his escape in September 1838.) Perhaps Ghosh got sloppy with details, or, more likely, he wanted to make clear to readers who might not know the name Frederick Bailey that it was Douglass who had an impact on Reid (and on Ghosh's conception of Reid). Ghosh also adds to the account something that never happened: Bailey/Douglass speaking directly to blacks to urge them to "scatter." Douglass thus becomes the direct inspiration for Reid in all sorts of ways, including his decision to join the *Ibis* in Baltimore. But Douglass has an impact on Reid beyond his decision to flee Baltimore. However implicated Reid becomes in British imperial practices and the hierarchies of the coolie ship, he remains a sympathetic character who keeps his distance from his British plantation-owner employers. As he remarks to one such employer who extolls slavery and indentured labor as the foundations of British freedom: "Well sir, if slavery is freedom then I'm glad I don't have to make a meal of it. Whips and chains are not much to my taste."[16] Not surprisingly, Reid is saved from certain death near the end of the novel by a sympathetic Asian coolie.

Douglass also has a key role in Chimamanda Ngozi Adichie's 2006 *Half of a Yellow Sun*, a novel about the Nigerian Civil War of 1967–70, but as in Updike's *Rabbit Redux*, he appears in the novel not as a person but as an autobiographical text. Ghosh works with the Douglass who helps to revise and enlarge conceptions of the Black Atlantic; Adichie presents a Douglass who achieves a global impact by virtue of his influential publications, especially the *Narrative*, which by the late 1960s has circulated to Africa. In *Half of a Yellow Sun*, the *Narrative* has an especially profound impact on the character Ugwu, who at the start of the novel is an uneducated village boy serving as a house servant to a Nigerian intellectual, but by the time of the war is something of an intellectual who, like his master, aligns himself with the Republic of Biafra. Still, Ugwu sees brutalities on both sides, and at a training camp for Biafran soldiers he vows to bear witness as a writer. As he searches "for bits of paper on which he could write down what he did from day to day," he discovers a copy of Douglass's *Narrative*, which entrances him. Adichie describes this magical moment: "He sat on the floor and read. He finished it in two days and started again, rolling the words round his tongue, memorizing some sentences." Two of the sentences he memorizes, from chapters 2 and 3, become conflated in his memory as a single passage: "*The slaves became as fearful of the tar as of the lash. They find less difficulty from the want of beds, than from the want of time to sleep.*"[17] This is the only passage (or set of sentences) quoted from the *Narrative*, and it's notable that Ugwu responds to parts of the autobiography that tend to be ignored. Unlike in *Rabbit Redux*, the quoted language is not about Douglass celebrating his active heroic self; the sentences are from communal moments when Douglass writes about his fellow slaves. For the community-minded Ugwu, the passage that he creates in memory is the essential Douglass, and it is the passage that inspires his own writing about the Nigerian-Biafran war.

Near the end of the novel, after Nigeria has reasserted its control by starving and killing Biafrans, Ugwu begins his history of the war. He discusses his ambitions with Richard Churchill, a white British expatriate who has his own aspirations to write such a history. Lying on a hospital bed after being wounded during an attack, Ugwu initiates the conversation with Churchill by telling him about his discovery:

> "I found a book at our camp. I was so sad and angry for the writer."
> "What book was it?"
> "The autobiography of a black American called Frederick Douglass."
> Mister Richard wrote something down. "I shall use this anecdote in my book."

As the exchange suggests, Richard has a kind of bloodsucker quality, taking in information as he works on his book. But in the end, it is Ugwu who produces the book on the civil war, in part because Richard comes to recognize, once he reads from Ugwu's manuscript, that he lacks the perspective of a true insider. When Richard expresses his admiration to

Ugwu, Ugwu offers this modest response: "It will be part of a big book. It will take me many more years to finish it and I will call it 'Narrative of the Life of a Country.'"[18] Given the inspiration for his writing, Ugwu suggests a revised understanding of Douglass's *Narrative of the Life of Frederick Douglass* as more communal than individualist, or else he's suggesting a willful reconceptualization of the *Narrative* as it informs his own writing. Shortly after being released from the hospital, Ugwu searches for his copy of the *Narrative*, which he concludes was burnt by the Nigerian army. But Douglass lives on in his memory, and it is Douglass who inspires him to write and eventually complete his Nigerian narrative, which is excerpted in eight short sections over the course of the novel.

For both Adichie and Ghosh, the *Narrative* is the essential Douglass text, and the man who was a slave in Maryland is the essential Douglass. But Douglass's life changed dramatically shortly after the publication of the 1845 *Narrative* when, in order to escape from fugitive slave hunters, he spent eighteen months in Ireland and Britain. That time abroad, during which his freedom was purchased by British abolitionists, led to a more cosmopolitan, radical, and independent Douglass, and the emergence of that Douglass is the subject of two recent novels: Richard Bradbury's *Riversmeet* (2007) and Colum McCann's *Transatlantic* (2013). In addition to imaginatively engaging Douglass's post-*Narrative* career, Bradbury and McCann point to the significance of US-Irish relations for nineteenth-century transatlantic studies.

To take up the better-known novel first: In *Transatlantic*, the National Book Award winner and Irish-American writer McCann tells the interrelated stories of Douglass's visit to Ireland and Britain during 1845–47; the first nonstop transatlantic flight in 1919; and former Maine senator George Mitchell's successful efforts to negotiate peace between Ireland and England in 1998. The section on Douglass comes early in the novel. In terms of historical fact, Douglass began his nearly two-year antislavery tour in the city of Dublin. Douglass at the time was still quite young (in his late twenties). Among the noteworthy details that we get in McCann's portrait of Douglass abroad is that he carries around with him a set of barbells and secretly works out in order to present himself as muscular and trim. (Douglass enjoyed lifting weights, though it's not clear that he actually took barbells on his transatlantic voyage.) McCann also nicely captures Douglass's excitement at finding himself celebrated abroad as an antislavery speaker, along with his desire to keep himself independent of those white abolitionists who regard him "as an elaborate poodle on a leash."[19]

The focus of McCann's attention, though, is on Douglass's growing realization that the potato blight is taking a toll on the Irish. Such a realization becomes central to the development of his transatlantic vision of human suffering and exploitation. For much of the Douglass section, the black abolitionist insists that the Irish poor are better off than American slaves, and that all the Irish have to do to solve their problems is cut back on their drinking and commit themselves to uplift. "The Irish had little or no order about themselves," Douglass concludes after viewing "staggering" filth, women in "less than rags," and "human waste slushed down the gutter." But as the sufferings of the Irish people intensify and as "rumors of a potato blight" seem increasingly on the mark, Douglass begins to feel uncertain about his assumption that US slaves belong in a special category apart from the Irish poor. As he loses confidence in this assumption, he tells himself: "The Irish were poor, but not enslaved. He had come here [to Ireland] to hack away at the ropes that held American slavery in place. Sometimes it withered him just to keep his mind steady."[20] He becomes especially unsteady when a starving Irish woman asks him to help her baby, who is clearly dead. Shocked, Douglass gives her money and quickly walks away, but later he asks an acquaintance to find the woman in order to give her baby a proper burial. McCann does not depict a thoroughly trans-formed Douglass, but by the end of his travels through Ireland Douglass is acutely aware that the blight is worsening and that the Irish poor are in need of assistance. As a result, Douglass offers his moral support when a poor Dublin woman, a hopeful emigrant, boards a ship for America.

In *Transatlantic*, McCann gives dramatic life to the insight that the Douglass who would return to the United States in 1847 and then have such an impact as a reformer was, in a sense, born in Ireland. A similar recognition, or argument, informs British writer Richard Bradbury's *Riversmeet*. In a scholarly article published in 1999, eight years before he published the novel, Bradbury asks what would have happened if Douglass during his Irish and British tour met the British black activist William Cuffay, a Chartist who regarded wage slavery and chattel slavery as similar forms of slavery. In history, Douglass and Cuffay apparently never met; in Bradbury's novel, Cuffay meets Douglass in 1846 and attempts to convince him of the shared oppression of Irish peasants, the British working class, and US slaves. At the center of the novel are Douglass's long conversations with Cuffay, reported both in Douglass's letters home to his wife, Anna, and in his diary entries (the letters and entries are all fictional). In one such conversation, Douglass tells Cuffay that "I have seen the awful poverty of the Irish for myself, and still I know that they do not live in bondage!"

Cuffay, described as "a small black man," responds, "Indeed, Mr. Douglass, are you so sure of that?" For a while Douglass maintains his certainty about the differences between the enslaved and the impoverished, but his position comes close to changing after Cuffay takes him on a tour of blighted areas of London. Douglass confesses to his diary: "[M]y hands are still shaking. . . . For my understandings of the world, the views that I have held close to since my escape from slavery and more especially since I took up the cause of my brothers and sisters in bondage, have been shaken to the core." Though he remains resistant to a complete conversion to Cuffay's point of view, he moves closer to seeing what Cuffay describes as "the analogy to be drawn between the lives of the poor here [in Britain] and the lives of the slaves in America."[21] And after Cuffay uses violence to save Douglass from a violent attack, Douglass begins to abandon his commitment to moral suasion. The novel has a lot of detail, sometimes a bit tedious, about Douglass's interactions with Cuffay, and it's ultimately informed by the desire of a Marxist scholar to imagine a Douglass who views the world primarily in terms of an international class struggle. Still, *Riversmeet* is a bold work that, like *Transatlantic*, helps us to better understand the Douglass who, by the time of his return to the United States in April 1847, had achieved a transatlantic vision of the challenges of social reform.

John Brown: Banks, Hill, Rhodes, McBride

As McCann and Bradbury both illustrate in their fictions, Douglass's trip to Britain and Ireland had radicalized him. In 1850, three years after his return, Douglass renounced William Lloyd Garrison's nonviolent approach to antislavery and aligned himself with the radical abolitionists Gerrit Smith and John Brown. John Stauffer argues that Douglass forged "interracial bonds of friendship and alliance" with these men "that were unprecedented in their own time and were probably not duplicated until well into the twentieth century."[22] Douglass's relationship with Brown, the man willing to use violence to create a multiracial democracy in the United States, will be the focus of the remainder of this chapter. In post-1960s novels that feature Brown and Douglass, writers look back to the mid-nineteenth century to consider what can only be taken as the unfulfilled promises of this interracial friendship. Whatever their perspective on the friendship – Russell Banks and Lawrence Hill see it as inspirational, while James McBride sees it as fundamentally flawed – their novels are impressive acts of historical imagination and critical thinking about race in America.

Before turning to the novels, it would be useful to review some of the known facts about the Douglass-Brown relationship. The men first met at Brown's house in Springfield, Massachusetts, in 1848. At that meeting, Brown told Douglass about his plan to end slavery through guerilla warfare in the Alleghany Mountains. Douglass found the plan intriguing, and he remained supportive of Brown when, during the mid-1850s, Brown and his sons slaughtered proslavery settlers in the Kansas Territory. In 1858 Brown stayed with Douglass for several weeks in his Rochester home as he wrote a Provisional Constitution for an America without slavery; Brown subsequently shared that constitution with antislavery whites and blacks in Chatham, Ontario. Brown and Douglass saw each other for the last time early in 1859, when the two men secretly met at a quarry in Chambersburg, Pennsylvania. Douglass brought along his black friend Shields Green, and Brown for the first time told Douglass about his plot to attack the federal arsenal at Harpers Ferry. According to Douglass in his 1881 *Life and Times*, he was taken aback by Brown's proposal, declaring that Brown would be entering a "steel trap." Thus he decides not to participate, even though Shields Green says at the end of the meeting, "I b'leve I'll go wid de ole man."[23] Green became one of the fifteen men in the group of twenty-two who died during or after the October 1859 attack; Brown was hanged in December. Because of his association with Brown, Douglass was forced to flee to England to avoid being arrested as an accomplice. As Douglass came to realize, the attack that he had initially regarded as foolhardy played a crucial role in pushing many Northerners to conceive of the Civil War as a war of emancipation. Twenty-two years after the attack, in 1881, Douglass delivered a laudatory speech on Brown at Storer College at Harpers Ferry. He then offered his fullest account of Brown in his 1881/1892 *Life and Times*.

Douglass's relationship with Brown and his connection to Harpers Ferry are the subjects of two well-received American novels: Russell Banks's 1998 *Cloudsplitter*, which was a finalist for the Pulitzer Prize, and James McBride's 2013 *The Good Lord Bird*, which won the National Book Award. I will focus on these two novels, but along the way I'm going to discuss the African American writer Jewell Rhodes's *Douglass' Women* (2002), which addresses issues of gender, and black Canadian writer Lawrence Hill's *Any Known Blood* (1997), which offers a hemispheric (North American) perspective on Brown's attack on Harpers Ferry. Canada has a place in Banks's and McBride's novels, as well.

Both Banks's *Cloudsplitter* and McBride's *The Good Lord Bird* tell the John Brown story somewhat slant. *Cloudsplitter*, a massive eight-hundred-page novel, is a first-person narrative told by Brown's third son, Owen

Brown, who in historical fact participated in the attack on Harpers Ferry and managed to survive. In the novel, Owen relates his father's history to the assistant of a Columbia University historian, Oswald Garrison Villard, who actually did publish an acclaimed biography of John Brown in 1910. Much of the novel focuses on John Brown's emerging antislavery radicalism, but at the novel's emotional and thematic core is the story of Owen Brown's attraction to the black wife of one of his father's black associates. At a key moment in the novel, Owen hands that man a loaded gun that is ready to go off, and the man is killed "accidentally." Banks in some respects has Updike's interest in exploring interracial desire, though because the desire is only on Owen's side, the narrator becomes implicated in white males' assumptions of mastery over black female bodies. Owen's eventual decision to join his father in the attack on Harpers Ferry speaks to his effort to expiate the guilt that ultimately informs his story.

McBride's *The Good Lord Bird* works with a very different, comic tone. As with *Cloudsplitter*, the novel has a retrospective narrator, who in this case focuses mainly on John Brown's mid-1850s Kansas years and the events leading to the October 1859 attack on Harpers Ferry. The story is told by one Henry Shackleford, whose memoir, we are informed in the novel's preface, has recently been rediscovered. At the beginning of the novel, Henry is a twelve-year-old slave in the Kansas Territory who meets John Brown when Henry's father is killed at a tavern just as Brown walks through the door. Henry is wearing a potato sack, which Brown mistakes for a dress. Thinking Henry is a girl, Brown offers the terrified young slave protection; and Henry, perhaps because he's terrified, or perhaps because he simply enjoys crossdressing, chooses to remain in the guise of a girl for the rest of the novel. Henry, now known as both Henrietta and "Little Onion" (the nickname Brown gives him), tells an over-the-top story about traveling with the Brown family from the time of their violent antislavery activities in the Kansas-Nebraska territories to the 1859 raid on Harpers Ferry. In the novel, McBride works with Henry's (Henrietta's/Little Onion's) vernacular voice to demythologize Brown while highlighting the day-to-day violence attending the battle over slavery. Henry, or Henrietta, or Little Onion (I'll go with the gender-neutral "Little Onion" for the rest of the chapter) initially finds Brown frightening but eventually comes to view his radicalism so sympathetically that Little Onion wonders why other blacks aren't supporting him. Banks, a white writer, explores white guilt and white privilege; McBride, a black writer, presses the case for blacks to actively resist racial injustice.

Douglass has an important place in both novels, and both novels limit him to two scenes: a scene of introduction, and then a second scene that draws on Douglass's account in *Life and Times* of his secret meeting with Brown at the Chambersburg quarry. In my view, McBride does a better job with the scene of introduction and Banks has more profound things to say about the decision Douglass made at Chambersburg not to participate in the attack. The novels' introductory scenes give a good sense of the authors' different approaches to their historical material.

In Banks's *Cloudsplitter*, Douglass doesn't actually appear until the midpoint of the novel, after the opening four-hundred-page account of Brown's emergence as a radical abolitionist. The moment that Banks uses to introduce Douglass is Owen Brown's recollection of Douglass's first visit to Brown and his family in Springfield, Massachusetts, in 1848. Brown at this meeting, both in history and in *Cloudsplitter*, shares with Douglass his plan for what he calls a "Subterranean Passway." Briefly, Brown's revolutionary idea, as Banks elaborates, is to establish a military force of blacks and whites in the Allegheny Mountains and fight a "sustained guerrilla war" that, as Brown explains to Douglass, would bring liberated slaves from the South to the mountains, would drive up the price of slaves (thereby making slavery "prohibitively expensive"), and would eventually force the South "to strike a deal that would free all slaves in exchange for their return home as paid workers." As described by Owen Brown, his father's "dream of a war of liberation and terror" has a thoroughly interracial dimension, for Brown imagines blacks and whites working together as guerrilla fighters to bring down the slave power. It's that interracial dimension that impresses Douglass, who is impressed, as well, that Brown is willing to surrender the leadership of such an operation to a black man (perhaps Douglass himself). Overall, what's astonishing to Douglass at this first meeting, at least as described by Owen, is his discovery of a white man who treats him and other blacks as equals. As Owen remarks, "I don't think that Mr. Douglass had ever heard a white man speak like this before, at least a white man whom he did not think crazy." Banks's depiction of Brown's ability to treat blacks as equals, and even to seem "black" himself in his rage against slavery, anticipates by several years Stauffer's elaboration of what he terms Brown's "black heart."[24]

This initial scene between Brown and Douglass also effectively suggests the give and take that must have characterized the discussions between these two strong personalities. For instance, Douglass, who throughout his life was opposed to black separatism, expresses his concerns that Brown's plan could produce a "little-land-locked Haiti separate from and surrounded by a white United States." In response, Brown promises that any sort of "temporary Negro republic would be dissolved" with the end of slavery. But even with such moments of intellectual exchange, the scene at times suffers from a hagiographic stiffness in its portrayal of Douglass as the great black leader of his time. Douglass is described as a "distinguished, intelligent . . . broad-shouldered, dark brown man with a forceful jaw and a great leonine mass of hair." We're told he has "a massive face and broad, high-forehead, a wonderful patrician look, but in an African way, as if he were a direct descendent of a long line of Ethiopian kings." "This was a man!" Owen exclaims. By the end of the scene, Douglass has been beatified by Banks (who seems to be working in conjunction with his narrator); and as Owen reverentially gazes at Douglass, it can seem that Douglass is consecrating the very scene that Banks has created for his readers. Owen writes: "I stole a glance down the table at Mr. Douglass, who was watching the scene as if from a great height with an expression of sweet approval on his broad face."[25] But even as he approves from his "great height," questions remain. Will Douglass actually join with Brown in his more militant antislavery activities? And is he, like Brown, prepared to die for the antislavery cause? These questions come to the fore in the endings of both *Cloudsplitter* and *The Good Lord Bird*. But first let's consider McBride's altogether different introduction of Douglass into his novel.

As in *Cloudsplitter*, Douglass is introduced relatively late into *The Good Lord Bird*, around halfway through. McBride chooses to introduce Douglass in a scene that takes place in 1858, ten years after that first meeting in Springfield. In historical fact, Brown had visited Douglass at his Rochester home in 1858 when Brown was still pressing his plan for guerilla warfare in the Allegheny Mountains, and he had perhaps also begun to formulate his plan to attack Harpers Ferry. In McBride's novel, Brown has not yet developed that plan; he decides to visit Douglass in Rochester mainly to get assurances of his continued support for his Allegheny passway. Brown is convinced that if he has Douglass's support, he will be able, in Brown's words, to "hive the bees." Brown actually used versions of that expression – "hive the bees" – as recounted by Douglass and others, and for comic effect McBride has Brown use that expression repeatedly – upwards of fifty times – over the course of the novel. So, with high hopes, Brown heads to Rochester with the narrator, Little Onion, to meet with the man that Brown calls "the king of the Negro people."[26]

As the phrase "the king of the Negro people" suggests, McBride through his narrator poses a challenge to the iconic Douglass, and to iconicity itself.[27] The Douglass we get in the novel thus bears little resemblance to the Douglass of the autobiographies. When Douglass meets Little Onion and Brown at the Rochester train station, for instance, Little Onion describes him as "a Negro unlike any I'd ever seen. He was a stout, handsome mulatto with long dark hair parted in the middle. His shirt was starched and clean. His suit was pressed and flat. His boots spotless. His face was shaved and smooth. He waited still as a statue, proud, erect. He stood like a king." At a time of black suffering, Douglass is presented as an aristocratic prig. McBride develops this characterization to comic effect when Little Onion (or Henrietta) greets Douglass with the informal, "Morning, Fred." Little Onion reports on Douglass's outraged response: "Why do you address me as Fred? Don't you know you are not addressing a pork chop, but rather a fairly considerable and incorrigible piece of the American Negro diaspora?" After reprimanding the person he thinks is a young black woman, Douglass turns to Brown and says, "I suspect there is a pretty little piece of pork chop under all them rags."[28]

McBride's satirical turn in this introductory scene focuses on Douglass in relation to sexuality and gender. Some additional historical background is in order. All of the evidence suggests that Douglass was attractive to white and black women alike. When he toured Ireland and Britain during the mid-1840s, one of his white sponsors even complained that Douglass was regularly "*petted* I may say by *ladies*." While in England in 1846, he became friendly with the English reformer Julia Griffiths, and she was so taken with Douglass that she followed him back to the United States to serve as the managing editor of his antislavery newspaper. She held this position for over four years while living with Douglass, his wife, and their children in Rochester. There is no evidence that Griffiths and Douglass were having an affair, but in the early 1850s, after Douglass publicly broke from Garrison, Garrison in his antislavery newspaper, the *Liberator*, accused Douglass of having an affair with Griffiths. In response, Douglass's wife, who was illiterate, wrote a letter to Garrison, which he published, saying that Griffiths and Douglass were business partners and that the accusations were groundless. (Douglass probably wrote the letter for Anna.) Embarrassed by these exchanges, Griffiths moved back to England. Several years later, a German woman named Ottilie Assing, inspired by Douglass's 1855 *My Bondage and My Freedom* (which she would translate from English to German), boarded a steamer to the United States and met Douglass in Rochester. They remained close friends for over twenty years. Assing didn't live with the Douglasses in the manner of Griffiths, but she traveled with Douglass, and the two were probably sexually involved. Douglass's wife, Anna, died in 1882, and in 1884 Douglass married not Assing but his white secretary, Helen Pitts. That same year Assing, suffering from cancer, killed herself. Douglass does not comment on his relationship with Assing in his final autobiography.[29]

To return to McBride's *The Good Lord Bird*: After meeting Douglass at the Rochester train station, Brown and Little Onion are invited to Douglass's house, where they remain for three weeks. In a great comic passage, Little Onion describes what he sees there in his distinctively vernacular voice: "Three weeks gived me plenty of time to get acquainted with the Douglass household, which was run by Mr. Douglass's two wives – a white one and a colored one. That was the first time I ever saw such a thing, two women married to one man, and both of 'em being a different race. Them two women hardly spoke to one another. When they did, you'd thunk a chunk of ice dropped into the room ... They hated each other's guts." They may hate each other, but they both love Douglass. As Little Onion comments on the workings of Douglass's Rochester home: "every inch of movement in that house, every speck of cleaning, cooking, dusting, working, writing, pouring of lye, and sewing of undergarments revolved around Mr. Douglass, who walked about the house like a king in pantaloons and suspenders, practicing his orations, his mane of dark hair almost wide as the hallways." Now, to say the obvious, Douglass was married to Anna Douglass and not to Ottilie Assing (who isn't named in this scene but in terms of chronology would be the white "wife"). Though Assing didn't live with Douglass in the way that's described here, she did make extended visits. McBride conflates the stories of Julia Griffiths and Ottilie Assing to give us a picture of Douglass, in the spirit of some recent feminist critiques, as overly invested in black manhood. McBride's portrayal of Douglass as a narcissistic ladies' man builds to a scene in which the increasingly inebriated Douglass attempts to seduce Little Onion/ Henrietta. Pressing his body against the narrator's, he tells him/her, "You simply *must* experience the sunlight coming over the Seine River." Then he turns to his most seductive mode: oration. As Little Onion recounts:

> The more stupefied he got, the more he forgot about the hanky-panky he had in mind and instead germinated on what he knowed – orating. First he orated on the plight of the Negro. He just about wore the Negro out. When he was done orating on them, he orated about the fowl, the fishes, the poultry, the white man, the red man, the aunties, uncles, cousins, the second cousins, his cousin Clementine, the bees, the flies, and by the time he worked down to the ants, the butterflies, and the crickets, he was stone-cold sloppy, clouded-up, sweet-blind drunk.

The chapter ends with Douglass passing out from his liquor, allowing Little Onion to escape from the black abolitionist leader as lecher.[30]

McBride is not alone among novelists calling attention to Douglass's somewhat problematic relationships with women. In 2002 the novelist Jewell Parker Rhodes attempted to bring such concerns to dramatic light in *Douglass' Women*. In Rhodes's novel, we learn about Douglass from Anna Murray Douglass and Ottilie Assing, as Rhodes moves back and forth between their first-person narrations, freely inventing scenes in order to indict Douglass as a callous libertine. Rhodes's sympathies lie with Anna, whom she regards as the neglected wife stuck with the children while Douglass takes to the road. Even though Douglass in historical fact didn't meet Assing until the late 1850s, she's depicted in the novel as having met Douglass in Boston in 1845, the year he published the *Narrative*, and as immediately falling in love with his muscular black body. The attraction is presented as mutual. When Douglass shortly after this meeting chooses to go to Britain to escape from fugitive slave hunters, Assing accompanies him. In Rhodes's telling, Douglass's British trip, the moment when he emerges as a transatlantic reformer independent of Garrison, is all about getting away from his black wife so he can have good sex with his white German mistress. This is presented not as comedy, in the way of McBride, but as an essential truth about Douglass, and thus there is virtually nothing in the novel about Douglass as an actual thinker. For what it's worth, the novel is written in a purple prose that only further heightens the sense that Rhodes has no interest in Douglass or Assing as intellectuals or political abolitionists. The following description from Assing's perspective of her time with Douglass in their London hotel room is representative of many such moments in the novel: "I stroked his manhood and felt it rise within my hand. Heat filled me ... His hands stroked my breasts. Then, his tongue reached up to flick my pink tip. I moaned. Douglass watched me ... I straddled him. Guided his brown shaft into my whiteness." As I say, Rhodes is clearly sympathetic to Anna, who has similarly great sex with Douglass early in the novel. What's troubling about the novel is that Rhodes wants us to believe that Douglass actually had an affair with Assing in England while Anna was back in Lynn, Massachusetts, with the children. But at this point in his career Douglass wasn't having an affair with anyone (he was mostly rooming with abolitionist-inclined families).[31] As for Douglass and John Brown: Consistent with Rhodes's unwillingness to present Douglass as a man of ideas, she depicts him as deciding not to participate in the raid on Harpers Ferry because Assing tells him not to.

Douglass's decision not to participate in Harpers Ferry is the culminating moment of the Douglass-Brown friendship in both McBride's *The Good Lord Bird* and Banks's *Cloudsplitter*. Both authors work closely with

Douglass's account in *Life and Times* of his secret meeting with Brown in order to explore why Douglass chose not to join Brown's small army of liberators. I find Banks's presentation of Douglass's decision-making more effective and moving than McBride's, so I'm going to conclude with Banks and return to where I left off with McBride.

In *The Good Lord Bird*, after the scene in which Little Onion escapes from Douglass's lascivious clutches, Brown begins to formulate plans for an attack on the federal arsenal at Harpers Ferry. He pitches these plans at a meeting in Canada (Chatham, Ontario) attended by Harriet Tubman and the black Canadian Osborne Anderson, who in historical fact became one of the twenty-one men who joined Brown at Harpers Ferry. Of course we know that Douglass decided not to join the group, and we also know that the raid did not lead to the immediate liberation of the slaves. So there's considerable pathos as we watch Brown, through Little Onion's increasingly admiring eyes, insist that Douglass will join them. Near the end of the novel, McBride's narrator supplies a four-page account of Brown's 1859 meeting with Douglass in Chambersburg, Pennsylvania, which draws on Douglass's account in *Life and Times*, but with a difference: Little Onion is there as a pledged participant and as a sort of judge prepared to render a verdict on Douglass for posterity.

According to Little Onion, Douglass's account of the Chambersburg meeting in his 1881 autobiography fails to get things right. Little Onion asserts: "I seen it differently." Still, Little Onion goes on to narrate the meeting almost exactly as Douglass describes it in *Life and Times*. As in Douglass's account, Douglass brings along his friend Shields Green and warns Brown that he will be walking into "a steel trap." As in Douglass's account, Douglass and Brown discuss the plan for a while before Douglass declines to participate. As in Douglass's account, Shields Green says, "I guess I'll go with the Old Man" (and thus goes to his death). Where Little Onion's account is different from Douglass's is in its moral emphases, and here McBride uses his crossdressed narrator to level some serious charges at Douglass. Little Onion says that the vainglorious Douglass is "like the colored president," and once again Little Onion depicts him as an aristocratic prig. As presented by Little Onion, Douglass's refusal to join Brown has nothing to do with pragmatic sense; instead, it reveals his hypocrisy, cowardice, and moral bankruptcy. Little Onion reports: "[S]tanding there in his frock coat, Mr. Douglass weren't up to it. He had too many highballs. Too many boiled pigeons and meat jellies and buttered apple pies. He was a man of parlor talk, of silk shirts and fine hats, linen suits and ties. He was a man of words and speech."[32] To be sure, all of this is invented in a novel that's hardly meant to be taken seriously as a factual rendition of history. Still, given the way that Douglass is presented in his two major scenes in the novel, McBride is arguably being unfair to a man who had a long history of not running away from physical confrontations while an abolitionist, whether in Pendleton, Indiana, in 1843, where he broke his hand fighting back against an antiabolitionist mob; in Boston during the 1850s, when he participated in violent street protests against the Fugitive Slave Act; or at Boston's Tremont Temple in 1860, when he stood up to racist assailants while giving a speech.[33] McBride's large point seems to be that, given his failure to join with Brown, Douglass might not be the most inspirational black hero for a time of crisis – whether in 1859 or 2013 (the year the hashtag #BlackLivesMatter was first used). At the very least, McBride, somewhat in the tradition of Sutton Griggs, suggests the dangers for black people of worshipping cultural icons. (I also wonder if the critique of Douglass as "colored president" might not be a veiled attack on the nation's first black president for failing to push a more activist, progressive agenda.) Even with the novel's celebration of Brown, McBride seems to be placing his hopes for the achievement of social justice in the United States on the workings of a larger black collectivity, to the point where someone like Douglass (or even Brown) would become almost incidental. By contrast, Russell Banks in *Cloudsplitter* continues to put some faith in Douglass.

Before considering Banks's account of the Chambersburg meeting, however, it would be useful to consider the black Canadian writer Lawrence Hill's more positive depiction of the Douglass-Brown relationship in his 1997 novel, *Any Known Blood*. Set during the 1990s, it is a long and complicated novel about the efforts of a black Canadian named Langston Cane the Fifth to understand his family history. In the novel's present – the 1990s – he learns about the historically close ties between Canadian and US blacks by moving back and forth between Ontario and Baltimore in search of documents about his family's past. Langston Cane the Fifth's major discovery in the archives is that his great-great-grandfather, Langston Cane the First, was the twenty-second person to join John Brown in his raid on Harpers Ferry (this is of course a fiction). Cane the First joins Brown in part because of his abolitionism and in part because he has been accused of bigamy in his Canadian town. Brown recruits him during a visit to Canada, and then this twenty-second participant, like the twenty-second participant Little Onion in McBride's novel, accompanies Brown to the Chambersburg quarry. *Any Known Blood* thus provides its own reimagining of that fateful moment when Douglass chooses not to join the raiders.

As in *Life and Times* and *The Good Lord Bird*, Douglass is accompanied by Shields Green and is initially unaware of why Brown summoned him to the quarry. Working with Cane the First's perspective, Hill presents Douglass as surprised by Brown's change of plans from creating a passway in the Allegheny Mountains to actually raiding a federal arsenal. Here's how Cane the First reports the encounter in the first-person narrative that Cane the Fifth discovers in an archive: "Douglass laughed and slapped the table. I sensed that I would rather have been working with him than with Brown." Cane's admiration increases when Douglass tells Brown: "You must have lost your mind." Once Douglass realizes that Brown is serious, he says the familiar, that Brown "would be walking into a death trap." In response, Brown says the familiar: "Come with me, Douglass. When I strike, the bees will begin to swarm, and I shall want you to help hive them." They have a long discussion, and, unlike in McBride, Douglass is anything but priggish or aristocratic in choosing not to join Brown's raid. In a scene that is quite moving, the narrator presents Douglass's decision as painful, and as coming with a human cost that Douglass and Brown both acknowledge. At their final parting, the men embrace, and Cane the First notes that Douglass "had tears in his eyes."[34]

In McBride, Douglass's refusal to join Brown is presented as the cowardice of a man who lives well and has little concern about his fellow African Americans. In Hill, Douglass is a complex man who loves Brown and wisely chooses not to martyr himself. Among the shrewd moves that Hill makes in his novel is to present Douglass in another key scene, twenty-two years after the raid on Harpers Ferry, in which Douglass celebrates Brown at Storer College. As mentioned, Douglass gave such a speech in 1881 at this college located at Harpers Ferry. In Hill's invented scene, the main character's great-grandfather, the son of the participant in Brown's raid on Harpers Ferry, is the valedictory speaker on the same day that Douglass lectures on Brown. Hill works with the transcript of Douglass's actual speech, which was surprisingly well received, as least as Douglass describes it in *Life and Times*. In the novel and in history, Douglass says at Storer College: "John Brown a madman? Mad, no. Obsessed, yes. But how could he not be obsessed, to overthrow a system that ruled with whip and chain? Obsessed, yes, a zealot, yes. And I say three cheers for that." The speech is consistent with speeches that Douglass made in the wake of Harpers Ferry, and it's consistent with the positive presentation of Brown in his 1881/1892 autobiography. In the novel and in history, the 1881 speech at Storer College concludes in this way: "My friends, much has been made of my accomplishments in life. But my accomplishments, next to John Brown's, have been proven meager in the extreme. I could live for the slave, but he [John Brown] could die for the slave."[35]

Douglass's recognition of both the suicidal nature of Brown's plan and its role in bringing about a war of emancipation is missing from McBride's novel, which has nothing to say about Douglass after Harpers Ferry. What's also missing from McBride is some recognition that Douglass was aware of his own limits and of Brown's selfless heroism, and that Douglass had a key role in the development of Brown's posthumous reputation. Not that novelists have to be "fair," but Hill's novel takes fuller account of the resonance of Douglass's interactions with Brown, such as the importance of their interracial friendship for both men from 1848 to 1859, and then, for Douglass, the importance of the memory of that friendship for many years after. We see a similar attention to historical resonance in Banks's John Brown novel.

In *Cloudsplitter*, the narrator, Owen Brown, who for most of the novel has been skeptical of his father's antislavery activities, at long last decides to throw in his lot with the Harpers Ferry raiders. As mentioned, Douglass has appeared just once in the novel, in the flashback to the moment in 1848 in Springfield, Massachusetts, when Brown apprises Douglass about his plan for guerilla warfare in the Allegheny Mountains. Hundreds of pages later, Owen now discloses what he calls "the Secret History of John Brown." In a brilliant novelistic move, Banks initially has Owen tell that history through counterfactuals, which is to say by presenting a historical account that we know didn't actually happen but that might have happened. Thus, as the novel builds toward Harpers Ferry, we see everything that John Brown had hoped for coming to fruition. In Owen's account, John Brown has the continued support of Douglass for the Alleghenies plan, and then gains his support for Harpers Ferry. Douglass's embrace of the plan will allow them both, as Owen remarks, to "hive the bees," bringing along "thousands" of blacks and even inspiring "thousands of non-slaveholding whites, too, God-fearing Southerners, who will come running to our side." As Owen presents his father's imaginings, the battle inspired by the raid on Harpers Ferry rages "until at last nothing remains of the Slavocracy but a smoldering pile of char!" That is what his father had expected, and the scene continues with an account of what at first seems to be the actual raid: "[W]e have, indeed, begun an insurrection, which surely, thanks to the presence of Frederick Douglass, will catch and burst into flame in the matter of mere days."[36]

But then comes a new chapter and the revelation, for those who think that Banks might be writing a counterfactual history, that Douglass declined to participate after all. I've recounted the story of the meeting at the Chambersburg quarry several times now, and Banks himself must have felt the story had become familiar, for he has Owen Brown tell the historian's assistant: "For you, like the rest of America, have read and believed Frederick Douglass's eloquent narrative of his life and are familiar with this version of the final meeting with Father and me in Chambersburg." The "and believed" leads one to think that Owen will be offering a different account of the meeting, but (mostly) he doesn't. He says about Douglass's testimony in the 1881/1892 *Life and Times*: "I have no quarrel with it – what Mr. Douglass says there is true; that for an entire day he and Father wrestled like angels, as the one struggled to keep the other from martyrdom, and the other fought to convince the one to save him from martyrdom by joining him there." But Banks does take his liberties as a fiction writer to add something new to the story. In recognition of Douglass's awareness of the problem of race throughout his long career, Banks in his reimagined version of the 1859 meeting in Chambersburg gives Douglass the thematic nub of the novel. In an exchange that's not in Douglass's *Life and Times*, Douglass, after hearing Brown proclaim that the raid on Harpers Ferry will produce an egalitarian United States, respectfully disagrees: "No, John," he says. "It's *race* that will settle it."[37]

Banks's overarching argument in the novel is that whatever happens with the raid, tensions will remain between blacks and whites because of the long (and unresolved) history of slavery and race in the United States. Banks underscores this theme when he has Douglass say to Brown near the end of their Chambersburg discussion, after his familiar warning that Harpers Ferry will turn out to be a "steel trap": "It's race, John. Skin color and hair and physiognomy. You say *us*, John, and you mean *all Americans willing to go to war to end slavery*. But every other American who says *us* means race, means *us white people*, or *us Negroes*. You are a noble, good man. But you are nearly alone in this country. Even me, when I say *us*, I mean *we negroes*." For what else could Douglass mean in a nation in which whites view blacks as them or other? Douglass thus chooses not to join, not out of cowardice but because "My love of my people forbids it." It is precisely his love for his people that leads him to reject a plan which at the time he believes ultimately fails to confront the problem of race in America – the very problem that he will continue to address long after Harpers Ferry. At this point Banks returns to Douglass's account in *Life and Times*, with Shields famously saying, "I believe I'll go with the Old Man." As the meeting comes to an end, Brown holds onto his hopes that "When I strike, the bees will begin to swarm, and I will need you to help hive them."[38] But of course the bees don't swarm. In the anticlimactic short closing scene of the novel, Owen Brown climbs a tree to watch the failed attack, and then makes his escape, only to tell his story of slavery and race in America to the historian's assistant fifty years later, around 1910.

But this is a novel for 1998, the year it was published, and for our own time, as well, which is true of all of the post-1960s novels I've been discussing, which consider Douglass in relation to the Civil Rights Movement, white racial anxiety, class, transnationalism, interracialism, gender and sexuality, militance, and the persistence of racial conflict in the United States. The anticlimactic close of *Cloudsplitter* gives it an unfinished feel, which is precisely Banks's thematic point about the social-reformist work that Douglass and Brown, both together and on their own, were attempting to accomplish. At the current historical moment, that work has a renewed urgency for novelists, critics, and readers alike. Flawed as Douglass may have been, there are few in American history who more powerfully addressed the problem of race in the United States, the Americas, and the larger Atlantic world. As Douglass suggests in his writings, and as post-1960s novelists have helped to teach us, our hopes for a multiracial democracy in the United States (and beyond) may well depend on continued efforts to address the long history of slavery and race in the overlapping contexts of the local and global.

Postscript

By the time this volume has been published, it will be old news that President Trump, in his awkward effort to launch African American History Month on February 1st, 2017, celebrated Douglass as "an example of somebody who's done an amazing job" and as a figure who "is being recognized more and more, I notice."[39] The antiracist, transnational, and historical Douglass disappears in these bromides – the Douglass who, for example, fought in the streets of Boston to help rescue blacks being remanded under the Fugitive Slave Act; or the Douglass who, as minister-consul to Haiti, supported Haiti's resistance to US efforts to place a naval base there.[40] Had Trump thought long and hard about Douglass's "lawless" and "un-American" socially-engaged actions, his more honest take would have been to say that the man his advisors told him to celebrate should have been imprisoned or fired.

I confess that while editing, revising, and developing new material for this volume, I have experienced moments of both exuberance and unease when struck by what can seem to be the prophetic insights of a number of nineteenth-century American writers. The authors considered in this volume forcefully address racial injustice, national exceptionalism, war, patriotism, imperialism, religion, citizenship, end-of-the-world scenarios, globalization, and the egalitarian promises of the US nation. Much of the political and aesthetic power of their writing derives from their engagement with the discourses and cultural politics of their own historical moment. My emphasis in *Race, Transnationalism, and Nineteenth-Century American Literary Studies* has been on the centripetal force of that moment. But as my discussion of post-1960s novelists' appropriations of Douglass has meant to suggest, that historical moment cannot be neatly confined to the nineteenth century. Arguably, what some call "the long nineteenth century" has never ended. Or at least that is the suggestion of novelists like Chimamanda Adichie and Russell Banks. Race and transnationalism have become central to American literary studies as practiced right now. But in crucial ways, we are just catching up to the insights of some of the most compelling writers of the nineteenth century.

Notes

Introduction

1. James Baldwin's "Everybody's Protest Novel" first appeared in the June 1949 *Partisan Review* and was reprinted in *Notes of a Native Son* (Boston: Beacon Press, 1955). On signifying, see Henry Louis Gates Jr., *The Signifying Monkey: A Theory of African-American Literary Criticism* (New York: Oxford University Press, 1988).

2. I address these questions in *Martin Delany, Frederick Douglass, and the Politics of Representative Identity* (Chapel Hill: University of North Carolina Press, 1997). See also Harriet Beecher Stowe, *Dred: A Tale of the Great Dismal Swamp*, ed. Robert S. Levine (2000; Chapel Hill: University of North Carolina Press, 2006).

3. See, for example, Jane Tompkins, *Sensational Designs: The Cultural Work of American Fiction, 1790–1860* (New York: Oxford University Press, 1985), ch. 5.

4. Robert S. Levine, *Conspiracy and Romance: Studies in Brockden Brown, Cooper, Hawthorne, and Melville* (Cambridge: Cambridge University Press, 1989). Standard works from the 1940s to the early 1960s include F. O. Matthiessen, *American Renaissance: Art and Expression in the Age of Emerson and Whitman* (New York: Oxford University Press, 1941); R. W. B. Lewis, *The American Adam: Innocence, Tragedy, and Tradition in the Nineteenth Century* (Chicago: University of Chicago Press, 1955); Richard Chase, *The American Novel and Its Tradition* (New York: Anchor, 1957); and Leo Marx, *The Machine in the Garden: Technology and the Pastoral Ideal in America* (New York: Oxford University Press, 1964). These works don't treat American literature in a complete historical vacuum and have moments of expansiveness. But one of the main goals of Americanist critical work of the time was to create a distinctively American literary tradition.

5. Sacvan Bercovitch, *The American Jeremiad* (Madison: University of Wisconsin Press, 1978); Walter Benn Michaels, *The Gold Standard and the Logic of Naturalism: American Literature at the Turn of the Century* (Berkeley: University of California Press, 1987).

6. *"Race," Writing, and Difference*, ed. Henry Louis Gates Jr. (Chicago: University of Chicago Press, 1986); Dana D. Nelson, *The Word in Black*

and White: Reading "Race" in American Literature, 1638–1867 (New York: Oxford University Press, 1992); Eric Sundquist, *To Wake the Nations: Race in the Making of American Literature* (Cambridge, MA: Harvard University Press, 1993).

7. William L. Andrews, *To Tell a Free Story: The First Century of Afro-American Autobiography, 1760–1865* (Urbana: University of Illinois Press, 1986); *Slavery and the Literary Imagination*, ed. Deborah E. McDowell and Arnold Rampersad (Baltimore: Johns Hopkins University Press, 1989); and Hortense Spillers, "Changing the Letter: The Yokes, the Jokes of Discourse, or Mrs. Stowe and Mr. Reed," *Slavery and the Literary Imagination*, ed. Deborah E. McDowell and Arnold Rampersad, 25–61. Robert B. Stepto's earlier *From Behind the Veil: A Study of Afro-American Narrative* (Urbana: University of Illinois Press, 1979) also caught the attention of mainstream Americanists.

8. Toni Morrison *Playing in the Dark: Whiteness and the Literary Imagination* (New York: Viking, 1992), 35, 33. *Playing in the Dark* expands on Morrison's "Unspeakable Things Unspoken: The Afro-American Presence in American Literature," *Michigan Quarterly Review* 28.1 (1989): 1–34.

9. Henry B. Wonham, *Criticism and the Color Line: Desegregating American Literary Studies* (New Brunswick: Rutgers University Press, 1996); Morrison, "Unspeakable Things Unspoken," 6; Robert S. Levine and Samuel Otter, eds. *Frederick Douglass and Herman Melville: Essays in Relation* (Chapel Hill: University of North Carolina Press, 2008).

10. Paul Gilroy, *The Black Atlantic: Modernity and Double Consciousness* (Cambridge, MA: Harvard University Press, 1993), ix; and on Martin Delany, see 19–40. On Delany's *Blake*, see Levine, *Martin Delany, Frederick Douglass*, ch. 4. Gilroy also influenced my conception of *Martin R. Delany: A Documentary Reader*, ed. Robert S. Levine (Chapel Hill: University of North Carolina Press, 2003). On oceanic studies and American literature, see, for example, Hester Blum, *The View from the Masthead: Maritime Imagination and Antebellum American Sea Narratives* (Chapel Hill: University of North Carolina Press, 2008).

11. *Cultures of U.S. Imperialism*, ed. Amy Kaplan and Donald E. Pease (Durham: Duke University Press, 1993); Amy Kaplan, *The Anarchy of Empire in the Making of U.S. Culture* (Cambridge, MA: Harvard University Press, 2002); and see Robert S. Levine, *Dislocating Race and Nation: Episodes in Nineteenth-Century American Literary Nationalism* (Chapel Hill: University of North Carolina Press, 2008), esp. 1–15. For examples of imperialism studies inspired by Kaplan and Pease's volume, see John Carlos Rowe, *Literary Culture and U.S. Imperialism* (New York: Oxford University Press, 2000); and Andy

Doolen, *Fugitive Empire: Locating Early American Imperialism* (Minneapolis: University of Minnesota Press, 2005).

12. Carolyn Porter, "What We Know That We Don't Know: Remapping American Literary Studies," *American Literary History* 6.3 (1994): 471, 521. See also José David Saldívar, *The Dialectics of Our America: Genealogy, Cultural Critique, and Literary History* (Durham: Duke University Press, 1991).

13. Surveying this work in her 2004 presidential address to the American Studies Association, Shelley Fisher Fishkin emphasized how productive these approaches had been for the study of race and American literature, remarking that as "the transnational becomes more central to American studies, the comparative study of race and racism will become more central to the field" ("Crossroads of Culture: The Transnational Turn in American Studies," *American Quarterly* 57.1 [2004]: 23). In his presidential address to the American Studies Association in 2007, Emory Elliott followed Fishkin in emphasizing the value of transnationalism for the study of race and for bringing an even greater diversity to American literary studies ("Diversity in the United States and Abroad: What Does It Mean When American Studies Is Transnational?," *American Quarterly* 59.1 [2007]: 1–22).

14. See, for example, Kirsten Silva Gruesz, *Ambassadors of Culture: The Transamerican Origins of Latino Writing* (Princeton, NJ: Princeton University Press, 2002); Anna Brickhouse, *Transamerican Literary Relations and the Nineteenth-Century Public Sphere* (Cambridge: Cambridge University Press, 2004); *Shades of the Planet: American Literature as World Literature*, ed. Wai Chee Dimock and Lawrence Buell (Princeton, NJ: Princeton University Press, 2007); *Imagining Our Americas: Toward a Transnational Frame*, ed. Sandhya Shukla and Heidi Tinsman (Durham, NC: Duke University Press, 2007); Colleen Glenney Boggs, *Transnationalism and American Literature: Literary Translation, 1773–1892* (New York: Routledge, 2007); *Hemispheric American Studies*, ed. Caroline F. Levander and Robert S. Levine (New Brunswick, NJ: Rutgers University Press, 2008); Laura Doyle, *Freedom's Empire: Race and the Rise of the Novel in Atlantic Modernity, 1640–1940* (Durham, NC: Duke University Press, 2008); Paul Jay, *Global Matters: The Transnational Turn in Literary Studies* (Ithaca, NY: Cornell University Press, 2010); *Globalizing American Studies*, ed. Brian T. Edwards and Dilip Parameshwar Gaonkar (Chicago: University of Chicago Press, 2010); Paul Giles, *The Global Remapping of American Literature* (Princeton, NJ: Princeton University Press, 2011); *Re-Framing the Transnational Turn in American Studies*, ed. Winfried Fluck, Donald E. Pease, and John Carlos Rowe (Hanover, NH: Dartmouth College Press, 2011); Caroline F. Levander, *Where Is American Literature?* (Oxford: Wiley-Blackwell, 2013); Lisa Lowe,

The Intimacies of Four Continents (Durham, NC: Duke University Press, 2015); and *The Cambridge Companion to Transnational American Studies,* ed. Yogita Goyal (Cambridge: Cambridge University Press, 2017). In some ways the founding text of the recent turn to transnational studies is Randolph S. Bourne, "Trans-National America," *Atlantic Monthly,* July 1916, 86–97. Recent work on temporality, which challenges nation-time as the organizing principle for literary study, has close connections to the transnational turn. See, for example, Wai Chee Dimock, *Through Other Continents: American Literature across Deep Time* (Princeton, NJ: Princeton University Press, 2006); Lloyd Pratt, *Archives of American Time: Literature and Modernity in the Nineteenth Century* (Philadelphia: University of Pennsylvania Press, 2010); and *Timelines of American Literature,* ed. Christopher Hager and Cody Marrs (Baltimore, MD: Johns Hopkins University Press, forthcoming).

15. In a special issue of the 2003 *PMLA,* for instance, Paul Giles predicted that transnationalism would eventually "sound the death knell for United States exceptionalism" ("Transnationalism and Classic American Literature," *PMLA* 118.1 [2003]: 75). Ralph Bauer takes a more cautious or measured approach, arguing that the transnational turn in American literary studies has "led not to a 'collapse' of national frameworks but to something that more closely resembles a palimpsest, where transnational geographical frameworks are superimposed on national ones without the latter becoming entirely erased" ("Of Turns and Paradigm Shifts: Humanities, Science, and Transnational American Studies," *Turns of Event: Nineteenth-Century American Literary Studies in Motion,* ed. Hester Blum [Philadelphia: University of Pennsylvania Press, 2016], 91).

16. Jared Hickman, "On the Redundancy of 'Transnational American Studies,'" *The Oxford Handbook of Nineteenth-Century American Literature,* ed. Russ Castronovo (New York: Oxford University Press, 2012), 269, 270; Winfried Fluck, "A New Beginning? Transnationalisms," *New Literary History* 42.3 (2011): 379; Winfried Fluck, "American Literary History and the Romance with America," *American Literary History* 21.1 (2009): 8, 7.

17. Yogita Goyal, "Introduction: The Transnational Turn," in *The Cambridge Companion to Transnational American Literature,* 7.

18. Fluck, "American Literary History and the Romance with America," 14.

19. Close reading is important to all of the chapters in this volume. On the importance of reading to historical criticism, see Paul B. Armstrong, "Form and History: Reading as an Aesthetic Experience and Historical Act," *Modern Language Quarterly* 69.2 (2008): 195–219; and Paul B. Armstrong, "In Defense of Reading: Or, Why Reading Still Matters in a Contextualist Age," *New Literary History* 42.1 (2011): 87–113.

20. See, for example, Rita Felski, "'Context Stinks!'" *New Literary History* 42.4 (2011): 573–91; and Eric Hayot, "Against Periodization; or, On Institutional Time," *New Literary History* 42.4 (2011): 739–56.
21. On this point, see Joel Pfister, *Surveyors of Customs: American Literature as Cultural Analysis* (New York: Oxford University Press, 2015).
22. In this regard, my book has been influenced by recent work on aesthetics and American literature. See, for example, Russ Castronovo, *Beautiful Democracy: Aesthetics and Anarchy in a Global Era* (Chicago: University of Chicago Press, 2007); and *American Literature's Aesthetic Dimensions*, ed. Cindy Weinstein and Christopher Looby (New York: Columbia University Press, 2012). For more on the topic, see Chapter 7, below.

Reading Slavery and Race in "Classic" American Literature

1. See volume 2 of Vernon L. Parrington's *Main Currents in American Thought,* which he titled *The Romantic Revolution in America, 1800–1860* (New York: Harcourt, Brace, and World, 1927).
2. See *American Literature: The Makers and the Making,* ed. Cleanth Brooks, R. W. B. Lewis, and Robert Penn Warren, 2 vols. (New York: St. Martin's Press, 1973), 1:1016.
3. Toni Morrison, "Unspeakable Things Unspoken: The Afro-American Presence in American Literature," *Michigan Quarterly Review* 28.1 (1989): 13, 11, 12; Morrison, *Playing in the Dark: Whiteness and the Literary Imagination* (New York: Viking Books, 1992), 44, 5. For important works on slavery and race inspired by Morrison's idea of haunting, see *Criticism and the Color Line: Desegregating American Literary Studies,* ed. Henry B. Wonham (New Brunswick: Rutgers University Press, 1996); and Teresa A. Goddu, *Gothic America: Narrative, History, and Nation* (New York: Columbia University Press, 1997).
4. Vincent Freimarck and Bernard Rosenthal, "Introduction," in *Race and the American Romantics* (New York: Schocken Books, 1971), 1, 2.
5. Morrison, *Playing in the Dark,* 90.
6. Stephen Best and Sharon Marcus, "Surface Reading: An Introduction," *Representations* 108.1 (2009): 1, 3, 9, 10, 11. For a sampling of the lively debate on Best and Marcus's essay, see Ellen Rooney, "Live Free or Describe: The Reading Effect and the Persistence of Form," *differences* 21.3 (2010), 112–39 (Rooney dissents, stating that the "unqualified reassertion of the givenness of what the text is allegedly saying about itself in 'Surface Reading' is itself puzzling" [124]); Elizabeth Weed, "'The Way We Read Now,'" *History of the Present* 2.1 (2012): 95–106 (Weed also dissents, defending ideological critique while scoffing at the notion of transparent

close reading); and Heather Love, "Close Reading and Thin Description," *Public Culture* 25.3 (2013): 401–434 (Love sees value in Best and Marcus's approach and champions an empirically based and interdisciplinary "thin description" that works with "slow, detailed reading" [419]).

7. James Fenimore Cooper, *The American Democrat* (1838; Baltimore: Penguin, 1969), 221, 222; Thomas Jefferson, *Notes on the State of Virginia* (1785; New York: Harper Torchbooks, 1964), 156.

8. Ezra Tawil, *The Making of Racial Sentiment: Slavery and the Birth of the Frontier Romance* (Cambridge: Cambridge University Press, 2006), 7, 20.

9. James Fenimore Cooper, *The Last of the Mohicans* (1826; New York: Penguin), 159.

10. See Eric Foner, *Free Soil, Free Labor, Free Men: The Ideology of the Republican Party before the Civil War* (New York: Oxford University Press, 1970).

11. Cooper, *The American Democrat*, 222; Cooper, *The Last of the Mohicans*, 159, 76. In their reading of Cora's key role in the novel, Nancy Armstrong and Leonard Tennenhouse discuss how Cooper offers the possibility of an interracial foundational fiction for the US nation only to take it away ("Recalling Cora: Family Resemblances in *The Last of the Mohicans*," *American Literary History* 28.2 [2016]: 223–46).

12. Cooper, *Last of the Mohicans*, 103, 284, 33. For an excellent discussion of whipping and race in the novel, see Geoffrey Sanborn, *Whipscars and Tattoos: The Last of the Mohicans, Moby-Dick, and the Maori* (New York: Oxford University Press, 2011), ch. 2.

13. John Carlos Rowe, "Poe, Antebellum Slavery, and Modern Criticism," in *Poe's Pym: Critical Explorations*, ed. Richard Kopley (Durham, NC: Duke University Press, 1992), 117. For a useful casebook, see *Romancing the Shadow: Poe and Race*, ed. J. Gerald Kennedy and Liliane Weissberg (New York: Oxford University Press, 2001).

14. Maurice S. Lee, *Slavery, Philosophy, and American Literature, 1830–1860* (Cambridge: Cambridge University Press, 2005), 37.

15. Edgar Allan Poe, *The Narrative of Arthur Gordon Pym of Nantucket* (1838; New York: Penguin, 1999), 48.

16. Ibid., 147, 163, 166, 162, 180.

17. Ibid., 220, 217.

18. Herman Melville, *Moby-Dick* (1851; New York: Norton, 2002), 21; Greg Grandin, *The Empire of Necessity: Slavery, Freedom, and Deception in the New World* (New York: Metropolitan Books, 2014), 54. For a classic reading of 1850s political debate on slavery and *Moby-Dick*, see Alan Heimert, "*Moby-Dick* and American Political Symbolism," *American Quarterly* 15.4 (1963): 498–534.

19. Herman Melville, Benito Cereno (1855), in *Billy Budd, Sailor and Selected Tales*, ed. Robert Milder (New York: Oxford University Press, 1997), 171, 177, 208, 247.

20. Toni Morrison, "Melville and the Language of Denial," *The Nation*, January 7, 2014, www.thenation.com/article/melville-and-language-denial.

21. Melville, *Benito Cereno*, 238, 241.

22. See Jean Fagin Yellin, "Hawthorne and the American National Sin," in *The Green American Tradition: Essays and Poems for Sherman Paul*, ed. H. Daniel Peck (Baton Rouge: Louisiana State University Press, 1989), 75–97; and Eric Cheyfitz, "The Irresistibleness of Great Literature: Reconstructing Hawthorne's Politics," *American Literary History* 6.3 (1994): 539–58.

23. Nathaniel Hawthorne, *Life of Franklin Pierce* (Boston: Ticknor, Reed, and Fields, 1852), 113; Hawthorne, "Chiefly about War-Matters. By a Peaceable Man" (1862), in Hawthorne, *Miscellaneous Prose and Verse*, ed. Thomas Woodson et al. (Columbus: Ohio State University Press, 1994), 420. See Leland S. Person, "The Dark Labyrinth of Mind: Hawthorne, Hester, and the Ironies of Racial Mothering," *Studies in American Fiction* 29.1 (2001): 33–48; and Jay Grossman, "'A' Is for Abolition?: Race, Authorship, *The Scarlet Letter*," *Textual Practice* 7.1 (1993): 13–30. The best study of Hawthorne and slavery is Larry J. Reynolds, *Devils and Rebels: The Making of Hawthorne's Damned Politics* (Ann Arbor: University of Michigan Press, 2010). See also Robert S. Levine, *Dislocating Race and Nation: Episodes in Nineteenth-Century American Literary Nationalism* (Chapel Hill: University of North Carolina Press, 2008), 119–47.

24. See, for example, Nathaniel Hawthorne, *The Blithedale Romance*, ed. Richard Millington (New York: Norton, 2011), 81.

25. Nathaniel Hawthorne, *The House of the Seven Gables* (1851; New York: Norton, 2006), 133.

26. For an important discussion of these racial and class tensions, see David R. Roediger, *The Wages of Whiteness: Race and the Making of the Working Class* (London: Verso, 1991).

27. Hawthorne, *House of the Seven Gables*, 136, 135, 149.

28. S. Margaret Fuller, *Woman in the Nineteenth Century* (New York: Greeley and McElrath, 1845), 18; Henry D. Thoreau, *Walden, Civil Disobedience, and other Writings*, ed. William Rossi (New York: Norton, 2008), 8, 258; Walt Whitman, *Leaves of Grass* (New York: Oxford University Press, 2008), 60. On Emerson and antislavery, see Len Gougeon, *Virtue's Hero: Emerson, Antislavery, and Reform* (Athens: University of Georgia Press, 1999); on Whitman, see Martin Klammer, *Whitman, Slavery, and the Emergence of Leaves of Grass* (University Park: Penn State University Press, 1995); and Ed Folsom, "Lucifer and Ethiopia: Whitman, Race, and Poetics before the Civil

War and After," in *A Historical Guide to Walt Whitman*, ed. David S. Reynolds (New York: Oxford University Press, 2001), 97–119.

29. For a revisionary reading of the ending of Twain's classic novel in relation to contemporaneous debates on slavery and race, see Brook Thomas, "*Adventures of Huckleberry Finn* and Reconstruction," *American Literary Realism* 50.1 (2017): 1–25.

Temporality, Race, and Empire in Cooper's *The Deerslayer*: The Beginning of the End

1. Charles E. Maier, *Among Empires: American Ascendency and Its Predecessors* (Cambridge, MA: Harvard University Press, 2006), ch. 2. Maier argues that, in empire building, frontier "marks insiders and outsiders and always becomes a contested fault line along which acts of violence – call it disorder or resistance, depending on your point of view – accumulate" (9). See also Thomas Bender, *A Nation among Nations: America's Place in World History* (New York: Hill and Wang, 2006), ch. 2; Sandra Gustafson, "Histories of Democracy and Empire," *American Quarterly* 59.1 (2007): 107–33; and, for a discussion of the "creole frontier" in Cooper in relation to "multiple experimental and alternative nationalisms of the early republic" (741), see Oana Godeanu-Kenworthy, "Creole Frontiers: Imperial Ambiguities in John Richardson's and James Fenimore Cooper's Fiction," *Early American Literature* 49.3 (2014): 741–70.

2. D. H. Lawrence, *Studies in Classic American Literature* (1923; New York: Viking, 1972), 54, 60.

3. On this point, see Alan M. Axelrad, "The Shock of Recognition: Twain and Lawrence Read Cooper," in *Reading Cooper, Teaching Cooper*, ed. Jeffrey Walker (New York: AMS Press, 2007), 46–75.

4. Thomas M. Allen, *A Republic in Time: Temporality and Social Imagination in Nineteenth-Century America* (Chapel Hill: University of North Carolina Press, 2008), 4.

5. Joshua David Bellin, *The Demon of the Continent: Indians and the Shaping of American Literature* (Philadelphia: University of Pennsylvania Press, 2001), 158; Philip Fisher, *Hard Facts: Setting and Form in the American Novel* (New York: Oxford University Press, 1985), 36, 35; Theresa Strouth Gaul, "Romance and the 'Genuine Indian': Cooper's Politics of Genre," *ESQ* 48.2 (2002): 159, 160. For similar arguments, see Eric Cheyfitz, "Savage Law: The Plot against American Indians in *Johnson and Graham's Lessee v. M'Intosh* and *The Pioneers*," in *Cultures of United States Imperialism*, ed. Amy Kaplan and Donald E. Pease (Durham, NC: Duke University Press, 1993), 109–28; Susan Scheckel, "'In the Land of His Fathers': Cooper, Land Rights, and

the Legitimation of American National Identity," in *James Fenimore Cooper: New Historical and Literary Contexts*, ed. W. M. Verhoeven (Amsterdam: Rodopi, 1993), 89–103; Lawrence Alan Rosenwald, *Multilingual America: Language and the Making of American Literature* (Cambridge: Cambridge University Press, 2008), 20–47; and Mark Rifkin, *When Did Indians Become Straight?: Kinship, the History of Sexuality, and Native Sovereignty* (New York: Oxford University Press, 2011), ch. 1.

6. See George Dekker and John P. McWilliams's comprehensive *Fenimore Cooper: The Critical Heritage* (London: Routledge and Keegan Paul, 1973).

7. However, for sharp dissents from the critical orthodoxy, see Geoffrey Rans, *Cooper's Leather-Stocking Novels: A Secular Reading* (Chapel Hill: University of North Carolina Press, 1991); Barbara Alice Mann, "Race Traitor: Cooper, His Critics, and Nineteenth-Century Literary Politics," in *A Historical Guide to James Fenimore Cooper*, ed. Leland S. Person (New York: Oxford University Press, 2007), 155–85; and Wayne Franklin, *James Fenimore Cooper: The Early Years* (New Haven, CT: Yale University Press, 2007).

8. Here I signify on Bellin's *The Demon of the Continent*.

9. For a different but complementary perspective on how Cooper often toned down and reexamined his US nationalism in the process of revision, see Joseph Rezek, *London and the Making of Provincial Literature: Aesthetics and the Transatlantic Book Trade, 1800–1850* (Philadelphia: University of Pennsylvania Press, 2015), ch. 5. Rezek focuses on Cooper's practice of revising his novels for British readers; for a striking example of how Cooper toned down the boisterous US nationalism of *The Pioneers*, the first novel in the Leatherstocking series, see esp. 141–48.

10. *Letters and Journals: James Fenimore Cooper*, 6 vols., ed. James Franklin Beard (Cambridge, MA: Harvard University Press, 1960–68), IV, 112; James Fenimore Cooper, *The Deerslayer; or, The First War Path*, ed. James Franklin Beard et al. (1841; Albany: State University of New York Press, 1987), 1, 5, 11 (this edition includes the two prefaces to *The Deerslayer*, along with the 1850 preface to the Leatherstocking novels).

11. Rans, *Cooper's Leather-Stocking Novels*, 55.

12. H. Daniel Peck, *A World by Itself: The Pastoral Moment in Cooper's Fiction* (New Haven, CT: Yale University Press, 1977), 159; William P. Kelly, *Plotting America's Past: Fenimore Cooper and the Leatherstocking Tales* (Carbondale: University of Southern Illinois Press, 1983), 168.

13. Cooper, *The Deerslayer*, 16, 146.

14. Bender, *A Nation among Nations*, 62; Gregory H. Nobles, *American Frontiers: Cultural Encounters and Continental Conquest* (New York: Hill and Wang, 1997), 63.

15. Cooper, *The Deerslayer*, 546.

16. On Fisher's critical concept of the "hard fact," see *Hard Facts*, esp. 3–21.

17. But for a more complex reading of "the stadialist model of progress" in Cooper, which underscores the losses that accompany progress, see George Dekker, *The American Historical Romance* (Cambridge: Cambridge University Press, 1987), 73–98.

18. James Fenimore Cooper, *The Last of the Mohicans: A Narrative of 1757*, ed. James Franklin Beard et al. (1826; Albany: State University of New York Press, 1983), 138.

19. John P. McWilliams, *Political Justice in a Republic: James Fenimore Cooper's America* (Berkeley: University of California Press, 1972), 278, 280.

20. See Mark Twain, "Fenimore Cooper's Literary Offenses," *North American Review* 161 (1895): 1–12.

21. See, for example, Richard Slotkin, *Regeneration through Violence: The Mythology of the American Frontier, 1600–1860* (Middletown, CT: Wesleyan University Press, 1973), ch. 13; and Leland S. Person, "The Historical Paradoxes of Manhood in Cooper's *The Deerslayer*," *Novel: A Forum on Fiction* 32.1 (1998): 76–98.

22. Dana D. Nelson, "Cooper's Leatherstocking Conversations: Identity, Friendship, and Democracy in the New Nation," in *A Historical Guide to James Fenimore Cooper*, ed. Leland S. Person (Oxford: Oxford University Press, 2007), 139; Cooper, *The Last of the Mohicans*, 31, 183.

23. Cooper, *The Deerslayer*, 59. All future page references to the 1987 State University of New York Press edition will be supplied parenthetically in the main body of the chapter.

24. George M. Fredrickson, *The Black Image in the White Mind: The Debate on Afro-American Character and Destiny, 1817–1914* (New York: Harper and Row, 1971), qtd. 104; on the romantic racialism of Kinmont and Stowe, see 97–129.

25. On Cooper's suspicion of racial categories, see also Geoffrey Sanborn, "James Fenimore Cooper and the Invention of the Passing Novel," *American Literature* 84.1 (2012): 1–29.

26. See Sandra Tomc, "'Clothes upon Sticks': James Fenimore Cooper and the Flat Frontier," *Texas Studies in Literature and Language* 51.2 (2009): 142–78.

27. See Thomas Cole's series of paintings *The Course of Empire* (1833–36), which may have been influenced by Cooper's early novels.

28. Cooper, *The Last of the Mohicans*, 344.

29. Cooper to Richard Bentley, letter of January 31, 1841, *Letters and Journals*, IV, 112. On the importance of women to the Leatherstocking series, see Nina Baym, "The Women of Cooper's Leatherstocking Tales," *American Quarterly* 23.5 (1971): 696–709; and Person, "Historical Paradoxes of Manhood."

30. Cheyfitz, "Savage Law," 120.

31. For an eloquent discussion of Cooper as a "creolized" American who drew on Native American culture and traditions for his ideals of deliberative democracy, see Sandra Gustafson, "Natty in the 1820s: Creole Subjects and Democratic Aesthetics in the Early Leatherstocking Tales," in *Creole Subjects in the Colonial Americas: Empires, Texts, Identities*, ed. Ralph Bauer and José Antonio Mazzotti (Chapel Hill: University of North Carolina Press, 2009), 465–90; and Sandra Gustafson, *Imagining Deliberative Democracy in the Early American Republic* (Chicago: University of Chicago Press, 2011), ch. 7.
32. See Fisher, *Hard Facts*, ch. 1.
33. Cooper, *Letters and Journals*, VI, 274–75.

Fifth of July: Nathaniel Paul and the Circulatory Routes of Black Nationalism

1. See Joanna Brooks, "The Early American Public Sphere and the Emergence of a Black Print Counterpublic," *William and Mary Quarterly*, 3rd series, 62.1 (2005): 67–92.
2. "Abolition of Slavery," *Freedom's Journal*, April 20, 1827, 2. For useful backgrounds on slavery and New York, see Shane White, *Somewhat More Independent: The End of Slavery in New York City* (Athens: University of Georgia Press, 1991).
3. A Nathaniel Paul letter and two of his speeches are the opening three selections in *The Black Abolitionist Papers. Volume I. The British Isles, 1830–1865*, ed. C. Peter Ripley et al. (Chapel Hill: University of North Carolina Press, 1985). The editors provide a brief biographical note on Paul, which helped to initiate my research. For an intriguing discussion of the Paul brothers in Boston during the first two decades of the nineteenth century, see John Saillant, "'This Week Black Paul Preach'd': Fragment and Method in Early African American Studies," *Early American Studies* 14.1 (2016): 48–81. Useful information about the Paul family can also be found in Lois Brown, *Pauline Elizabeth Hopkins: Black Daughter of the Revolution* (Chapel Hill: University of North Carolina Press, 2008). Nathaniel Paul was Pauline Hopkins's maternal great-granduncle, but she claimed him as a direct descendent.
4. Sterling Stuckey, ed., *The Ideological Origins of Black Nationalism* (Boston: Beacon Press, 1972), 6, 1.
5. Paul Gilroy, *The Black Atlantic: Modernity and Double Consciousness* (Cambridge, MA: Harvard University Press, 1993), 4, 35. In response to Gilroy, Joseph Rezek has called for an even greater emphasis on book history in studies of the early black Atlantic; see his "The Orations on the Abolition of the Slave Trade and the Uses of Print in the Early Black

Atlantic," *Early American Literature* 45.3 (2010): 655–82; and "The Print Atlantic: Phillis Wheatley, Ignatius Sancho, and the Cultural Significance of the Book," *Early African American Print Culture*, ed. Lara Langer Cohen and Jordan Alexander Stein (Philadelphia: University of Pennsylvania Press, 2012), 19–39. As I elaborate in this chapter, many of Paul's speeches were published in British and American newspapers and circulated widely.

6. Nathaniel Paul, *An Address, Delivered on the Celebration of the Abolition of Slavery, in the State of New-York, July 5, 1827* (Albany, NY: John B. Van Steenbergh, 1827), 12, 11, 18–19. On black elevation, see Frederick Cooper, "Elevating the Race: The Social Thought of Black Leaders, 1827–1850," *American Quarterly* 24.5 (1972): 604–25; and Robert S. Levine, *Martin Delany, Frederick Douglass, and the Politics of Representative Identity* (Chapel Hill: University of North Carolina Press, 1997), ch. 1.

7. Martin Robison Delany, *The Condition, Elevation, Emigration, and Destiny of the Colored People of the United States* (1852; rpt. New York: Arno Press, 1969), 12.

8. Paul, *An Address, Delivered on the Celebration of the Abolition of Slavery*, 3, 12, 8, 13.

9. Ibid., 6, 10, 11, 21, 23.

10. Ibid., 16, 15, 14.

11. Nathaniel Paul, *An Address, Delivered at Troy, on the Celebration of the Abolition of Slavery, in the State of New York, July 6, 1829 – Second Anniversary* (Albany, NY: John B. Van Steenbergh, 1829), 6–7, 8, 10, 16.

12. On Wilberforce, see William H. Pease and Jane H. Pease, *Black Utopia: Negro Communal Experiments in America* (Madison: The State Historical Society of Wisconsin, 1963), ch. 3; and Robin W. Winks, *The Blacks in Canada: A History* (1971; rpt. Montreal: McGill-Queen's University Press, 1997), 153–62.

13. Austin Steward, *Twenty-Two Years a Slave, and Forty Years a Freeman*, ed. Jane H. Pease and William H. Pease (1857; rpt. Reading, MA: Addison-Wesley, 1969), 114.

14. "Colony in Upper Canada," *Liberator*, September 17, 1831, 150; R., "Rev. Nathaniel Paul," *Liberator*, January 14, 1832, 5, 6.

15. "Rev. Nathaniel Paul," *Liberator*, August 25, 1832, 135.

16. "The Rev. Nathaniel Paul in Scotland," *Liberator*, February 7, 1835, 22.

17. Manisha Sinha, *The Slave's Cause: A History of Abolitionism* (New Haven, CT: Yale University Press, 2016), 221; Henry Mayer, *William Lloyd Garrison and the Abolition of Slavery* (New York: St. Martin's, 1998), 162. Mayer patronizingly refers to Paul's speeches as the fulfillment of "assignments" (162) given by British abolitionists. The evidence suggests that Paul was an eloquent and independent speaker who was able to develop arguments on his own or in

consultation with his abolitionist colleagues. For excellent discussions of Paul's work with British abolitionists in attacking Cresson, see Blackett's *Building an Antislavery Wall*, 53–69; and Ousmane K. Power-Greene, *Against Wind and Tide: The African American Struggle against the Colonization Movement* (New York: New York University Press, 2014), 63–80. In addition to his lectures, Paul published a pamphlet that reprinted anti-ACS resolutions and addresses by African Americans; see Nathaniel Paul, *Reply to Mr. Joseph Phillips' Enquiry, Respecting "The Light in which the Operations of the American Colonization Society Are Viewed by the Free People of Colour in the United States"* (London: 1832). Paul would continue to defend Garrison from Cresson's and other colonizationists' attacks even after Garrison returned to the United States, asserting in a letter printed in the *Liberator*: "It is, however, almost beyond endurance, to hear these men talk of your having slandered your country while in England. To slander America, with regard to her treatment of her slaves, and free colored people, would be tantamount to slandering his Satanic majesty, by calling him wicked!" (*Liberator*, April 12, 1834, 15).

18. Nathaniel Paul to William Lloyd Garrison, letter of April 10, 1833, *Liberator* June 22, 1833, rpt. in *Black Abolitionist Papers*, ed. Ripley, 38, 39. Garrison and Paul would together visit Thomas Clarkson in the summer of 1833, and at that meeting, according to Garrison, Paul convinced Clarkson to withdraw his support for the American Colonization Society (ACS). See R. J. M. Blackett, *Building an Antislavery Wall: Black Americans in the Atlantic Abolitionist Movement, 1830–1860* (Baton Rouge: Louisiana State University Press, 1983), 67.

19. "Speech by Nathaniel Paul, Delivered at Exeter Hall, London, England, 13 July 1833," *Black Abolitionist Papers*, ed. Ripley, 45, 46–47. See also *Speeches Delivered at the Anti-Colonization Meeting in Exeter Hall, London* (Boston, 1833), 13–15.

20. Nathaniel Paul, "Compensation for Slaves," *Liberator*, August 31, 1833, 137, 138.

21. "Speech by Nathaniel Paul, Delivered at Exeter Hall," *Black Abolitionist Papers*, 44, 46, 48; Gilroy, *The Black Atlantic*, 46; Paul to Garrison, letter of April 10, 1833, *Black Abolitionist Papers*, 38.

22. "Wilberforce Colony," *Liberator*, April 13, 1833, 57. See also "Caution to the Public," *Liberator*, March 9, 1833, 40.

23. "Israel Lewis," *Liberator*, July 16, 1836, 113.

24. Steward, *Twenty-Two Years a Slave*, 152; "Rev. Nathaniel Paul," *Liberator*, December 19, 1835, 204.

25. Steward, *Twenty-Two Years a Slave*, 115.

26. Garrison's letter of December 17, 1835, to Lewis Tappan describing how he borrowed money from Tappan is cited in Benjamin Quarles, *Black Abolitionists* (New York: Oxford University Press, 1969), 21, and is available

in the Lewis Tappan Papers at the Library of Congress, Washington, DC. That said, in a letter of June 1856 from William Lloyd Garrison to Austin Steward, Garrison asserts: "I borrowed no money, nor had I any occasion to ask a loan of my friend, Paul" (*Twenty-Two Years a Slave*, 205).

27. Steward, *Twenty-Two Years a Slave*, 159, 160–61. The story of Paul's putative decline into poverty, illness, and obscurity is also rehearsed by Winks, *The Blacks in Canada*, 161. For brief remarks on Paul as a vital abolitionist in the late 1830s, see Quarles, *Black Abolitionists*, 47, 87.

28. See *The Friend of Man*, March 14, 1838, 3; and *The Colored American*, June 27, 1839, 2.

29. As Louis Brown notes, Anne Aday lived on into the 1840s and then vanished into obscurity. After Paul's death, she remained in New York and was befriended by Garrison and other abolitionists; see Brown's *Pauline Elizabeth Hopkins*, 247–48.

30. Winks, *The Blacks in Canada*, 160. In *Black Utopia*, Pease and Pease similarly conclude that "Paul was a rascal, but not a criminal" (60).

American Studies in an Age of Extinction: Poe, Hawthorne, Katrina

1. See Melani McAlister, "Rethinking the 'Clash of Civilizations': American Evangelicals, the Bush Administration, and the Winding Road to the Iraq War," in *Race, Nation, and Empire in American History*, ed. James. T. Campbell, Matthew Pratt Guterl, and Robert G. Lee (Chapel Hill: University of North Carolina Press, 2007), 352–74.

2. Doug Struck, "Emissions Growth Must End in 7 Years, U.N. Warns: Report Lays out Stark Choices to Avoid the Death of Species," *The Washington Post*, November 18, 2007, A10; Juliet Eilperin, "Carbon Output Must Near Zero to Avert Danger, New Studies Say," *The Washington Post*, March 10, 2008, A1; Elizabeth Kolbert, *The Sixth Extinction: An Unnatural History* (New York: Henry Holt, 2014), 17–18; Lauren McCauley, "NASA: The Earth Is Running out of Water," *Common Dreams*, June 16, 2015, www.commondreams.org/news/2015/06/16/nasa-earth-running-out-water.

3. See Ernest Lee Tuveson, *Redeemer Nation: The Idea of America's Millennial Role* (Chicago: University of Chicago Press, 1968), esp. 1–34. For a consideration of millennialism in the comparative context of the Americas, see Thomas O. Beebee, *Millennial Literatures of the Americas, 1492–2002* (New York: Oxford University Press, 2009).

4. Donald E. Pease and Robyn Wiegman, "Futures," in *The Futures of American Studies*, ed. Donald E. Pease and Robyn Wiegman (Durham, NC: Duke University Press, 2002), 22.

5. Walter Benjamin, "Theses on the Philosophy of History," in *Illuminations*, ed. Hannah Arendt (New York: Schocken, 1969), 254, 263; Pease and Wiegman, "Futures," 3, 38. Benjamin's "Theses" was completed in 1940 and first published in 1950. For discussions of Benjamin in the larger context of messianic thought, see *Messianic Thought outside Theology*, ed. Anna Glazova and Paul North (New York: Fordham University Press, 2014). On Benjamin and American studies scholarship, see *States of Emergency: The Object of American Studies*, ed. Russ Castronovo and Susan Gillman (Chapel Hill: University of North Carolina Press, 2009).

6. Benjamin, "Theses on the Philosophy of History," 257, 261.

7. Kolbert, *The Sixth Extinction*, 3; Alan Weisman, *The World without Us* (New York: St. Martin's, 2007), 4, 15, 119. Weisman's bestselling book has been translated into over thirty languages. Two Weisman-inspired films appeared in 2008: *Life without People*, which was the History Channel's most widely viewed program of January 2008, and *Aftermath: Population Zero*, which aired on the National Geographic channel in March 2008.

8. Jack Miles, "Global Requiem: The Apocalyptic Moment in Religion," in *Religion and Cultural Studies*, ed. Susan L. Mizruchi (Princeton, NJ: Princeton University Press, 2001), 194, 196, 208.

9. Whitney R. Cross, *The Burned-Over District: The Social and Intellectual History of Enthusiastic Religion in Western New York, 1800–1850* (1950; New York: Harper Torchbooks, 1965), 287. On the European tradition of premillennialism, dating back to the medieval period, see Norman Cohn, *The Pursuit of the Millennium: Revolutionary Millenarians and Mystical Anarchists of the Middle Ages* (1957; rev. ed., New York: Oxford University Press, 1970).

10. See Gary Scharnhorst, "Images of the Millerites in American Literature," *American Quarterly* 32.1 (1980): 19–36. Scharnhorst reports that there were over one hundred Millerite tent-meetings in the early 1840s with a cumulative attendance of around five hundred thousand worshipers and the curious (21).

11. Jan Stievermann, "The Discursive Construction of American Identity in Millennialist Tracts during the War of 1812," in *Millennial Thought in America: Historical and Intellectual Contexts, 1630–1860*, ed. Bernd Engler, Joerg O. Fichte, and Oliver Scheiding (Trier: Wissenschaftlicher Verlag, 2002), 283, 297. Seminal studies of American millennialism and nationalism include Tuveson, *Redeemer Nation*; and James West Davidson, *The Logic of Millennial Thought: Eighteenth-Century New England* (New Haven, CT: Yale University Press, 1977).

12. There was also transatlantic interest in Miller; on Millerites in Great Britain, see Penelope J. Corfield, *Time and the Shape of History* (New Haven, CT: Yale University Press, 2007), 113–21.

13. William Miller, *Evidence from Scripture and History of the Second Coming of Christ, about the Year 1843: Exhibited in a Course of Lectures* (Troy, NY: Elias Gates, 1838), 22, iii, 111, 166, 16, 51, vii. The slightly revised and expanded edition was published in Boston in 1842 by Joshua V. Himes.
14. Miller, *Evidence from Scripture and History*, iii, 267, 278.
15. Scharnhorst agues for the direct influence of Miller on the tale ("Images of the Millerites," 21–22). See also Douglass Robinson, "Poe's Mini-Apocalypse: 'The Conversation of Eiros and Charmion'," *Studies in Short Fiction* 19.4 (1982): 329–37.
16. Edgar Allan Poe, "The Conversation of Eiros and Charmion," *Edgar Allan Poe, Poetry and Tales*, ed. Patrick F. Quinn (New York: Library of America, 1984), 359.
17. Benjamin, "Theses on the Philosophy of History," 263.
18. Miller, *Evidence from Scripture and History*, 166.
19. Poe, "Conversation," 359, 363. On apocalyptic endings in Poe's writings, see Paul John Eakin, "Poe's Sense of an Ending," *American Literature* 45.1 (1973): 1–22. For an influential analysis of connections between fictional narrative endings and conceptions of the Last Judgment, see Frank Kermode, *The Sense of an Ending: Studies in the Theory of Fiction, with a New Epilogue* (1967; New York: Oxford University Press, 2000), 3–31.
20. Edgar Allan Poe, "The Philosophy of Composition," in *Edgar Allan Poe, Essays and Reviews*, ed. G. R. Thompson (New York: Library of America, 1984), 13. There is also a materialist, physical-science dimension to Poe's sense of an ending, which comes across most clearly in his 1848 prose poem *Eureka*, where he posits that the Godhead is the force within the matter of the universe that is forever imploding and thus moving toward "*Inevitable Annihilation*" (Poe, *Poetry and Tales*, 1261 [Poe's emphasis]).
21. Poe, "Conversation," 361, 359, 360, 361, 362, 363. According to Martin Rees, the statistics suggest that we face our own dire possibilities of being hit by a runaway comet or asteroid. The last major hit was sixty-five million years ago, probably resulting in the extinction of the dinosaurs. Because, as Rees writes, a "ten-kilometre asteroid, harbinger of worldwide catastrophe and major extinctions, is expected to hit Earth once every fifty to one-hundred-million years," we could say that in some ways we're fifteen millions years overdue; see Martin Rees, *Our Final Hour: A Scientist's Warning: How Terror, Errors, and Environmental Disaster Threaten Humankind's Future in this Century—On Earth and Beyond* (New York: Basic Books, 2003), 90–91.
22. Poe, "Conversation," 362; Benjamin, "Theses on the Philosophy of History," 263.
23. Poe, "Conversation," 361, 363.

24. For a classic account of Poe's rejection of the American literary nationalists of his time, see Perry Miller, *The Raven and the Whale: The War of Words and Wits in the Era of Poe and Melville* (New York: Harcourt, Brace, and World, 1956).

25. In addition to the two Hawthorne sketches I discuss in this chapter, see also "The Christmas Banquet" (1844), which has an allusion to Miller, and "Earth's Holocaust" (1844), which focuses on book burning. James Hewitson argues that Hawthorne makes use of Miller to attack reformism, thus presenting Hawthorne as considerably more skeptical about reform than he actually was during the 1840s (James Hewitson, "'To Despair at the Tedious Delay of the Final Configuration': Hawthorne's Use of the Figure of Father Miller," *ESQ: A Journal of the American Renaissance* 53.1 [2007]: 89–111). Hewitson ignores Scharnhorst's much more nuanced analysis of Hawthorne's and other American writers' responses to Miller (see "Images of the Millerites"). For discussions of the influence of millennial thought on Hawthorne's writings of the 1840s, see also Jonathan A. Cook, "New Heavens, Poor Old Earth: Satirical Apocalypse in Hawthorne's *Mosses from an Old Manse,*" *ESQ: A Journal of the American Renaissance* 39.4 (1993): 208–51; and Beebee, *Millennial Literatures of the Americas*, 110–15. On Hawthorne as a conflicted reformer during the 1840s and 1850s, see Robert S. Levine, *Dislocating Race and Nation: Episodes in Nineteenth-Century American Literary Nationalism* (Chapel Hill: University of North Carolina Press, 2008), ch. 3.

26. Nathaniel Hawthorne, "The Hall of Fantasy," in Nathaniel Hawthorne, *Tales and Sketches*, ed. Roy Harvey Pearce (New York: Library of America, 1982), 734, 738, 741, 740, 741–42.

27. Ibid., 742, 743.

28. Hawthorne, "The New Adam and Eve," *Tales and Sketches*, 746, 758, 759.

29. Ibid., 759, 760. The Bunker Hill Monument was dedicated on June 17, 1843, right around the time that Hawthorne published "The New Adam and Eve."

30. Hawthorne, "New Adam and Eve," 760, 761, 762.

31. Ibid., 762, 763.

32. Pease and Wiegman, "Futures," 37. For a representative critique of Pease and the so-called New Americanists as presentist in their politics, see G. R. Thompson and Eric Carl Link, *Neutral Ground: New Traditionalism and the American Romance Controversy* (Baton Rouge: Louisiana State University Press, 1999).

33. Wai Chee Dimock, "World History according to Katrina," *States of Emergency*, 156; Wai Chee Dimock "Afterword: The Hurricane and the Nation," *ESQ: A Journal of the American Renaissance* 50.1–3 (2004): 224, 227, 226. See also Anna Brickhouse, "'L'Ouragan de Flammes' ('The Hurricane of Flames'): New Orleans and Transamerican Catastrophe, 1866/2005," *American Quarterly*

59.4 (2007): 1097–1127; and Kirsten Gruesz, "The Gulf of Mexico System and the 'Latinness' of New Orleans," *American Literary History* 18.3 (2006): 468–497.

34. Christopher Lloyd, *Rooting Memory, Rooting Place: Regionalism in the Twenty-First-Century American South* (New York: Palgrave Macmillan, 2015), 54; for his insightful discussion of Spike Lee's *When the Levees Broke*, see 70–84.

35. See also, for example, the chapters on Katrina in Katherine Henniger, *Ordering the Façade: Photography and Contemporary Southern Women's Writings* (Chapel Hill: University of North Carolina Press, 2007); and Anna Hartwell, *Rewriting Exodus: American Futures from Du Bois to Obama* (London: Pluto Press, 2011).

36. Benjamin, "Theses on the Philosophy of History," 262.

The Slave Narrative and the Revolutionary Tradition of African American Autobiography

1. John Sekora, "Black Message/White Envelope: Genre, Authenticity, and Authority in the Antebellum Slave Narrative," *Callaloo* 32 (1987): 509, 502, 497, 510; James Olney, "'I Was Born': Slave Narratives, Their Status as Autobiography and Literature," *Callaloo* 20 (1984): 64. See also Robert B. Stepto, *From Behind the Veil: A Study of Afro-American Narrative* (Urbana: University of Illinois Press, 1979), ch. 1.

2. Benjamin Franklin, *The Autobiography and Other Writings*, ed. Kenneth Silverman (New York: Penguin, 1986), 80.

3. Eric J. Sundquist, *To Wake the Nations: Race in the Making of American Literature* (Cambridge, MA: Harvard University Press, 1993), 21; William L. Andrews, *To Tell a Free Story: The First Century of Afro-American Autobiography, 1760–1865* (Urbana: University of Illinois Press, 1986), 1; Xiomara Santamarina, *Belabored Professions: Narratives of African American Working Womanhood* (Chapel Hill: University of North Carolina Press, 2005), 40. On the collaborative nature of the slave narrative, see also Barbara McCaskill, "Collaborative American Slave Narratives," in *The Oxford Handbook of the African American Slave Narrative*, ed. John Ernest (New York: Oxford University Press, 2014), 298–312.

4. Theodore Parker, "The American Scholar" (1849), in Theodore Parker, *The American Scholar*, ed. George Willis Cooke (Boston: American Unitarian Association, 1907), 37.

5. Michaël Roy, "Cheap Editions, Little Books, and Handsome Duodecimos: A Book-History Approach to Antebellum Slave Narratives," *MELUS* 40.3 (2015): 70. See also Teresa A. Goddu, "The Slave Narrative as Material Text," in *Oxford Handbook of the African American Slave Narrative*, 149–64; and the essays collected in *Early African American Print Culture*, ed. Lara

Langer Cohen and Jordan Alexander Stein (Philadelphia: University of Pennsylvania Press, 2012).

6. For an invaluable overview of Franklin's influence on subsequent writers, including African American writers, see Carla Mulford, "Figuring Benjamin Franklin in American Cultural Memory," *New England Quarterly* 72.3 (1999): 415–43.

7. On the impact of spiritual autobiography on black writing, see Katherine Clay Bassard, *Spiritual Interrogations: Culture, Gender, and Community in Early African American Writing* (Princeton, NJ: Princeton University Press, 1999); and Yolanda Pierce, "Redeeming Bondage: The Captivity Narrative and the Spiritual Autobiography in the African American Slave-Narrative Tradition," in *The Cambridge Companion to the African American Slave Narrative*, ed. Audrey Fisch (Cambridge: Cambridge University Press, 2007), 83–98. For a discussion of the topic with respect to classic white autobiography, see Daniel B. Shea's *Spiritual Autobiography in Early America* (Princeton, NJ: Princeton University Press, 1968).

8. For examples, see "Franklin's Birthday," the *North Star*, January 14, 1848, 1; and "Franklin," January 28, 1848, the *North Star*, 1.

9. Franklin, *Autobiography*, 21.

10. James M. Cox, *Recovering Literature's Lost Ground: Essays in American Autobiography* (Baton Rouge: Louisiana State University Press, 1989), 16. See also Christopher Looby, "'The Affairs of the Revolution Occasion'd the Interruption: Writing, Revolution, Deferral, and Conciliation in Franklin's Autobiography," *American Quarterly* 38.1 (1986): 72–96.

11. Venture Smith, *A Narrative of the Life and Adventures of Venture, a Native of Africa: But Resident above Sixty Years in the United States of America. Related by Himself* (1798), in *Unchained Voices: An Anthology of Black Authors in the English-Speaking World of the Eighteenth Century*, ed. Vincent Carretta (Lexington: University Press of Kentucky, 1996), 369, 382, 369, 372. For an insightful reading of Smith's *Narrative*, see Robert S. Desrochers Jr., "'Not Fade Away': The Narrative of Venture Smith, an African American in the Early Republic," *Journal of American History* 84.1 (1997): 40–66; and the essays in *Venture Smith and the Business of Slavery and Freedom*, ed. James Brewer Stewart and James O. Horton (Amherst: University of Massachusetts Press, 2010).

12. William Grimes, *Life of William Grimes, the Runaway Slave, Brought down to the Present Time, Written by Himself* (1825; rev. ed. 1855), in *Five Black Lives*, ed. Arna Bontemps (Middleton, CT: Wesleyan University Press, 1971), 120.

13. Andrews, *To Tell a Free Story*, 52.

14. Douglass, *Narrative*, 39, 106, 151. On the collaborative nature of the *Narrative*, see Robert S. Levine, *The Lives of Frederick Douglass* (Cambridge, MA: Harvard University Press, 2016), ch. 1.

15. On Franklin and Douglass, see Rafia Zafar, "Franklinian Douglass: The Afro-American as Representative Man," in *Frederick Douglass: New Literary and Historical Essays*, ed. Eric J. Sundquist (Cambridge: Cambridge University Press, 1990), 99–117.

16. Douglass, *Narrative*, 124, 35, 151.

17. Frederick Douglass, *My Bondage and My Freedom*, ed. William L. Andrews (Urbana: University of Illinois Press, 1987), 17, 9, 11, 9. On the black communitarian emphases of *Bondage*, see Levine, *Lives of Frederick Douglass*, ch. 3.

18. Douglass, *Bondage*, 22.

19. William Wells Brown, *Narrative of William W. Brown, a Fugitive Slave. Written by Himself* (1847), rpt. in *Slave Narratives*, ed. William L. Andrews and Henry Louis Gates Jr. (New York: Library of America, 2002), 420, 398; Franklin, *Autobiography*, 92; Brown, *Narrative*, 391, 399.

20. Henry Bibb, *Narrative of the Life and Adventures of Henry Bibb, an American Slave, Written by Himself* (1849), rpt. in Andrews and Gates, *Slave Narratives*, 442, 373; Brown, *Narrative*, 386.

21. Bibb, *Narrative*, 437, 441, 444.

22. Ibid., 452, 459, 552, 553.

23. Maurice O. Wallace, "'I Rose a Freeman': Power, Property, and the Performance of Manhood in the Slave Narrative," in *Oxford Handbook of the African American Slave* Narrative, 275, 274; Kimberly Drake, "Rewriting the American Self: Race, Gender, and Identity in the Autobiographies of Frederick Douglass and Harriet Jacobs," *MELUS* 22.4 (1997): 96. See also Nellie Y. McKay, "The Narrative Self: Race, Politics, and Culture in Black Women's Autobiography," in *Women, Autobiography, Theory: A Reader*, ed. Sidonie Smith and Julia Watson (Madison: University of Wisconsin Press, 1998), 96–107. And for an influential critique of the masculinist bent of Douglass's *Narrative*, see Deborah E. McDowell, "In the First Place: Making Frederick Douglass and the Afro-American Narrative Tradition," in *Critical Essays on Frederick Douglass*, ed. William L. Andrews (Boston: G. K. Hall, 1991), 192–213.

24. Joanne M. Braxton, *Black Women Writing Autobiography: A Tradition within a Tradition* (Philadelphia: Temple University Press, 1989), 23, 30, 29. See also Xiomara Santamarina, "Black Womanhood in North American Women's Slave Narratives," in *Cambridge Companion to the African American Slave Narrative*, 232–45; and Doveanna S. Fulton, "'There Is Might in Each': Slave

Narratives and Black Feminism," in *Oxford Handbook of the African American Slave Narrative*, 248–59.

25. *Narrative of Sojourner Truth, a Northern Slave, Emancipated from Bodily Servitude by the State of New York, in 1828* (1850), rpt. in Andrews and Gates, *Slave Narratives*, 600; Harriet A. Jacobs, *Incidents in the Life of a Slave Girl. Written by Herself* (1861), ed. Jean Fagan Yellin (Cambridge, MA: Harvard University Press, 1987), 26, 85.

26. *Narrative of Sojourner Truth*, 573, 594.

27. Jacobs, *Incidents*, 3, 54, 128, 114; Henry David Thoreau, *Walden and Resistance to Civil Government*, ed. William Rossi (New York: Norton, 1992), 235; Jacobs, *Incidents*, 183, 201.

28. Wallace, "'I Rose a Freeman,'" 274.

29. My phrasing is meant to suggest a degree of skepticism about Kenneth Warren's claim that African American literature is bounded by the rise of Jim Crow during the 1890s, on the one side, and the early Civil Rights Movement, on the other; see his forceful but I think overargued *What Was African American Literature?* (Cambridge, MA: Harvard University Press, 2011).

"Whiskey, Blacking, and All": Temperance and Race in William Wells Brown's *Clotel*

1. Letter from William Wells Brown, *Frederick Douglass' Paper*, August 26, 1853, 2. For the editorial in support of the Maine Law, see *Frederick Douglass' Paper*, March 18, 1852, 2. By 1855, thirteen states had adopted their own versions of the Maine Law, though by the Civil War most such laws had been repealed. For a good discussion of the politics of the Maine Law, see Ian R. Tyrrell, *Sobering Up: From Temperance to Prohibition in Antebellum America, 1800– 1860* (Westport, CT: Greenwood, 1979), ch. 10. On Douglass and Stowe, see Robert S. Levine, *Martin Delany, Frederick Douglass, and the Politics of Representative Identity* (Chapel Hill: University of North Carolina Press, 1997), ch. 2. On Brown and Stowe, see Peter A. Dorsey, "De-authorizing Slavery: Realism in Stowe's *Uncle Tom's Cabin* and Brown's *Clotel*," *ESQ* 41.4 (1995): 257–88.

2. William Wells Brown, *Clotel; or, The President's Daughter: A Narrative of Slave Life in the United States* (1853), ed. Robert S. Levine (Boston: Bedford/ St. Martin's, 2011), 187, 191. Subsequent citations from the novel and its prefatory "Narrative" are from this edition and will be noted parenthetically in the main body of the text.

3. Paul Gilmore, *The Genuine Article: Race, Mass Culture, and American Literary Manhood* (Durham, NC: Duke University Press, 2001), 66.

4. Geoffrey Sanborn, *Plagiarama! William Wells Brown and the Aesthetics of Attractions* (New York: Columbia University Press, 2016), 79, 81.

5. William Wells Brown, *The American Fugitive in Europe: Sketches of Places and People Abroad* (Boston: John P. Jewett, 1855), 189. While abroad from 1849 to 1854, Brown attended numerous temperance conventions and was voted a life member of the Edinburgh Temperance Society (William Edward Farrison, *William Wells Brown: Author and Reformer* [Chicago: University of Chicago Press, 1969], 180). For additional information on Brown and temperance, see Ezra Greenspan's *William Wells Brown: An African American Life* (New York: Norton, 2014), esp. 447–49.

6. Josephine Brown, *Biography of an American Bondman, by His Daughter* (Boston: R. F. Wallcut, 1856), 52. She notes about her father: "As one of the pioneers in the Temperance cause, among the colored people in Buffalo [circa 1840–43], he did good service. He regarded temperance and education as the means best calculated to elevate the free people of color" (52).

7. As Donald Yacovone and others have documented, temperance groups were formed by free blacks in the late eighteenth century; by the late 1820s temperance was central to the emergent black press and black convention movement of the period. See Donald Yacovone, "The Transformation of the Black Temperance Movement, 1827–1854: An Interpretation," *Journal of the Early Republic* 8.3 (1988): 281–97; and Patrick Rael, *Black Identity and Black Protest in the Antebellum North* (Chapel Hill: University of North Carolina Press, 2002), 65–72.

8. "Minutes and Proceedings of the Third Annual Convention, for the Improvement of the Free People of Colour in These United States, Held by Adjournments in the City of Philadelphia (1833)," rpt. in *Minutes and Proceedings of the National Negro Conventions, 1830–1864*, ed. Howard Holman Bell (New York: Arno, 1969), 18; William Whipper, "Presidential Address to the Colored Temperance Society of Philadelphia," rpt. in *The Black Abolitionist Papers: The United States, 1830–1846*, ed. C. Peter Ripley et al. (Chapel Hill: University of North Carolina Press, 1991), 125–26; "Proceedings of the State Convention of the Colored Freemen of Pennsylvania, Held in Pittsburgh, on the 23rd, 24th, and 25th of August, 1841, for the Purpose of Considering Their Condition, and Means of Improvement," in *Proceedings of the Black State Conventions, 1840–1865*, ed. Philip S. Foner and George E. Walker (Philadelphia: Temple University Press, 1979), I:109; *Northern Star and Freeman's Advocate*, 1 (1842): 18. On Delany's interest in temperance during the 1830s, see Victor Ullman, *Martin R. Delany: The Beginnings of Black Nationalism* (Boston: Beacon Press, 1971), 25–30.

9. Frederick Douglass, "Intemperance and Slavery: An Address Delivered in Cork, Ireland, on 20 October 1845," in *The Frederick Douglass Papers: Series*

One: Speeches, Debates, and Interviews, ed. John W. Blassingame et al. (New Haven, CT: Yale University Press, 1979), I:56. By the 1840s, according to Yacovone, "temperance and abolitionism had become virtually synonymous" ("Transformation of the Black Temperance Movement," 290). For a fuller discussion of Douglass and temperance, see Levine, *Martin Delany, Frederick Douglass*, ch. 3.

10. Theodore Weld, *American Slavery as It Is: Testimony of a Thousand Witnesses* (New York: American Anti-Slavery Society, 1839), 115; William Wells Brown, *A Lecture Delivered before the Female Anti-Slavery Society of Salem, at Lyceum Hall, Nov. 14, 1847* (Boston: Massachusetts Anti-Slavery Society, 1847), 4. As a historian of antebellum temperance observes, these reformers believed that to "be free, it was necessary to curb appetites, to subordinate passions to reason, to control animalistic impulses through the development of moral ideas" (W. J. Rorabaugh, *The Alcoholic Republic: An American Tradition* [New York: Oxford University Press, 1979], 200).

11. Josephine Brown, *Biography*, 11. For a good discussion of Brown's concerns about the sexual exploitation of slave women, see Ann duCille, *The Coupling Convention: Sex, Text, and Tradition in Black Women's Fiction* (New York: Oxford University Press, 1993), 17–29.

12. W. Wells Brown, *Three Years in Europe; or, Places I Have Seen and People I Have Met* (London: Charles Gilpin, 1852), 274.

13. On Brown's use of "rumors" about the relationship between Jefferson and his slave Sally Hemmings, see William Edward Farrison's classic essay "Clotel, Thomas Jefferson, and Sally Hemmings," *CLA Journal* 17.2 (1973): 147–74. On the significance of Brown's historical and cultural sources, see also Russ Castronovo, *Fathering the Nation: American Genealogies of Slavery and Freedom* (Berkeley: University of California Press, 1995), 162–70; John Ernest, *Resistance and Reformation in Nineteenth-Century African-American Literature: Brown, Wilson, Jacobs, Delany, Douglass, and Harper* (Jackson: University of Mississippi Press, 1995), ch. 1; and Sanborn, *Plagiarama!*

14. See Lydia Maria Child, "The Quadroons," in *Fact and Fiction: A Collection of Stories* (New York: C. S. Francis, 1847), 61–76. On Child's antislavery fiction, see Carolyn L. Karcher, "Rape, Murder, and Revenge in 'Slavery's Pleasant Homes': Lydia Maria Child's Antislavery Fiction and the Limits of Genre," *Women's Studies International Forum* 9.4 (1986): 323–32.

15. See, for example, T. S. Arthur, *Temperance Tales; or, Six Nights with the Washingtonians*, 2 vols. (Philadelphia: W. A. Leary, 1848), esp. "The Broken Merchant" and "The Tavern Keeper."

16. See, for example, William C. Nell, *Services of Colored Americans in the Wars of 1776 and 1812* (1851; rpt. New York: AMS, 1976).

17. On John Randolph and the fate of the approximately five-hundred slaves emancipated at his death in 1833, see William H. Pease and Jane H. Pease, *Black Utopia: Negro Communal Experiments in America* (Madison: State Historical Society of Wisconsin, 1963), 26–27.

18. See, for example, George Fitzhugh, *Slavery Justified, by a Southerner* (Fredericksburg, VA: Recorder Printing Office, 1850).

19. For an insightful discussion of this scene, see Christopher Mulvey, "The Fugitive Slave and the New World of the North: William Wells Brown's Discovery of America," in *The Black Columbiad: Defining Moments in African American Literature and Culture*, ed. Werner Sollors and Maria Diedrich (Cambridge, MA: Harvard University Press, 1994), esp. 99–102. This myth of origins would continue to speak to Brown's post–Civil War concerns. In *The Rising Son; or, The Antecedents and Advancement of the Colored Race* (1874; rpt. New York: Negro Universities Press, 1970), Brown refers to the founders of Jamestown, now representative of the white racists opposing Reconstruction, as intemperate drinkers who "had with them their 'native beverage,' which, though not like the lager of the present time, was a drink over which they smoked and talked of 'Faderland,' and traded for the negroes they brought" (265). On temperance and Northern "free labor" rhetoric, see Eric Foner, *Free Soil, Free Labor, Free Men: The Ideology of the Republican Party before the Civil War* (New York: Oxford University Press, 1971), esp. 230–42. Consistent with his own commitment to free-labor ideals, Brown in *Clotel* calls attention to the ways in which slavery "reflects discredit on industry" (119), thus leading poor Southern whites to become, in the words of the New York missionary Hontz Snyder, "worthless, drunken, good-for-nothing[s]" (118).

20. Here and throughout *Clotel*, Brown pays close attention to spatial geographies; on this aspect of the novel, see Martha Schoolman, *Abolitionist Geographies* (Minneapolis: University of Minnesota Press, 2014), ch. 3; and Judith Madera, *Black Atlas: Geography and Flow in Nineteenth-Century African American Literature* (Durham, NC: Duke University Press, 2015), ch. 1.

21. In December 1848, the light-skinned Ellen Craft escaped from slavery in Georgia with the dark-skinned William Craft by masquerading as a slave master accompanied by his valet. Brown befriended the Crafts in 1849, lectured with them on numerous occasions in Britain, and modeled *Clotel*'s cross-dressing escape on the Crafts' escape. Brown discusses the Crafts in a letter to William Lloyd Garrison printed in the *Liberator*, January 12, 1849, 7. According to R. J. M. Blackett, when Brown and the Crafts lectured together, they regularly advocated temperance reform (*Beating against the Barriers:*

Biographical Essays in Nineteenth-Century Afro-American History [Baton Rouge: Louisiana State University Press, 1986], esp. 97).

22. Thomas Jefferson, *Notes on the State of Virginia* (New York: Harper Torchbooks, 1964), 124, 132–33.

23. On black writers' hesitations about representing black violence, see Raymond Hedin, "The Structuring of Emotion in Black American Fiction," *Novel* 16.1 (1982): 35–54.

24. Brown, *American Fugitive*, 83–86; William Wells Brown, *St. Domingo: Its Revolution and Its Patriots. A Lecture, Delivered before the Metropolitan Athenaeum, London, March 16, and at St. Thomas' Church, Philadelphia, December 20, 1854* (Boston: Bela Marsh, 1855), 13; William Wells Brown, *The Black Man, His Antecedents, His Genius, and His Achievements* (1863; rpt. New York: Arno, 1969), 85, 71, 61, 72. See also Brown's discussion of Nat Turner in William Wells Brown, *The Negro in the American Rebellion: His Heroism and His Fidelity* (1867; rpt. New York: Kraus Reprint Co., 1969), 20–24. As William L. Andrews notes, for many antislavery whites Madison Washington was a more appealing figure than Turner because Washington was seen "as singularly reasonable, self-controlled, and humane" (William L. Andrews, "The Novelization of Voice in Early African American Narrative," *PMLA* 105.1 [1990]: 28). Douglass presented Madison Washington in just this way in his 1853 novella, *The Heroic Slave*.

25. Harriet Beecher Stowe, *Dred: A Tale of the Great Dismal Swamp*, ed. Robert S. Levine (Chapel Hill: University of North Carolina Press, 2006), 406, 445–46.

26. On the strange ways in which marriage can seem a form of incest in domestic novels of the 1850s, see Cindy Weinstein, *Family, Kinship, and Sympathy in Nineteenth-Century American Literature* (Cambridge: Cambridge University Press, 2004), esp. chs. 1 and 6.

27. Picquilo's presence makes this first version of the novel the most subversive of the three book versions of *Clotel/le*. The subsequent versions eliminate Picquilo. For an excellent discussion of Brown's tendency to present resistance as the province of his male characters (while keeping his female characters circumscribed by sentimental plots that seem to demand their deaths), see M. Giulia Fabi, "The 'Unguarded Expressions of the Feelings of the Negroes': Gender, Slave Resistance, and William Wells Brown's Revisions of *Clotel*," *African American Review* 27.4 (1993): 639–54.

28. William Wells Brown, *Clotelle; or, The Colored Heroine* (Boston: Lee and Shepard, 1867), 106. For a powerful reading of this scene, see Jennifer James, *A Freedom Bought with Blood: African American War Literature from the Civil War to World War II* (Chapel Hill: University of North Carolina Press, 2007), ch. 1. The comments on Brown and Harper were made by W. C. Nell in the *Liberator* of July 31, 1857, cited in Farrison, *William Wells Brown*, 288.

29. Alonzo D. Moore, "Memoir of the Author," in Brown, *The Rising Son*, 25. On Brown and Hopkins, see Farrison, *William Wells Brown*, 436; and Louis Brown, *Pauline Elizabeth Hopkins: Black Daughter of the Revolution* (Chapel Hill: University of North Carolina Press, 2008), 299–300, 326–27, 345–51.
30. Brown, *The Negro in the American Rebellion*, 52. Brown similarly uses temperance to address white racism in the North, blaming the 1863 Draft Riots on an "infuriated band of drunken men, women, and children" (193).
31. William Wells Brown, *My Southern Home; or, The South and Its People*, ed. John Ernest (Chapel Hill: University of North Carolina Press, 2011), 176, 170.
32. Brown, *My Southern Home*, 127, 176, 186, 185, 183.

Beautiful Warships: The Transnational Aesthetics of Melville's *Israel Potter*

1. Key works include Russ Castronovo, *Beautiful Democracy: Aesthetics and Anarchy in a Global Era* (Chicago: University of Chicago Press, 2007); *Melville and Aesthetics*, ed. Samuel Otter and Geoffrey Sanborn (New York: Palgrave Macmillan, 2011); and *American Literature's Aesthetic Dimensions*, ed. Cindy Weinstein and Christopher Looby (New York: Columbia University Press, 2012).
2. See Wai Chee Dimock, *Shades of the Planet: American Literature as World Literature* (Princeton, NJ: Princeton University Press, 2007).
3. Elaine Scarry, *On Beauty and Being Just* (Princeton, NJ: Princeton University Press, 1999), 30, 106, 107.
4. Mark Canuel, "Doing Justice in Aesthetics," *Representations* 95.1 (2006): 97. See also Irene Kacandes, "Beauty on My Mind: Reading Literature in the Age of Cultural Studies," in *The Aesthetics of Cultural Studies*, ed. Michael Bérubé (Malden, MA: Blackwell, 2005), 156–74.
5. Immanuel Kant, *Critique of the Power of Judgment*, ed. Paul Guyer (Cambridge: Cambridge University Press, 2000), 130. For a useful discussion of Kant and the sublime, see Paul Crowther, *The Kantian Sublime: From Morality to Art* (Oxford: Clarendon, 1989). On Melville and the Kantian sublime, see John Stauffer, "Interracial Friendship and the Aesthetics of Freedom," in *Frederick Douglass and Herman Melville: Essays in Relation*, ed. Robert S. Levine and Samuel Otter (Chapel Hill: University of North Carolina Press, 2008), 134–58; and Nancy Fredricks, *Melville's Art of Democracy* (Athens: University of Georgia Press, 1995), 14–41.
6. Herman Melville, *Pierre; or, The Ambiguities*, ed. Robert S. Levine and Cindy Weinstein (New York: Norton, 2017), 206, 205; Herman Melville, *Israel Potter: His Fifty Years of Exile*, ed. Harrison Hayford, Hershel Parker, and G. Thomas Tanselle (Evanston and Chicago: Northwestern University Press

and The Newberry Library, 1982), vii. All future page references to *Israel Potter* are to this edition and will be supplied parenthetically in the main body of the chapter.

7. Elizabeth Maddock Dillon, "Sentimental Aesthetics," *American Literature* 76.3 (2004): 503.

8. Immanuel Kant, "Idea for a Universal History with a Cosmopolitan Purpose," in Immanuel Kant, *Kant: Political Writings*, ed. Hans Reiss (Cambridge: Cambridge University Press, 1991), 46; Friedrich von Schiller, *On the Aesthetic Education of Man: In a Series of Letters*, ed. Elizabeth M. Wilkinson and L. A. Willoughby (Oxford: Oxford University Press, 1967), 56, 215.

9. Kant, *Critique of the Power of Judgment*, 141; Friedrich von Schiller, *Naïve and Sentimental Poetry and On the Sublime*, ed. Julia A. Elias (New York: Frederick Ungar, 1966), 206; Kant, "Idea for a Universal History," 41, 51–52. On Kant, Schiller, and revolutionary politics, see H. S. Reiss, "Introduction," *Kant: Political Writings*, 1–40; Stephen Boos, "Rethinking the Aesthetic: Kant, Schiller, and Hegel," in *Between Ethics and Aesthetics: Crossing the Boundaries*, ed. Dorata Glowacka and Stephen Boos (Albany: State University of New York Press, 2002), 15–27; and Dillon, "Sentimental Aesthetics."

10. Russ Castronovo, "Transnational Aesthetics," in *The Cambridge Companion to Transnational American Literature*, ed. Yogita Goyal (Cambridge: Cambridge University Press, 2017), 80.

11. See Merton M. Sealts Jr., *Melville's Reading: Revised and Enlarged Edition* (Columbia: University of South Carolina Press, 1988), 53, 71, 83, 107, 210–11.

12. Melville, *Pierre*, 244.

13. On this phase of Melville's career, see Marvin Fisher, *Going Under: Melville's Short Fiction and the American 1850s* (Baton Rouge: Louisiana State University Press, 1977).

14. Andrew Delbanco suggests that "a weariness of tone kept *Israel Potter* from rising above the level of minor work" (*Melville: His World and Work* [New York: Knopf, 2005], 228). But it would be more accurate to say that one of the novel's subjects is "weariness of tone" – a weariness with the self-congratulatory nationalism of the various post-Revolutionary histories and autobiographies that Melville appropriates for his novel. In addition to the 1824 *Life and Remarkable Adventures of Israel R. Potter*, Melville drew on such texts as Ethan Allen's *A Narrative of Colonel Ethan Allen's Captivity* (1799), Robert C. Sands's *Life and Correspondence of John Paul Jones* (1830), James Fenimore Cooper's *The History of the Navy of the United States* (1839), and the writings of Benjamin Franklin. For a fuller discussion of textual, biographical, and cultural backgrounds, see my introduction to Herman Melville, *Israel*

Potter: His Fifty Years of Exile (New York: Penguin, 2008), vii–xxxv. I have drawn on some of the material in that introduction for this chapter.

15. In this respect, Melville arguably extends one of the key arguments of Kant's third *Critique*. As elaborated by Robert Kaufman in "Red Kant, or The Persistence of the Third Critique in Adorno and James," *Critical Inquiry* 26.4 (2000): 682–724, Kant makes clear in the third *Critique* "that the aesthetic ought to be distinguished from aestheticization" (684), and that the value of aesthetics during the revolutionary moment in particular lay in its ability "to defamiliarize the given and hence to allow for the perception of the real or new" (703). From a different perspective, David Faflik argues that Melville sought to write a "little history" that "downsizes our historical point of view by (dis)orienting us by design toward the local, the ephemeral, the pedestrian" ("Melville's Little Historical Method," *J19: The Journal of Nineteenth-Century Americanists* 5.1 [2017]: 55).

16. On the inventiveness and sheer inaccuracy of the 1824 *Life and Remarkable Adventures of Israel R. Potter*, see David Chacko and Alexander Kulcsar, "Israel Potter: Genesis of a Legend," *William and Mary Quarterly*, 3rd series, 41.3 (1984): 365–89. According to their research, Potter probably did not fight in the Battle of Bunker Hill and may have even been a British spy who chose to remain in England for nearly five decades. The autobiography was published, and in all probability ghost-written, by Henry Trumbull, who was cashing in on the market for narratives by Revolutionary veterans. Melville would have known that Trumbull was notorious for his production of wildly inaccurate histories, biographies, and autobiographies.

17. Daniel Webster, "The Bunker Hill Monument: An Address Delivered at the Laying of the Corner-Stone of the Bunker Hill Monument of Charlestown, Massachusetts, on the 17th of June, 1825," in *The Great Speeches and Orations of Daniel Webster, with an Essay on Daniel Webster as a Master of English Style*, ed. Edwin P. Whipple (Boston: Little, Brown, 1879), 128. Completed in 1843, the monument commemorated the first significant military conflict between the colonial army and British forces, which took place on June 17, 1775, in Charlestown, Massachusetts. See John Hay's excellent "Broken Hearths: Melville's *Israel Potter* and the Bunker Hill Monument," *The New England Quarterly* 89.2 (2016): 192–221. On monumentalism and nation building in antebellum culture, see Dana Luciano, *Arranging Grief: Sacred Time and the Body in Nineteenth-Century America* (New York: New York University Press, 2007), 169–214. For a discussion of the theme in Melville in particular, see Edgar A. Dryden, *Monumental Melville: The Formation of a Literary Career* (Stanford: Stanford University Press, 2004). Nathaniel Philbrick's *Bunker Hill: A City, a Siege, a Revolution* (New York: Viking, 2013) is a useful but conventionally nationalistic history.

18. *Life and Remarkable Adventures of Israel R. Potter* (1824), rpt. in Melville, *Israel Potter*, 287.

19. Peter J. Bellis, "Israel Potter: Autobiography as History as Fiction," *American Literary History* 2.4 (1990): 621.

20. For an informative discussion of this early phase of Israel Potter's career, see Hester Blum, "Atlantic Trade," in *A Companion to Herman Melville*, ed. Wyn Kelley (Oxford: Blackwell, 2006), 116–20.

21. As Jeffrey Insko points out, Melville's recourse to the present tense in the novel works to create "a kind of unknowing, letting go of the certainties and comforts provided by, say, providence, or progress, or normative ideas about time as an ameliorative force" ("Melville's Weak Present Tense," presented at the 2016 C19 conference at Penn State; my thanks to Insko for sharing his paper). On the complex temporality of the novel, see also Joshua Tendler, "A Monument upon a Hill: Antebellum Commemoration Culture, the Here-and-Now, and Democratic Citizenship in Melville's *Israel Potter*," *Studies in American Fiction* 42.1 (2015): 29–50.

22. On Melville's exploration in *Israel Potter* of "the possibilities for a deindividuated protagonist" (120), see Russell Reising, *Loose Ends: Closure and Crisis in the American Social Text* (Durham, NC: Duke University Press, 1996), 117–85; and on the slipperiness of identity in the novel, see Gale Temple, "Fluid Identity in *Israel Potter* and *The Confidence-Man*," *A Companion to Herman Melville*, 451–66. Clothes are central to Stephen Matterson's analysis of the self and modernity in *Israel Potter*; see his *Melville: Fashioning in Modernity* (New York: Bloomsbury, 2014), ch. 4. As a number of critics have observed, Melville's aesthetic of clothes owes a good deal to his reading of Thomas Carlyle's *Sartor Resartus* (1833–34).

23. For Kant's reflections on these sometimes interrelated topics, see "Idea for a Universal History with a Cosmopolitan Purpose" (1784), "An Answer to the Question: 'What Is Enlightenment?'" (1784), and "Perpetual Peace: A Philosophical Sketch" (1795), wherein Kant links war to "savage and lawless freedom" (*Political Writings*, 105).

24. Nathaniel Hawthorne, "My Kinsman, Major Molineaux," in Nathaniel Hawthorne, *Tales and Sketches*, ed. Roy Harvey Pearce (New York: The Library of America, 1982), 86.

25. To some extent Melville anticipates Jean Baudrillard's emphasis on the importance of spectacle to war; see *The Spirit of Terrorism* (London: Verso, 2003).

26. Dryden, *Monumental Melville*, 52.

27. Hennig Cohen, ed., *The Battle-Pieces of Herman Melville* (New York: Thomas Yoseloff, 1963), 227; Melville, "A Utilitarian View of the Monitor's Flight," in *Battle-Pieces*, 71. On connections between *Israel Potter* and *Battle-Pieces*, see

Stephanie A. Smith, "Union Blues: Melville's Poetic In(ter)ventions," *Genre* 47.1 (2014): 21–53.

28. Daniel Herwitz, *Aesthetics: Key Concepts in Philosophy* (London: Continuum, 2008), 71, 72.

29. Kant, "An Answer to the Question: 'What Is Enlightenment?,'" 55.

30. Schiller, *On the Aesthetic Education of Man*, 215.

31. Castronovo, *Beautiful Democracy*, 91. Castronovo writes of how during the 1877 labor clashes in the United States the "strikers and soldiers often seemed like grand spectacles, as crowds gathered on overlooks to watch – and participate – in the melee" (86).

32. My reading here has been influenced by Christopher Castiglia and Russ Castronovo, "Aesthetics and the End(s) of Cultural Studies," *American Literature*, 76.3 (2004): esp. 428. For a different perspective on Melville's presentation of the battle between the *Bonhomme Richard* and the *Serapis*, see Faflik, who argues that the scene works with "narrative half-starts and deflations that *belittle* in every connotation of the word" ("Melville's Little Historical Method," 66).

33. For an excellent reading of *Israel Potter* that emphasizes the importance of the closing chapters, see George Dekker, *The American Historical Romance* (Cambridge: Cambridge University Press, 1987), 190–97. For a discussion of the novel as a critique of class politics, see Carolyn L. Karcher, *Shadow over the Promised Land: Slavery, Race, and Violence in Melville's America* (Baton Rouge: Louisiana State University Press, 1980), 102–108. On the novel's transatlantic perspective, see Paul Giles, "'Bewildering Intertanglement': Melville's Engagement with British Culture," in *The Cambridge Companion to Herman Melville*, ed. Robert S. Levine (Cambridge: Cambridge University Press, 1998), esp. 238–42.

34. On slavery and *Israel Potter*, see Karcher, *Shadow over the Promised Land*, 102–108; and my introduction to the Penguin edition of *Israel Potter*, xxiv-xxvi.

35. Schiller, *On the Aesthetic Education of Man*, 37.

36. Kant, *Critique of the Power of Judgment*, 151. The editors of this edition adopt boldface to indicate Kant's use of larger Gothic type at those places where he wished to provide extra emphasis to his ideas.

37. Schiller, *On the Aesthetic Education of Man*, 61.

38. On Kant, the sublime, and Franklin, see Elizabeth Maddock Dillon, "Fear of Formalism: Kant, Twain, and Cultural Studies in American Literature," *Diacritics* 27.4 (1997): esp. 55, 57.

Antebellum Rome: Transatlantic Mirrors in Hawthorne's
The Marble Faun

1. See Robert Weisbuch, *Atlantic Double-Cross: American Literature and British Influence in the Age of Emerson* (Chicago: University of Chicago Press, 1986); Paul Giles, *Transatlantic Insurrections: British Culture and the Formation of American Literature, 1730–1860* (Philadelphia: University of Pennsylvania Press, 2001); and Leonard Tennenhouse, *The Importance of Feeling English: American Literature and the British Diaspora, 1750–1850* (Princeton, NJ: Princeton University Press, 2007). Other important transatlantic work includes Elisa Tamarkin, *Anglophilia: Deference, Devotion, and Antebellum America* (Chicago: University of Chicago Press, 2008); Laura Doyle, *Freedom's Empire: Race and the Rise of the Novel in Atlantic Modernity, 1640–1940* (Durham, NC: Duke University Press, 2008); and Christopher Hanlon, *America's England: Antebellum Literature and Atlantic Sectionalism* (New York: Oxford University Press, 2013).

2. Nathaniel Hawthorne, *The Letters, 1857–1864*, ed. Thomas Woodson et al. (Columbus: Ohio State University Press, 1987), 262; Nathaniel Hawthorne, *The Marble Faun*, ed. Roy Harvey Pearce et al. (Columbus: Ohio State University State Press, 1968), 3. All future page references to this edition will be provided parenthetically in the main body of the text. Mid-twentieth-century critics helped to establish the primacy of the Fortunate Fall theme in *The Marble Faun*; see, for example, F. O. Matthiessen, *American Renaissance: Art and Expression in the Age of Emerson and Whitman* (1941; New York: Oxford University Press, 1974), 308–12; Richard Harter Fogle, *Hawthorne's Fiction: The Light and the Dark* (Norman: University of Oklahoma Press, 1952), 162–83; Roy R. Male, *Hawthorne's Tragic Vision* (1957; New York: Norton, 1964), 157–77; and Hyatt Waggoner, *Hawthorne: A Critical Study* (Cambridge, MA: Harvard University Press, 1963), 209–25. For a discussion of the limits of reading the novel in relation to a Fortunate Fall thematics, see Evan Carton, *The Marble Faun: Hawthorne's Transformation* (New York: Twayne, 1992), 37–45. But for an effort to reinvigorate the theme via Schiller and Nietzsche, see Robert Milder, *Hawthorne's Habitations: A Literary Life* (New York: Oxford University Press, 2013), ch. 10.

3. For a good discussion of the politics and historicism of Milton's allegory of the fall, particularly with reference to America, see Keith W. F. Stavely, *Paradise Lost and the New England Tradition, 1630–1890* (Ithaca, NY: Cornell University Press, 1987).

4. On this point, see Joshua Parker, "War and Union in Little America: The Space of Hawthorne's Rome," *Nathaniel Hawthorne Review* 40.2 (2014): 60–84. From a more critical (and I think reductive) perspective, John Carlos Rowe argues that Hawthorne, "in a politically conservative manner," "makes

consistently superficial observations about the great political events taking place around him" and in his Italian writings tends to "'Americanize' international and transnational issues" in the manner of a US imperialist (John Carlos Rowe, "Nathaniel Hawthorne and Transnationality," *Hawthorne and the Real: Bicentennial Essays*, ed. Millicent Bell [Columbus: Ohio State University Press, 2005], 89, 98).

5. On antebellum political nativism, see Ray Allen Billington, *The Protestant Crusade, 1800–1860: A Study of the Origins of American Nativism* (1938; New York: Quadrangle, 1964). The best recent accounts of nativism and literary culture are Jenny Franchot, *Roads to Rome: The Antebellum Protestant Encounter with Catholicism* (Berkeley: University of California Press, 1994); and Susan M. Griffin, *Anti-Catholicism and Nineteenth-Century Fiction* (Cambridge: Cambridge University Press, 2004).

6. Nathaniel Hawthorne, "Churches and Cathedrals," in *Hawthorne as Editor: Selections from His Writings in the American Magazine of Useful and Entertaining Knowledge*, ed. Arlin Turner (1941; Port Washington: Kennikat, 1972), 205, 203–4. My understanding of Hawthorne's attitude toward his reading public is indebted to the classic work of Nina Baym, who observes that "it was part of Hawthorne's strategy through this part of his career [1834–39] to accede to the presumed view of his readers, and never assert either his superiority or his disagreement. By such a strategy he hoped to gain the goodwill of those on whom his success as an author depended" (Baym, *The Shape of Hawthorne's Career* [Ithaca, NY: Cornell University Press, 1976], 81). On Hawthorne and nativist rhetoric, with special reference to the early tales and *The Blithedale Romance*, see Robert S. Levine, *Conspiracy and Romance: Studies in Brockden Brown, Cooper, Hawthorne, and Melville* (Cambridge: Cambridge University Press, 1989), ch. 3.

7. Nathaniel Hawthorne, *The Scarlet Letter*, ed. William Charvat (Columbus: Ohio State University Press, 1962), 144; Nathaniel Hawthorne, *The French and Italian Notebooks*, ed. Thomas Woodson (Columbus: Ohio State University Press, 1980), 59. On Lowell and *The Scarlet Letter*, see Henry G. Fairbanks, "Hawthorne and Confession," *Catholic Historical Review* 43.1 (1957), 40; and Ernest Baugham, "Public Confession and *The Scarlet Letter*," *New England Quarterly* 40.4 (1967): 168–83. Franchot argues that *The Scarlet Letter* is "[p]erhaps the finest antebellum romance of Catholicism" (*Roads to Rome*, 260).

8. Henry James, *Hawthorne* (1879; Ithaca: Cornell University Press, 1956), 133.

9. *Pope, or President? Startling Disclosures of Romanism as Revealed by Its Own Writers. Facts for Americans* (New York: Delisser, 1859), 45.

10. Charles Eliot Norton, *Notes of Travel and Study in Italy* (Boston: Ticknor, 1859), 164. The confessional scene in Charlotte Brontë's Roman novel, *Villette*

(1853), may have influenced Hawthorne's. Like Hilda, Lucy Snowe turns to the confessional at a moment of psychological need, and finds relief in an institution that is nonetheless depicted as contributing to Roman Catholic authoritarian control; see Griffin, *Anti-Catholicism and Nineteenth-Century Fiction*, 150–53.

11. James Jackson Jarves, *Italian Sights and Papal Principles: Seen through American Spectacles* (New York: Harper, 1856), 271. On the Gothic revival, particularly as mediated through Ruskin, see Roger B. Stein, *John Ruskin and Aesthetic Thought in America, 1840–1900* (Cambridge, MA: Harvard University Press, 1967). For a pioneering study of Hawthorne and the Gothic, see Dennis Berthold, "Hawthorne, Ruskin, and the Gothic Revival: Transcendent Gothic in *The Marble Faun*," *ESQ* 20.1 (1974): 15–32. On American travelers in Rome, see William L. Vance, "The Sidelong Glance: Victorian Americans and Baroque Rome," *New England Quarterly* 58.4 (1985): 501–32; Franchot, *Roads to Rome*, ch. 2; Richard L. Millington, "Where Is Hawthorne's Rome? *The Marble Faun* and the Cultural Space of Middle-Class Leisure," in *Roman Holidays: American Writers and Artists in Nineteenth-Century Italy*, ed. Robert K. Martin and Leland S. Person (Iowa City: University of Iowa, 2002), 9–27; and Steven Mailloux, "Narrative as Embodied Intensities: The Eloquence of Travel in Nineteenth-Century Rome," *Narrative* 21.2 (2013): 125–39. For a useful account of connections between nativism and the political debates of the 1850s, see James M. McPherson, *Battle Cry of Freedom: The Civil War Era* (New York: Oxford University Press, 1988), 117–44; and on the familial ideology informing the burgeoning total institutions of the period, see Levine, *Conspiracy and Romance*, 173–84.

12. John Ruskin, *Modern Painters*, ed. E. T. Cook and Alexander Wedderburn (London: Allen, 1903), 95; James Jackson Jarves, *Art Studies: The Old Masters of Italy: Painting* (New York: Derby, 1861), viii.

13. George B. Forgie, *Patricide in the House Divided: A Psychological Interpretation of Lincoln and His Age* (New York: Norton, 1979).

14. Richard H. Brodhead more ominously argues that Hilda embodies the "militant high-cultural spirit" that would come to dominate American Victorian literary culture; see Richard H. Brodhead, *The School of Hawthorne* (New York: Oxford University Press, 1986), 79.

15. William Ellery Channing, *Conversations in Rome: Between an Artist, a Catholic, and a Critic* (Boston: Crosby, 1847), 136; Hawthorne, *French and Italian Notebooks*, 54.

16. On Cenci, see Louise K. Barnett, "American Novelists and the 'Portrait of Beatrice Cenci,'" *New England Quarterly* 53.2 (1980): 168–83; and Rowe, "Nathaniel Hawthorne and Transnationality," 100–102. For an illuminating

discussion of Miriam as anti–Roman Catholic plotter, see Arnold Goldman, "The Plot of Hawthorne's *The Marble Faun*," *Journal of American Studies* 18.3 (1984): 383–404. Critics are divided on Hawthorne's attitude toward Miriam. I join with those who regard Hawthorne as in many respects sympathetic to, and even at times aligned with, her transgressiveness. David Leverenz, for example, persuasively argues that *The Marble Faun* "gains much of its narrative energy from covertly doubling a dangerously creative female character" with "the not quite controlling male narrator" ("Working Women and Creative Doubles: Getting to *The Marble Faun*," *Hawthorne and the Real*, 153–54). Michael Broek argues that Miriam "may be reconsidered Hawthorne's internationalized Hester, or, more aptly, his mature Pearl" (Michael Broek, "Hawthorne, Madonna, and Lady Gaga: *The Marble Faun*'s Transgressive Miriam," *Journal of American Studies* 46.3 [2012]: 625). In his influential study, Leland S. Person notes that "Hawthorne embodied his deepest creative impulse in his strongest female characters" (*Aesthetic Headaches: Women and a Masculine Poetics in Poe, Melville, and Hawthorne* [Athens: University of Georgia Press, 1988], 172; on Miriam, see also 160–71).

17. Qtd. in Christopher Hibbert, *Rome: The Biography of a City* (New York: Norton, 1985), 250; Margaret Fuller Ossoli, *At Home and Abroad, or Things and Thoughts in America and Europe*, ed. Arthur B. Fuller (1856; Port Washington, NY: Kennikat, 1971), 327; Theodore Dwight, *The Roman Republic of 1849; with Accounts of the Inquisition and the Siege of Rome, and Biographical Sketches* (New York: Dien, 1851), 16. On Fuller and the Roman Revolution, see Thomas R. Mitchell, *Hawthorne's Fuller Mystery* (Amherst: University of Massachusetts Press, 1998), ch. 8; Brigitte Bailey, "Fuller, Hawthorne, and Imagining Urban Spaces in Rome," *Roman Holidays*, 175–190; and Larry J. Reynolds, "Righteous Violence: The Roman Republic and Margaret Fuller's Revolutionary Example," in *Margaret Fuller: Transatlantic Crossings in a Revolutionary Age*, ed. Charles Capper and Cristina Giorcelli (Madison: University of Wisconsin Press, 2007), 172–92.

18. Paul Baker, *The Fortunate Pilgrims: Americans in Italy, 1800–1860* (Cambridge, MA: Harvard University Press, 1964), 164. For useful studies of Jewish themes in the novel, see Augustus M. Kolich, "Miriam and the Conversion of the Jews in Nathaniel Hawthorne's *The Marble Faun*," *Studies in the Novel* 33.1 (2001): 430–44; and David Greven, "Hawthorne and the Gender of Jewishness: Anti-Semitism, Aesthetics, and Sexual Politics in *The Marble Faun*," *Journal of American Culture* 35.2 (2012): 133–52.

19. Ann Taves, *The Household of Faith: Roman Catholic Devotions in Mid-Nineteenth-Century America* (Notre Dame, IN: University of Notre Dame Press, 1986), 109.

20. For an illuminating metafictional discussion of Kenyon as surrogate victim at carnival, see Jonathan Auerbach, "Executing the Model: Painting, Sculpture, and Romance-Writing in Hawthorne's *The Marble Faun*," *ELH* 47.1 (1980), 102–20. On metafictional themes in the romance, see also Evan Carton, *The Rhetoric of American Romance: Dialectic and Identity in Emerson, Dickinson, Poe, and Hawthorne* (Baltimore, MD: Johns Hopkins University Press, 1985), 252–64.

21. Baym, *The Shape of Hawthorne's Career*, 246.

22. On Hawthorne's conflicted response to revolutionism, see Larry J. Reynolds, *European Revolutions and the American Literary Renaissance* (New Haven, CT: Yale University Press, 1988), ch. 5.

23. Hawthorne, *The Scarlet Letter*, 232; Nathaniel Hawthorne, *The Letters, 1853–1855*, ed. Thomas Woodson et al. (Columbus: Ohio State University Press, 1987), 188; Hawthorne, *French and Italian Notebooks*, 502.

24. On Hawthorne's concerns that American ships were becoming overly populated with intoxicated foreigners, see John Byers, ed., "Consular Despatches of Nathaniel Hawthorne," *Essex Institute Historical Collections* 113 (1977): 239–322, esp. 313–15. On flogging, see Hawthorne's notebook entry of November 16, 1855 (*The English Notebooks*, ed. Randall Stewart [New York: MLA, 1941], 267); and his letter of October 8, 1857, to Elizabeth P. Peabody (*Letters, 1857–1864*, 116). For an analysis of the relationship between nautical and land-bound politics, see Myra C. Glenn, *Campaigns against Corporeal Punishment: Prisoners, Sailors, Women, and Children in Antebellum America* (Albany: State University Press of New York, 1984).

25. Accordingly, we might modify just a bit the critical insistence on Hawthorne's magisterial powers of sympathy. His inability to offer affectional sympathy to America's black slaves is well known. Despite Hawthorne's opposition to the Fugitive Slave Law, he wrote his friend Zachariah Burchmore on July 15, 1851: "I have not, as you suggest, the slightest sympathy for the slaves; or, at least, not half so much as for the laboring whites, who, I believe, as a general thing, are ten times worse off than the Southern negros [sic]" (*The Letters, 1843–1853*, ed. Thomas Woodson et al. [Columbus: Ohio State University Press, 1985], 456). On sympathy in *The Marble Faun*, see John Michael, "History and Romance, Sympathy, and Uncertainty: The Moral of the Stones in Hawthorne's *Marble Faun*," *PMLA* 103.2 (1988): 150–61.

26. Nathaniel Hawthorne, *The Life of Franklin Pierce* (1852; Cambridge, MA: Riverside, 1900), 102–03; Hawthorne, *Letters, 1857–1864*, 227, 355; Hawthorne, *French and Italian Notebooks*, 463.

27. Dennis Berthold takes a very different, and more literal, approach to the political implications of this scene, noting that "Archduke Maximillian's ill-fated idea of an Italian confederation under papal rule was closer to Pierce's

position on states' rights than Lincoln's insistence on union; the anti-Catholic Garibaldi, not the pope, represented national unity" (Dennis Berthold, "Italy, the Civil War, and the Politics of Friendship," *Hawthorne and Melville: Writing a Relationship*, ed. Jana L. Argersinger and Leland S. Person [Athens: University of Georgia Press, 2008], 142). My argument is less about such historical actualities and more about cultural nostalgia and desires, as explored by George Forgie and others, for a unifying father on the order of George Washington. Or, to put this differently, my argument is about the longings and anxieties informing US anti-Catholicism of the period, which I've been arguing both inform and are the subject of *The Marble Faun*.

28. Nathaniel Hawthorne, "Chiefly about War-Matters. By a Peaceable Man," *The Atlantic Magazine: A Magazine of Literature, Art, and Politics* 10 (July 1862): 47, 45.

29. Hawthorne, *The Life of Franklin Pierce* (1852); Nathaniel Hawthorne, *Miscellaneous Prose and Verse*, ed. Thomas Woodson, Claude M. Simpson, and L. Neal Smith (Columbus: Ohio State University Press, 1994), 352; and see Robert S. Levine, *Dislocating Race and Nation: Episodes in Nineteenth-Century American Literary Nationalism* (Chapel Hill: University of North Carolina Press, 2008), 129–33. Hawthorne did remain suspicious of aggressively self-righteous abolitionists advocating what Larry J. Reynolds terms "righteous violence" (*Devils and Rebels: The Making of Hawthorne's Damned Politics* [Ann Arbor: University of Michigan Press, 2008], 209).

30. Hawthorne, "Chiefly about War-Matters," 50.

31. Blythe Ann Tellefsen, "'The Case with My Dear Native Land': Nathaniel Hawthorne's Vision of America in *The Marble Faun*," *Nineteenth-Century Literature* 54.4 (2000): 459, 474, 472; Arthur Riss, *Slavery and Liberalism in Nineteenth-Century American Literature* (Cambridge: Cambridge University Press, 2006), 159. For a different perspective on "Chiefly about War-Matters," see Brenda Wineapple, who describes the essay as "Swiftian, corrosive and funny" (*Hawthorne: A Life* [New York: Knopf, 2003], 349).

32. Nancy Bentley, in an excellent discussion of race in *The Marble Faun*, argues that Hawthorne's approach is mainly ethnographic; see Nancy Bentley, *The Ethnography of Manners: Hawthorne, James, Wharton* (Cambridge: Cambridge University Press, 1995), ch. 2. For a complex discussion of slavery and race in the novel from the perspective of sculpture and pain, see Tim Armstrong, *The Logic of Slavery: Debt, Technology, and Pain in American Literature* (Cambridge: Cambridge University Press, 2012), 122–28.

33. Hawthorne, "Chiefly about War-Matters," 50. Carton writes perceptively on this relatively neglected passage in Hawthorne's essay; see *The Marble Faun: Hawthorne's Transformation*, 114–15.

Edward Everett Hale's and Sutton E. Griggs's Men without a Country

1. On the phenomenal popularity of "The Man without a Country," see Brook Thomas, *Civic Myths: A Law-and-Literature Approach to Citizenship* (Chapel Hill: University of North Carolina Press, 2007), 55–57; Hsuan L. Hsu, "Contexts for Reading 'The Man without a Country,'" in *Two Texts by Edward Everett Hale: "The Man without a Country" and Philip Nolan's Friends*, ed. Hsuan L. Hsu and Susan Kalter (Lanham, MD: Lexington Books, 2010), 1–16; and Hsuan L. Hsu, "'The Man without a Country': Treason, Expansionism, and the History of a 'Bestselling' Short Story," in *Must Read: Rediscovering American Bestsellers: From Charlotte Temple to The Da Vinci Code*, ed. Sarah Churchwell and Thomas Ruys Smith (London: Bloomsbury, 2012), 131–51.
2. Edward Everett Hale, "The Man without a Country," in *If, Yes, and Perhaps* (Boston: Ticknor and Fields, 1868), 206. This is the first book publication of Hale's 1863 story, with the first printing of his introduction. Hale titled subsequent editions of this volume *The Man without a Country and Other Tales*.
3. Hale, "The Man without a Country," 235–36.
4. Ibid., 241.
5. Carrie Hyde, "Outcast Patriotism: The Dilemma of Negative Instruction in 'The Man without a Country'," *ELH* 77.4 (2010): 916, 915, 919.
6. Edward Everett Hale, *The Man without a Country and Other Tales* (Boston: Roberts Brothers, 1886), 8.
7. See Hyde, "Outcast Patriotism," 915–39. In a provocative essay on Griggs's depiction of black patriotism in a racialist, Uncle Tom tradition, Stephen Knadler notes similarities between Griggs's novel and "The Man without a Country" with respect to their depictions of Texas as a site for conspiracy (Stephen Knadler, "Sensationalizing Patriotism: Sutton Griggs and the Sentimental Nationalism of Uncle Tom" (*American Literature* 79.4 [2007]: 673–99).
8. Hale, "The Man without a Country," 203, 205, 222, 224. On Hale and national fantasy, see Elizabeth Duquette, *Loyal Subjects: Bonds of Nation, Race, and Allegiance in Nineteenth-Century America* (New Brunswick, NJ: Rutgers University Press, 2010), 49–51.
9. Hale, "The Man without a Country," 199.
10. Ibid., 203, 206, 212, 230, 199.
11. Sutton E. Griggs, *Imperium in Imperio* (1899; New York: Modern Library, 2003), 6, 5, 6, 3, 4, 3.
12. On pioneering aspects of Griggs's narrative strategies in *Imperium in Imperio*, see Raymond Hedin, "Probable Readers, Possible Stories: The Limits of Nineteenth-Century Black Narrative," in *Readers in History: Nineteenth-*

Century American Literature and the Contexts of Response, ed. James L. Machor (Baltimore, MD: Johns Hopkins University Press, 1993), esp. 197–200. Critics are divided about whether Griggs's use of Berl as narrator is successful. Finnie D. Coleman states that "this experiment fails miserably at a number of levels" (Coleman, *Sutton Griggs and the Struggle against White Supremacy* [Knoxville: University of Tennessee Press, 2007], 45). For an important defense of Griggs's narrative strategy, see Eric Curry, "'The Power of Combinations': Sutton Griggs' *Imperium in Imperio* and the Science of Collective Efficiency," *American Literary Realism* 43.1 (2010): 23–40.

13. Griggs, *Imperium in Imperio*, 7, 37, 44, 33, 49, 50.
14. Ibid., 91, 95, 99, 109.
15. Ibid., 74.
16. Hale, "The Man without a Country," 237, 231.
17. For a richly textured account of the histories of blacks in the southern borderlands that Griggs both drew on and contributed to in his portrayal of the Imperium's home base in Waco, Texas, see Caroline Levander, "Sutton Griggs and the Borderlands of Empire," in *Jim Crow, Literature, and the Legacy of Sutton E. Griggs*, ed. Tess Chakkalakal and Kenneth W. Warren (Athens: University of Georgia Press, 2013), 21–48.
18. Griggs, *Imperium in Imperio*, 138, 125.
19. On the importance of oratory in the novel, see Maria Karafilis, "Oratory, Embodiment, and US Citizenship in Sutton E. Griggs's *Imperium in Imperio*," *African American Review* 40.1 (2006): 125–43.
20. Griggs, *Imperium in Imperio*, 145, 152.
21. Ibid., 162.
22. [Edward Everett Hale], *How to Conquer Texas before Texas Conquers Us* (Boston: Redding, 1845), 13.
23. Griggs, *Imperium in Imperio*, 167, 168.
24. Ibid., 168, 172, 173–74; Hale, "The Man without a Country," 233.
25. Coleman, *Sutton Griggs*, 69.
26. Griggs, *Imperium in Imperio*, 176, 177.
27. Ibid., 175, 139. As critics have pointed out, the fictional Felix Cook, a postmaster, is based on the black postmaster Frazier Baker, who was murdered in South Carolina in 1898.
28. Griggs, *Imperium in Imperio*, 176.
29. Hale added these sentences in his introduction to a republication of the story in *New Outlook* 59 (1898): 116; this new introduction accompanied subsequent reprintings of *The Man without a Country and Other Tales*.
30. Hsu, "The Man without a Country: Treason, Expansionism," 146. In his essay Hsu shows how the story was used to rally support for the US military during the two world wars and the Korean War.

31. Sutton E. Griggs, *Unfettered: A Novel* (Nashville, TN: Orion, 1902), 156.

32. Qtd. in Willard B. Gatewood Jr., *Black Americans and the White Man's Burden, 1898–1903* (Urbana: University of Illinois Press, 1975), 249. On Griggs and the Spanish-American War, see Susan Gillman, *Blood Talk: American Race Melodramas and the Culture of the Occult* (Chicago: University of Chicago Press, 2003), 73–116; and for a useful discussion of Griggs and US empire, see also John Gruesser, "Empires at Home and Abroad in Sutton E. Griggs's *Imperium in Imperio*," in *Jim Crow, Literature, and the Legacy of Sutton E. Griggs*, 49–68.

33. Sutton E. Griggs, *Overshadowed: A Novel* (Nashville, TN: Orion Pub, 1901), 102, 127.

34. Ibid., 214, 216, 217. For a reading of the novel that emphasizes its more optimistic vision of the future possibilities for postbellum southern blacks, see Andreá N. Williams, "Moving up a Dead-End Ladder: Black Class Mobility, Death, and Narrative Closure in Sutton Griggs's *Overshadowed*," in *Jim Crow, Literature, and the Legacy of Sutton E. Griggs*, 88–110.

35. See, for example, Arlene E. Elder's critical remarks on Astral in *The "Hindered Hand": Cultural Implications of Early African-American Fiction* (Westport, CT: Greenwood, 1978), 82–84.

36. Griggs writes at the end of the *Guide to Racial Greatness; or, The Science of Collective Efficiency* (Memphis, TN: National Public Welfare League, 1923): "The greatest of all agencies capable of bringing about transformation is the individual" (218).

37. Hale, "The Man without a Country," 204, 240–41.

Frederick Douglass in Fiction: From Harriet Beecher Stowe to James McBride

1. See Paul John Eakin, *Fictions in Autobiography: Studies in the Art of Self-Invention* (Princeton, NJ: Princeton University Press, 1985). Some of the material in this and the next paragraph draws on my *The Lives of Frederick Douglass* (Cambridge, MA: Harvard University Press, 2016), ch. 1.

2. For a fuller discussion of Douglass's and Stowe's textual conversations, see Robert S. Levine, *Martin Delany, Frederick Douglass, and the Politics of Representative Identity* (Chapel Hill: University of North Carolina Press, 1998), esp. chs. 2 and 4.

3. Harriet Beecher Stowe, *Uncle Tom's Cabin*, ed. Elizabeth Ammons (New York: Norton, 2010), 407. See also Robert S. Levine, "*Uncle Tom's Cabin* in *Frederick Douglass' Paper*: An Analysis of Reception," *American Literature* 64.1 (1992): 71–93.

4. María Amparo Ruiz de Burton, *Who Would Have Thought It?*, ed. Amalia María de la Luz Montes (New York: Penguin, 2009), 20; Jesse Alemán, "'Thank God, Lolita Is Away from those Horrid Savages': The Politics of Whiteness in *Who Would Have Thought It?*," in *María Amparo Ruiz de Burton: Critical and Pedagogical Perspectives*, ed. Amelia María de la Luz Montes and Anne Elizabeth Goldman (Lincoln: University of Nebraska Press, 2004), 102, 99; Ruiz de Burton, *Who Would Have Thought It?*, 304. Grant's snub of Douglass occurred in 1871, a time when the two were on friendly terms and Douglass was serving on his Dominican Republic commission. For a discussion of Douglass's relationship with Grant, see Robert S. Levine, *Dislocating Race and Nation: Episodes in Nineteenth-Century American Literary Nationalism* (Chapel Hill: University of North Carolina Press, 2008), 200–17. On comparative racialization and late nineteenth-century American literary studies, see Hsuan L. Hsu, *Sitting in Darkness: Mark Twain's Asia and Comparative Racialization* (New York: New York University Press, 2015), and Edlie L. Wong, *Racial Reconstruction: Black Inclusion, Chinese Exclusion, and the Fictions of Citizenship* (New York: New York University Press, 2015).

5. Sutton E. Griggs, *The Hindered Hand: or, The Reign of the Repressionist* (1905; New York: AMS, 1969), 307, 42, 43, 44, 313.

6. Pauline E. Hopkins, *Contending Forces: A Romance Illustrative of Negro Life North and South* (1900; New York: Oxford University Press, 1988), 86; James Weldon Johnson, *The Autobiography of an Ex-Colored Man* (1912; New York: Library of America Paperback Classics, 2011), 30, 64; Ralph Ellison, *Invisible Man* (1952; New York: Vintage, 1972), 369; David Messmer, "Trumpets, Horns, and Typewriters: A Call and Response between Ralph Ellison and Frederick Douglass," *African American Review* 43.4 (2009): 589. And see *The Life and Writings of Frederick Douglass*, 5 vols., ed. Philip S. Foner (New York: International Publishers, 1950). My focus in this chapter is on Douglass in fiction; for an excellent discussion of Douglass in visual art and theater, see Celeste-Marie Bernier, *Characters of Blood: Black Heroism in the Transatlantic Imagination* (Charlottesville: University of Virginia Press, 2012), ch. 5.

7. This and the prior paragraph draw from Levine, *Lives of Frederick Douglass*, ch. 1; see also Waldo E. Martin Jr., "Images of Frederick Douglass in the Afro-American Mind: The Recent Black Freedom Struggle," in *Frederick Douglass: New Literary and Historical Essays*, ed. Eric J. Sundquist (Cambridge: Cambridge University Press, 1990), 271–86. For their views on Douglass, see Martin Luther King Jr., "The Ethical Demands of Integration" (1962), *A Testament of Hope: The Essential Writings of Martin Luther King, Jr.*, ed. James Melvin Washington (San Francisco: Harper and Row, 1986), 119; and Malcolm X, *By Any Means Necessary* (1970; New York: Pathfinder, 1992), 124.

8. The four novels are *Rabbit, Run* (1960), *Rabbit Redux* (1971), *Rabbit Is Rich* (1981), and *Rabbit at Rest* (1990). Updike also published an epilogue to the series, "Rabbit Remembered" (2000), which first appeared in the *New Yorker*.

9. On Rabbit as a hipster, see Michael Szalay, *Hip Figures: A Literary History of the Democratic Party* (Stanford, CA: Stanford University Press, 2012), ch. 3. On the hipster figure during this time, see also Lee Konstantinou, *Cool Characters: Irony and American Fiction* (Cambridge, MA: Harvard University Press, 2016).

10. Updike thus anticipated the work of Martin Jr., who, in "Images of Frederick Douglass," was one of the first critics to discuss the importance of Douglass to the 1960s.

11. John Updike, *Rabbit Redux* (New York: Knopf, 1971), 229, 278. For a helpful reading of this scene, see Lawrence Buell, *The Dream of the Great American Novel* (Cambridge, MA: Harvard University Press, 2014), 60–67.

12. See, for example, the 1990 essay by Jenny Franchot, "The Punishment of Esther: Frederick Douglass and the Construction of the Feminine," in *Frederick Douglass: New Literary and Historical Essays*, 141–65.

13. Updike, *Rabbit Redux*, 281, 282, 283, 337. On the sexual dynamic at work here, see Sally Robinson, *Marked Men: White Masculinity in Crisis* (New York: Columbia University Press, 2000), 32–39. Robinson concludes that "Skeeter escapes relatively intact and leaves in his wake a white male body conscious of its own impotence and even figurative deadness" (38). See also Szalay, *Hip Figures*, ch. 3. Arguably, Updike in his portrayal of Rabbit's attraction to Skeeter is extending the insights of James Baldwin, who writes in *The Fire Next Time* (1963; New York: Vintage, 1993): "The white man's unadmitted – and apparently to him, unspeakable – private fears and longings are projected onto the Negro. The only way he can be released from the Negro's tyrannical power over him is to consent, in effect, to become black himself" (96).

14. On the limits of Mailer's racial politics, see Konstantinou, *Cool Characters*, 49–51; and on Styron's disturbing presentation of Nat Turner's sexuality, which, as Szalay argues, focuses on Turner's "imagined possession of white women" (198), see *Hip Figures*, ch. 5. At a key moment in Saul Bellow's *Mister Sammler's Planet* (New York: Fawcett World Library, 1970), the protagonist is confronted by a black pickpocket and exhibitionist, whose penis – described as "a large tan-and-purple uncircumscribed thing – a tube, a snake; . . . suggesting the fleshly mobility of an elephant's trunk" (48) – is linked to what Bellow portrays, somewhat in the manner of Updike's presentation of Skeeter's ejaculating penis, as a metaphor for the frighteningly seductive "black" sexual energies of the 1960s. Indicative of Updike's continuing fascination with Douglass, one of the epigraphs for Updike's 1990 *Rabbit at Rest* comes from Douglass's *Life and Times*.

15. Paul Gilroy, *The Black Atlantic: Modernity and Double Consciousness* (Cambridge, MA: Harvard University Press, 1993), 4; Jacob Crane, "Beyond the Cape: Amitav Ghosh, Frederick Douglass, and the Limits of the Black Atlantic," *Postcolonial Text* 6.4 (2011): 5. For a critic who addresses the larger geographical frame that Ghosh explores in his *Ibis* novels, see Lisa Lowe, *The Intimacies of Four Continents* (Durham, NC: Duke University Press, 2015).

16. Amitav Ghosh, *Sea of Poppies* (2008; New York: Picador, 2009), 50, 78. On Reid's troubling implication in British imperial power, see Kesi Augustine, "Zachary Reid's Transoceanic Performance of White Gentility in *Sea of Poppies*," *Journal of African American Studies* 20.1 (2016): 120–32.

17. Chimamanda Ngozi Adichie, *Half of a Yellow Sun* (New York: Anchor, 2006), 451, 452.

18. Ibid., 495, 530. On Adichie and Douglass, see Bernier, *Characters of Blood*, 296.

19. Colum McCann, *Transatlantic* (New York: Random House, 2013), 59.

20. Ibid., 44, 68, 85.

21. Richard Bradbury, *Riversmeet* (London: Muswell, 2007), 171, 169, 171, 194, 177. See also Bradbury's "Frederick Douglass and the Chartists," in *Liberating Sojourn: Frederick Douglass and Transatlantic Reform*, ed. Alan J. Rice and Martin Crawford (Athens: University of Georgia Press, 1999), 169–86.

22. John Stauffer, *The Black Hearts of Men: Radical Abolitionists and the Transformation of Race* (Cambridge, MA: Harvard University Press, 2001), 1.

23. Frederick Douglass, *Life and Times of Frederick Douglass* (1892; New York: Collier Books, 1962), 319, 320.

24. Russell Banks, *Cloudsplitter* (1998; New York: HarperPerennial, 1999), 401, 405, 401, 409. See also Stauffer's *The Black Hearts of Men*.

25. Banks, Cloudsplitter, 406, 401, 403, 410.

26. James McBride, *The Good Lord Bird* (New York: Riverhead, 2013), 215. In his 1881/1892 *Life and Times of Frederick Douglass*, Douglass reports that Brown said: "When I strike, the bees will begin to swarm, and I shall want you to help hive them" (320).

27. On this point see Andrew Delbanco, "Mysterious, Brilliant, Frederick Douglass," *New York Review of Books*, April 7, 2016, 47–50. Delbanco writes: "Perhaps the closest any writer has come to dispensing with Douglass the monument and imagining Douglass the man is James McBride, in his rollicking 2013 novel *The Good Lord Bird*" (50).

28. McBride, *The Good Lord Bird*, 215, 216. For an earlier comic take on Brown and Douglass, see George MacDonald Fraser's *Flashman and the Angel of the Lord* (1994; New York: Plume, 1996).

29. J. B. Estlin to Samuel May, letter of January 12, 1847, in *British and American Abolitionists: An Episode in Transatlantic Understanding*, ed. Clare Taylor (Edinburgh: Edinburgh University Press, 1974), 305. On Douglass and Assing, see Maria Diedrich, *Love across the Color Lines: Ottilie Assing and Frederick*

Douglass (New York: Hill and Wang, 1999), and Leigh Fought, *Women in the World of Frederick Douglass* (New York: Oxford University Press, 2017), 148–51, 207–16. Unlike Diedrich, Fought rejects the idea that Assing and Douglass were sexually involved.

30. McBride, *The Good Lord Bird*, 219, 220, 224, 227–28. For critiques of Douglass's investment in black manhood at the expense of the voices and perspectives of black women, see, for example, Richard Yarborough, "Race, Violence, and Manhood: The Masculine Ideal in Frederick Douglass's 'The Heroic Slave,'" in Frederick Douglass: New Literary and Historical Essays, 166–88; Deborah E. McDowell, "In the First Place: Making Frederick Douglass and the Afro-American Narrative Tradition," in *Critical Essays on Frederick Douglass*, ed. William L. Andrews (Boston: G. K. Hall, 1991), 192–213; and Meina Yates-Richard, "'What Is Your Mother's Name?': Maternal Disavowal and Black Women's Pain in Black Nationalist Literature," *American Literature* 88.3 (2016): esp. 481–85.

31. Jewell Parker Rhodes, *Douglass' Women* (New York: Atria Books, 2002), 157. In *Love across Color Lines*, Diedrich emphasizes Douglass's and Assing's shared intellectual and political interests.

32. McBride, *The Good Lord Bird*, 329, 330, 331, 327, 331.

33. For a short story that highlights Douglass's heroism in taking on the mob at Pendleton, Indiana, see Charles Johnson's "A Lion at Pendleton," *Soulcatcher and Other Stories* (New York: Harcourt, 1998), 83–92. On Douglass's willingness to use violence against the slave power, see Robert S. Levine, "Frederick Douglass, War, Haiti," *PMLA* 124.5 (2009): 1864–68.

34. Lawrence Hill, *Any Known Blood* (1997; HarperCollins Canada, 2008), 475, 476. For a discussion of *Any Known Blood* in the context of black Canadian diasporic writing, see Winfried Simmerling, *The Black Atlantic Reconsidered: Black Canadian Writing, Cultural History, and the Presence of the Past* (Montreal: McGill-Queen's University Press, 2015), 160–70.

35. Hill, *Any Known Blood*, 422. For Douglass's account of this speech, see *Life and Times*, Second Part, ch. 16.

36. Banks, *Cloudsplitter*, 678, 705, 725.

37. Ibid., 727, 735.

38. Ibid., 732, 736, 737, 736. For an excellent discussion of race in *Cloudsplitter* and other novels by Banks, see Evan Carton, "White Boy (American Hunger) and the Angel of History: Russell Banks's Identity Knowledge," *American Literary History* 27.4 (2015): 740–67.

39. Dana Milbank, "Trump's Awkward Discovery of Frederick Douglass," *Washington Post*, February 2, 2017, A2.

40. On Douglass and Haiti, see Robert S. Levine, *Dislocating Race and Nation: Episodes in Nineteenth-Century American Literary Nationalism* (Chapel Hill: University of North Carolina Press, 2008), ch. 4.

Index

Abolitionism. *See also* antislavery; slave narratives;
    temperance
  in England, 53–55, 59–61, 207–8
  Paul, N., and, 46–47, 56–59
ACS. *See* American Colonization Society
Aday, Anne, 58, 60–61, 209
Adichie, Chimamanda Ngozi, 11, 176, 195
  Half of a Yellow Sun, 177–79
aesthetics
  art as stabilizing force for, 119
  Catholicism and, 136–37
  of defamiliarization, 120
  Israel Potter, 132–33
  of monumentalization, 120
  revolution and, 118–20
  transnational, 118, 131
Africa, 50, 51
African American literature, 5–6, 11. *See also*
    Brown, William Wells; Griggs, Sutton E.;
    Morrison, Toni; slave narratives; slavery
  Civil Rights Movement as influence on, 216
  Jim Crow as influence on, 216
Alemán, Jesse, 170
allegory, in nineteenth-century American
    literature, 4–5
*The American Adam: Innocence, Tragedy, and
    Tradition in the Nineteenth Century* (Lewis,
    R. W. B.), 12
American Civil War, 148–50
  in *Imperium in Imperio*, 159
  "The Man without a Country" the and, 153–54
American Colonization Society (ACS), 50, 51,
    55–59
The American Democrat (Cooper), 15–16, 17, 201
The American Fugitive in Europe (Brown,
    W. W.), 100, 109–10
The American Jeremiad (Bercovitch), 3
American literature. *See* African American
    literature; canonicity; nineteenth-century
    American literature; twentieth- and
    twenty-first century American literature

American Literature: The Makers and the Making
    (Lewis, R. W. B.), 12–13
American Moral Reform Society, 101
The American Novel and Its Tradition (Chase),
    2–3, 12, 23
American Renaissance (Matthiessen), 12
American Revolution, 51
  autobiography initiated during, 85, 94, 97
  Franklin's commitment to, 86–87
  in *Israel Potter: His Fifty Years of Exile*, 118–23
  slave narratives and, 87–88, 96–97
American Slavery as It Is (Weld), 102
*The Anarchy of Empire in the Making of U.S.
    Culture* (Kaplan), 6–7
Anderson, Osborne, 189
André, John, 153
Andrews, William, 4, 84
antebellum Rome. *See* Rome, nineteenth-century
anti-Catholicism, 135–36, 138, 139
  in *The Marble Faun*, 142–43, 230–31
antislavery, as literary topic. *See also* slave
    narratives; Brown, W. W.
  for Emerson, 26
  in Hawthorne works, 25–26
  in Melville works, 21–23
  in nineteenth-century literature, 4–5, 26–27
  Paul, N., on, 61–62
  for Stowe, 25–26
Any Known Blood (Hill), 182, 190–91
apocalypse
  global warming as, 72
  Hurricane Katrina as, 81
  as literary theme
    in "The Conversation of Eiros and
      Charmion," 71–74
    in *The Narrative of Arthur Gordon Pym*, 72
Appiah, Anthony, 3
Armstrong, Nancy, 201
art. *See* aesthetics
Art Studies: The Old Masters of Italy (Jarves), 139
Arthur, T. S., 104

239